DATE DUE			
OCT 8 '78			

Shakespeare's Use of Music

HAKESPEARE'S
USE OF MUSIC:
THE HISTORIES
AND TRAGEDIES

by

JOHN H. LONG

UNIVERSITY OF FLORIDA PRESS
GAINESVILLE·1971

To Bertie, with love

SHAKESPEARE'S USE OF MUSIC: A TRILOGY

☆ A STUDY OF THE MUSIC AND ITS
PERFORMANCE IN THE ORIGINAL
PRODUCTION OF SEVEN COMEDIES

☆☆ THE FINAL COMEDIES

☆☆☆ THE HISTORIES
AND TRAGEDIES

Acknowledgments

ACKNOWLEDGE WITH GRATITUDE THE GENEROSITY of the following libraries and publishers in permitting me to reproduce materials in their custody: the Bodleian Library; the Trustees of the British Museum; Cambridge University Library; the Folger Shakespeare Library; the Huntington Library, San Marino, California; the New York Public Library, Music Division; the Royal Musical Association; Stainer & Bell Limited; the Board of Trinity College, Dublin; and the Wellesley College Library.

Contents

viii)

Introduction

NCE MORE I OFFER THE RESULTS OF A STUDY OF Shakespeare's use of music—in this volume, his use of performed music in the histories and tragedies. With two exceptions, the plays considered are those usually placed in these two categories: I have placed *Troilus and Cressida* among the tragedies although it is sometimes classified as a comedy, and I have omitted consideration of *King John* because it contains insufficient music to warrant study. By the term "use of music" I mean the dramatic functions served by the performed music in those productions of the plays occurring between 1590 and 1615. As in the first two volumes of this three-part series—*Shakespeare's Use of Music: ... Seven Comedies* and *Shakespeare's Use of Music: The Final Comedies*—I once more attempt to determine the functions of the performed music, the manner of performance, the original music scores or notation used (when possible), and the significance of these data to peripheral problems of interpretation, text, staging, and stage history.

I have tried to meet the interests of a broad audience including students of Elizabethan music, drama in performance, and literature, as well as the producers of Shakespeare faced with practical problems. I hope this book may evoke that sense of kinship and close relationship of the arts which, accompanied by an alert eye for the practical, was one of the remarkable characteristics of the English Renaissance.

For my texts I have used modern editions, the First Folio of 1623, and relevant quartos. All quotations, unless otherwise noted, are from G. B. Harrison's edition of the plays. Line numbers follow the Globe edition.

In selecting the musical examples, I have chosen scores existing before 1650 which chronologically and otherwise are appropriate to the music called for in each of the plays. In some cases, particularly the ballads, the original tunes are given; in others, I have tried to approximate what I believe to have been the type and "mood" of the music originally used in the earliest productions of the dramas. My criteria for choosing music not specifically described in the play-texts are two. In selecting the form or type of piece, especially for instrumental music, I follow the conventional practices of Shakespeare's day. In determining the mood or emotion produced by a given piece of music, I have been guided by the titles attached to programmatic compositions of the period. This procedure may seem too simple, but I am convinced that such titles provide the most accurate criterion we have. Titles frequently give some indication of the emotional response expected by the composer; melodic or harmonic patterns, however, cannot be trusted to induce the same emotion now as they did around the beginning of the seventeenth century. We often associate the minor keys with sadness or nostalgia; the Elizabethans, it seems, made no such association.

In making transcriptions of the early music, I have tried to be as literal as possible. Editorial emendations or alterations have been enclosed in brackets. Musical compositions associated closely with Shakespeare, and several examples of early music previously unpublished, have been photographically reproduced when clarity permitted. I do not supply complete instrumental or vocal parts for the producer. When possible, however, I have given cantus and bassus voices, from which inner voices can be realized without great effort.

The bibliography includes some basic titles listed in the first two volumes of this study, but it is largely a supplement, not a full listing of source material.

For a discussion of the musical instruments, musical forms, notation, and songs of Shakespeare's time, and my methodology in treating these subjects, I suggest that the reader turn to the first volume of this series and to the many excellent studies on these topics.

When I began this study in 1948, the literature consisted of four books—Elson's *Shakespeare in Music*, Naylor's *Shakespeare and Music . . .*, Cowling's *Music on the Shakespearean Stage*, and Noble's *Shakespeare's Use of Song . . .* —and a few excellent articles scattered among various books and learned journals. These works are still of value, though they lack the benefits of research contributed by recent musicologists and literary scholars. In the years following the publication of the first volume of this series in 1955, excellent scholars have done significant work with the subject. For example, Peter Seng, whose dissertation on the songs in Shakespeare's plays and subsequent book *The Vocal Songs in the Plays of Shakespeare* now surpass the preceding work by Noble; John P. Cutts, whose

La Musique de Scène de la Troupe de Shakespeare... and many other publications resurrect, in the main successfully, much of the dramatic music of the period; Frederick Sternfeld, whose book *Music in Shakespearean Tragedy* provides an excellent bibliography, photographic reproductions of Shakespearean music, and stimulating comments on the subject; and Gretchen Finney, whose book *Musical Backgrounds for English Literature: 1580–1650* and other articles provide a rich store of knowledge about the symbolic and connotative qualities of Renaissance music.

I am happy to acknowledge the able assistance given me by many individuals and institutions, in particular the following: T. Walter Herbert of the University of Florida; Moelwyn Merchant of the University of Exeter; the directors and staffs of the Folger Shakespeare Library, the Music Division of the New York Public Library, the Music Division of the Library of Congress, the Henry E. Huntington Library; the Library of the Royal College of Music; the British Museum; the Bodleian Library; the Library of the University of North Carolina at Greensboro; and the Library of Greensboro College. I am also grateful for the money grant given me in 1957 by the Trustees of the John Simon Guggenheim Foundation, and in 1965 by the Research Committee of Greensboro College, which have enabled me to complete my research.

For her exacting work in preparing the musical notation for publication I am indebted to Mrs. Betty Marzan. For my wife, Bertie, who typed the final draft and indexed and cross-indexed hundreds of ballad titles and tunes, my gratitude is exceeded only by my love.

Errors that, despite such able assistance, may appear can be attributed only to the author.

JOHN H. LONG

ONE

The Music of Men's Lives

HOMAS DEKKER RECORDED: "I SPENT MY HOWRES in reading of Histories, and for the laying out of a little time receiued larger interest then the greatest vsurers doe for their money. By looking on those perspectiue glasses, I beheld kingdomes and people a farre off, came acquainted with their manners, their pollicics, their gouernement, their risings, and their downefalls: was present at their battailes, and (without danger to my selfe) vnlesse it were in greeuing to see States so ouerthrowne by the mutabilitie of Fortune, I saw those Empires vtterly brought to subuersion, which had beene terrours and triumphers ouer all the nations vppon earth. . . . Hast thou an ambition to be equall to Princes! read such bookes, as are the *Chronicles* of Ages, gone before thee: there maiest thou find lines drawne (if vertue be thy guide) to make thee paralell with the greatest Monarch: wouldst thou be aboue him, there is ye scale of him ascending. Huntst thou after glory? marke in those pathes how others haue run, and follow thou in the same course. Art thou sicke in minde? (and so to be diseased, is to be sicke euen to ye death) there shalt thou finde physicke to cure thee. Art thou sad? where is sweeter musicke then in reading? Art thou poore? open those closets, and inualuable treasures are powred into thy hands."[1] So Thomas Dekker described the pleasures he found in reading histories. Nor was he being extravagant when he referred to the reading of histories as sweet music; he was but reflecting the same association of ideas, common in the Renaissance, as did Shakespeare when he had John of Gaunt, *1 Henry IV*, refer to the "music of men's lives"—*musica humana* as the theorists called it—the harmony of the four humors that was but an echo of the divine harmony of God and His angels. Analysis of Dekker's remarks, therefore, helps clarify the reason for much of the music in Shakespeare's histories and tragedies and produces evidence for the popularity of the chronicles and histories both in books and on the stage. And since the Elizabethan concept of history was essentially tragic, Dekker's comments partially explain

1. T. Dekker, "Worke for Armorours" (1609), in *The Non-Dramatic Works of Thomas Dekker* 4:100–102.

the popularity of stage tragedies. The theme of Mutability, the inexorable force that swept away kingdoms and threw down the monuments of princes, is a common denominator that often makes it difficult to make a clear distinction between Elizabethan history plays and tragedies. Another element the two have in common is the lofty pageantry so often the setting for both.

The music in Shakespeare's chronicle plays (*Henry VI, Richard III, Richard II, Henry IV, Henry V*, and *Henry VIII*) owes its origin and dramatic uses, in large measure, to the chronicles of Hall, Holinshed, Froissart, and others from whose works the plays were derived. The moralistic-didactic qualities of these chronicles carry over into their dramatic counterparts and may easily be discerned in the choice of incidents, characters, and prevailing tones of the plays. But it is the pageantry, ceremony, and color so dear to the chronicler, as to the dramatist, that shapes the types and uses of music in these plays.

The chronicler could, and frequently did, dismiss in a few sentences the havoc caused by a great plague, yet write with loving attention to the smallest details page after page describing a royal masque or pageant. The addiction to color and spectacle which Chaucer displayed while describing the tournament in "The Knight's Tale" also pervades the Renaissance chronicles. For example, here is a brief excerpt from Holinshed's account of a masque Henry VIII gave in honor of Cardinal Wolsey:

> On a time the king came suddenlie thither (the palace of the Cardinal) in a maske with a dozen maskers all in garments like Sheepheards, made of fine cloth of gold, and crimosin sattin paned, & caps of the same, with visards of good physnomie, their haires & beards either of fine gold-wire silke, or black silke, hauing sixteene torchbearers, besides their drums and other persons with visards, all clothed in sattin of the same color. And before his entring into the hall, he came by water to the water gate without anie noise. ... Then went he [the Cardinal] incontinent downe into the hall, whereas they receiued them with twentie new torches, and conueid them up into the chamber, with such a noise of drums and flutes, as seldome had been heard the like. ... Thus passed they foorth the night with banketting, dansing, and other triumphs, to the great

comfort of the king, and pleasant regard of the nobilities
there assembled.[2]

The same love of pageantry is apparent in the commoners' chronicles, the ballads. Many Tudor ballads are popularized versions of
incidents taken from the chroniclers, shorn of the lofty rhetoric and
even more highly romanticized than the originals. But while the
ballads often lack style and fact, they retain in good measure the
ceremony, ritual, and pomp that gave pleasure to both chronicler and
commons. The reporter of Queen Elizabeth's visit to review the army
at Tilbury did not draw his matter from a chronicle, but he had an
eye for spectacle when he described the royal train in his ballad "The
Queens visiting the Campe at Tilburie":

> The Sargeant trumpet with his mace,
>   and nyne with trumpets after him:
> Bare headed went before her grace,
>   in coats of scarlet colour trim.
> The king of Heralds tall and comely,
>   was the next in order duely,
> With the famous Armes of *England*,
>   wrought with rich embroidered gold:
> On finest veluet blew and crimson,
>   that for siluer can be sold.
>
> With Maces of cleane beaten gold,
>   the Queenes two Sargeants then did ride,
> Most comely men for to behold,
>   in veluet coates and chaines beside.
> The Lord generall then came riding,
>   and Lord marshall hard beside him.
> Richly were they both atired,
>   in princelie garments of great price:
> Bearing still their hats and fethers
>   in their handes in comely wise.
>
> Then came the Queene on pranceing steede
>   atired like an Angell bright:
> And eight braue footemen at her feete,
>   whose Ierkins were most rich in sight.
> Her Ladies, likewise of great honor,

2. R. Holinshed, *The Third volume of Chronicles . . .* (1587), pp. 921–22.

> most sumpteuously did waite vpon her.
> With pearles and diamonds braue adorned,
> 　　　and in costly cales of gold:
> Her Guarde in scarlet then ride after,
> 　　　with bowes and arrowes stoute and bold.[3]

These two general sources, the chronicles and the chronicle-ballads, determine to a large extent the music and its uses in Shakespeare's two chronicle-tetralogies. We will examine the ballads and their influences more closely below; now let us return to the chronicle-histories.

The chronicles are confined, for the most part, to royal events—the affairs of state, public ceremonies, military campaigns, religious observances, and, not to be overlooked, the court amusements and pleasures. In drawing from the chronicles, the playwright apparently considered ceremony and ritual important elements to be preserved as much as possible on his stage. Likewise, the military councils and campaigns had prime value for the dramatist. To both chronicler and dramatist, the art of rhetoric, or lofty speech, was a matter worth close attention.

Frequently these three general categories overlap; that is, a military matter might be discussed during a royal reception in highly rhetorical language. In any event, these three elements—military feats, ceremony (whether solemn or playful), and rhetoric—largely explain the varied uses and types of music employed in the plays. In his efforts to translate historical events into plays, the dramatist often used music to indicate offstage battles and the characters' shifting fortunes. Likewise, the ceremonious processions and councils were made impressive and solemn by the playhouse musicians. Music was also used rhetorically, that is, to underscore emotional speeches made by the actors.

In discussing the military music, we should make a distinction between the music actually employed on the battlefield—drum or trumpet signals directing the movements of troops—and the ceremonious music associated with the art of war—the marches, dead marches, and at least one dance form.[4] It is to the first category that

3. T. Deloney, "Strange Histories" (1602), in *The Works of Thomas Deloney*, pp. 476–77.

4. In Christ Church Library MS 431 there is a program piece for virginals which includes several examples of military music. Titled "Mr. Birds battle," it contains "The souldiers sumuns," "The marche of the foote men," "The

the terms "alarum" and "retrait," for example, apply; and to the second, such terms as "marche," "dead marche," and "almain." Francis Markham gave the following, rather full account of the music used by an army in the field in his *Fiue Decades of Epistles of Warre* (1622):

> To proceed then in my Range of Martiall dependants, the next which doth precede those which I haue ouerpassed, are the *Drumme* and *Phiph*, which for as much as like the former they are Officers of power, and not of command, therefore I may in no wise giue them place before the Commaunders, only I will allow them according to their place in March, and their greatnesse in entertainment to be the best of priuate Souldiers; and as they are Instruments of direction and incouragement to others: so are they by superior officers to be directed themselues. Now albe I doe ioyne these two Officers together, and that in Ranke and pay they are all one, yet it is to be vnderstood, that the *Phiph* is but onely an Instrument of pleasure, not of necessitie, and it is to the voice of the *Drum* the Souldier should wholly attend, and not to the aire of the whistle; for the one (which is the *Drumme*) speakes plainely and distinctly, the other speakes loud and shrill, but yet curiously and confusedly, and therefore the *Drumme* being the very tongue and voyce of the Commander, he is to haue an exceeding carefull and diligent eare vnto all the wordes of direction . . . for to mistake and do contrary, as to beat a Retrait when he is commanded to Charge, or to beat a Charge when men are to retire, were a thing of that danger, that the armie might perish by the action . . . Of which Beatings of the *Drum*, these are the most behouefull and vsefull for euery raw Souldier to learne. First, in the morning the discharge or breaking vp of the *Watch*, then a preparation or Summons to make them repaire to their Colours; then a beating away before they begin to march; after that a *March* according to the nature and custom of the country (for diuers countries haue diuers Marches) then a *Charge*, then a *Retrait*, then a *Troupe*, and lastly a *Battalion*, and a *Battery*, besides other sounds which de-

---

march of the horsemen," "The Trumpetts," "The Irish march," "The bagpipe and the drume," several "changes," and "The march to the fight." The manuscript is unfinished. The complete suite is given in W. Byrd, *The Collected Works of William Byrd*, vol. 18.

pending on the phantastikenes of forrein nations are not so vseful: ... It is the Office of the *Drumme* to make all Proclamations ... and when any dies, the *Drumme* with a sad solemnitie must bring him to his graue, for it is the only mourner for the lost, and the greatest honor of Funerals: whence it comes that any man dying (aboue the degree of a common Souldier) the *Drum* performing the last dutie, may for his fee challenge the Sword of the deceased. ... It is also the Office and dutie of the *Drumme* to carry Ransomes. ... It is he that must trucke and compound for Prisoners ... he may vpon tolleration from the *Generrall,* carrie Challenges and Defiances from one enemie to another, and either for Honour of Ladies loues make composition for single Encounters, provided it bee vpon foot ... but if it be vpon Horseback, then it is the office of the *Trumpet,* and the *Drumme* hath no interest in it.[5]

Markham made it clear that the drum was used for directing foot soldiers on the battlefield as well as in the camp. The fife joined the drum to provide music for marches or for entertainment. However, the dead march was played by the drum alone, probably muffled.[6] While Markham scarcely mentioned the trumpet, his remark at the conclusion of the quotation implies that this instrument was used only by the cavalry. Later, we will see that the trumpet was mainly associated with the aristocracy and royalty.

No notation of cavalry trumpet signals has been found that is both distinctly Renaissance and English. In the Brit. Mus. Harleian MS 6461, fols. 58[b] and 69, however, there is a collection of trumpet signals for cavalry taken from Mersenne's *Traité de l'Harmonie Vniverselle* ... (2. 12), first published in 1635 (see Appendix I). The descriptive titles of each of these signals are written in a curious mixture of French, Latin, and Greek. Most calls are for movements equivalent to those of the infantry, as "La charg conflictus" (The Charge to Battle), "La Retraite Receptui Cavitur" (Retreat—Rein in Horses), and "La quet vigilid" (Recall of the Watch). Others are peculiar to the cavalry, as "Bouteselle ad Ephippia" (Boots and Saddles?) and "Ascentio in equos indicatur A cheval" (Mount Horses). It seems probable that military men, regardless of nationality, understood these signals. Chivalry was still international, and the mil-

5. Pages 57–58.
6. Markham, *Fiue Decades of Epistles of Warre,* p. 59.

itary campaigns waged by the English during Shakespeare's lifetime, particularly in the Low Countries, were fought by troops from many countries—France, Austria, Switzerland, Holland, England, Ireland, Spain, Germany—amid frequently shifting alliances. International field signals were necessary. As Markham noted, national peculiarities in military music appear in the marches but not in the field signals. We might therefore assume that the trumpet signals recorded by Mersenne differed little from those used by the English cavalry.

The entertainment Markham mentioned may refer to military displays like the one described in William Bariffe's *Mars, his Trivmph* (1639). According to the title page, this is "The Description of an Exercise performed the XVIII of October, 1638, in Merchant-Taylors Hall by Certain Gentlemen of the Artillery Garden London." It includes a parade, figure-marching, and manuals-of-arms and concludes with a mock battle between "Christians" and "Saracens," all set to music. In its mixed elements of military exercises, tournament, and masque, it provides an interesting example of more formal and ceremonious forms of military music.

A consort of cornets began the entertainment with an overture. Then,

> The Cornets having once play'd over, the *Targettiers* 9. in a company marched into the Hall . . . drawing into *figures* 9. *against* 9. performing 10. severall *forms*, making their *figures*, all according to distinct sounds of their musick. . . . Next marched into the Hall, Captain *Mulli-Aben-Achmat* with his *Saracens* in great state, their musick was a Turky Drumme, and a hideous noise making *pipe* (made of a *Buffolas* horn:). . . . Lastly, Captain *Iohn Ven* led in the Moderne Armes his Drums beating a lofty *English march.* . . . The second time of their coming from the lower end of the Hall, the Drums *beat a Troop*, the *Pikes advance*, and *Ranks close forwards to their distance of order.* . . . After some small respite . . . the *phife* and *drumme* play the posture [manual-of-arms] tune once over. When the musick began the second time, the *Muskettiers* in the *front* and *pikes* in the *reere*, begun the postures as followeth. . . . Having thus performed their *postures*, the *Phife* and *Drum* play the *falling of*[f] *Tune*; in the interim whereof the Muskettiers perform their *Saluting posture*, and *wheel* of[f]

by *division*, two to the *right*, and two to the *left*, placing themselves in the reere of the Pikes.[7]

We thus see English military music in both its warlike and ceremonious forms. We might suppose that field signals included the following: "The Breaking Up of the Watch," a "Call to the Colors," then a "Beating Away" (Preparative?), then a "march," "alarum," "charge," "retrait," "troupe" (assembly). These, excepting the "alarum," were the "Beatings of the *Drum* . . . most behouefull & vsefull for euery raw Souldier to learne," according to Markham. We might infer that these signals were familiar to most playgoers, and hence most suitable for dramatic purposes. Markham's omission of the term "alarum," so frequently encountered in Elizabethan plays, also suggests that it may not have been a definite signal, but rather any noise—bells, trumpet blasts, or drum rolls—which would serve to indicate an enemy attack.

These drum signals must have been transmitted aurally. Naylor discovered the only notation I have found—an old English drum march revived, he noted, in the reign of Charles I[8] (see Appendix II). National differences appeared in the marches: Markham observed that "diuers countries haue diuers Marches." The French marched to a slower tempo than the English. Thomas Dekker, in his "Seven Deadly Sinnes of London" (1603?), mentioned "the *Worshipfull Sir*, (that leades a Gentlemans life, and dooth nothing) though he comes but slowly on (as if hee trodde a French March). . . ."[9] The Danes apparently marched to a quicker tempo. In Dekker's *The Magnificent Entertainment* (1604), "to delight the Queene with her owne country Musicke, nine Trumpets, and a Kettle Drum, did very sprightly & actiuely sound the *Danish march*: Whose cunning and quicke stops, by that time they had toucht the last Ladyes eare in the traine, behold, the King was aduanced vp so hie as to Cheapside. . . ."[10]

When a drum and fife played the military march, that is, when it became more completely a musical composition, it sometimes was called an "almain." The almain, as a ballroom dance form, gained popularity in the Elizabethan period; the lutenists' books include

7. Pages 1–6.
8. E. Naylor, *Shakespeare and Music, with Illustrations from the Music of the 16th and 17th Centuries,* pp. 200–201.
9. *The Non-Dramatic Works* 2:51.
10. E2–E2ᵛ.

many examples. But it never entirely lost its association with the military, and in the combination of popular dance and military march we may observe a blend typical of the Renaissance.

The Elizabethans apparently considered the almain a popular or folk dance. Probably because of its name, they thought it of German or Lowland origin. Thomas Morley described the "Alman":

> The Alman is a more heavy dance than this [the galliard] (fitly representing the nature of the people whose name it carrieth) so that no extraordinary motions are used in dancing of it. It is made of strains, sometimes two, sometimes three, and every strain is made by four; but you must mark that the four of the Pavan measure is in Dupla Proportion to the four of the Alman measure, so that as the usual Pavan containeth in a strain the time of sixteen semibreves, so the usual Alman containeth the time of eight, and most commonly in short notes.[11]

Morley wrote nothing about the almain as a military march or dance, but some of his contemporaries, perhaps of a more classical bent, saw in the almain an appropriate modern version of the ancient Greek Pyrrhic dance. Dekker, describing Rome under the emperors in "A Strange Horse-Race," mentioned the theaters:

> In these they sometimes saw playes tragicall, or comicall, with all sorts of musicke, *Doricke, Chromaticke,* soft and delicate, *Lidian, Nipolydian* mournfull, fit for Tragedies: and to these sorts of music they had all sorts of Dauncing; And *Hyporchema* (in time of a pestilence) a daunce to *Apollo* in the Campe; the Pyrichian, which was a daunce in Armour: In the Chamber (as wee now haue) dances, with wanton gesticulation. All which, as well *Musicke* as *Daunces,* they borrowed from the Greekes.[12]

Despite the misplaced semicolon, we can see that the Pyrrhic dance was a military dance performed by warriors in armor. Hence, in George Peele's *The Arraignment of Paris* (1584) appears the stage direction *Pallas' Show. Hereupon did enter Nine Knights in armour, treading a warlike almain, by drum and fife* . . . (act 2, scene 2). And

---

11. *A Plain and Easy Introduction to Practical Music,* p. 297.
12. *The Non-Dramatic Works* 3:319–20.

we may be fairly certain that the "Knights' Dance" in *Pericles* (act 2, scene 3), in which the knights dance in armor, is also an almain. Finally, we may note that Bariffe's work, quoted above, uses "tune" and "almain" interchangeably where the tunes are obviously marches. Bariffe referred to three separate tunes—"The Posture tune," "The Tune for the Motions," and "The Falling of[f] Tune"; also he called two of them the "Posture Almayne" and "the *Almaine* tune for the *motions*."[13] Fortunately, Bariffe included the musical notation for the three tunes (see Appendix III); a glance will show them to be almains, written for the fife. A military drum was most likely used, not the kettledrum usually reserved for royal or state occasions.[14]

Because they seldom controlled troop movements, the "flourish," "sennet," and "tucket" (see Appendix IV)[15] signify, at least on the stage, ceremonious rather than military music. These terms call attention to the presence of authority or the dignity of government. The word "flourish" on the stage, as in actuality, implies kingship or royalty, as many critics have observed. It is, Portia states in *The Merchant of Venice*, "the flourish when true subjects bow / To a new-crowned monarch" (act 3, scene 2). But, to make a slight distinction, the flourish may also announce the presence of princes, dukes, or other titled persons, provided they exercise or represent sovereignty. In this sense, the flourish provides an aural sign of "presence," that intangible but recognizable aura of authority that surrounds power and command in their noblest forms. This distinction may enable us to decide where the authority really rests in those dramatic scenes where two opponents, both kings or princes, contend for a kingdom, as often occurs in Shakespeare's first historical tetralogy. If the playwright indicates a flourish for one king and none for the other, we may assume that the first king wields the kingly power.

The flourish was as much a part of the kingly trappings as the crown; therefore, a royal train usually included a group of trumpeters

13. *Mars, his Trivmph*, pp. 10, 15, 18.
14. For a recent account of Renaissance military music, see C. Titcomb, "Baroque Court and Military Trumpets and Kettledrums: Technique and Music." See also Titcomb's doctoral dissertation, "The Kettledrums in Western Europe: Their History Outside the Orchestra."
15. For extended discussion of these terms as they appear in Elizabethan dramatic literature, see Naylor, *Shakespeare and Music*; G. Cowling, *Music on the Shakespearian Stage*; and J. Manifold, *The Music in English Drama*

varying in number according to the stateliness of the occasion. The queen was accompanied by nine trumpeters when she reviewed the troops at Tilbury, as our ballad tells us, and Dekker reported that nine trumpets and a kettledrum sounded a Danish march for Queen Anne at the coronation of James I. For lesser occasions fewer trumpets were used—perhaps four or five. In any event, one of the trumpeters was the sergeant, the officer in charge of all the royal trumpeters and kettledrummers.[16]

The royal trumpeters, and presumably the kettledrummers, formed an exclusive and haughty group. As a part of the monarch's "menie," they possessed special perquisites and probably gave themselves considerable airs. They came mostly from a few families knit closely by blood ties or marriage, and they obtained their offices by hereditary right. They belonged to an exclusive guild and were not members of the Municipal Company of Waits. Like their monarch, they were above the trade.

But the royal trumpeters could stoop, and they frequently did so. Having virtually a royal monopoly, when trumpet flourishes or marches were needed for impressive occasions, they could command a good fee for the services they rendered beyond the call of duty. It was one of the sergeant's duties to arrange for his men to fill engagements in the city, that is, for other than the king's service. For this he also exacted a suitable fee. If a new lord mayor were being installed, or if a playing company needed a brace of trumpeters for a coronation scene, the royal trumpeters were called upon, sometimes to the detriment of their service to the king. A royal decree of James I proclaims:

> And ovr will & pleasure is that no drum trumpett nor fife shall sound at any plaies dumb-shewes or modells without the lycence of our said serjant. And our sergeant or his deputies shall have out of every playhouse to his or their owne use twelve pence the daie or every daie in which they shall play, the same to be truelie paide to him or his

---

from *Shakespeare to Purcell.* Carpenter has noted that the term "fluryshe" introduces the "kinge of Mobe land" in the mystery play *Balaam* (see "Music in the English Mystery Plays," in J. Long, ed., *Music in English Renaissance Drama,* p. 19).

16. For an account of the organization of the royal trumpeters and drummers in the courts of Elizabeth and James, see H. Lafontaine, ed., *The King's Musick: A Transcript of Records . . . 1460–1700*; and W. Woodfill, *Musicians in English Society from Elizabeth to Charles I.*

deputies without anie trouble or deniall, our owne playors excepted.[17]

The sennet was apparently a processional march usually performed by a group of trumpets, sometimes by hautboys or cornets. No musical score described as a sennet survives, if indeed one ever existed; in this matter we have run into a minor mystery. There are stage directions in many Elizabethan plays calling for sennets. It is also clear that the sennets were used for entrances and exits by large groups of actors, usually in some ceremonious scene. Some plays, notably several by Dekker, have stage directions calling for sennets during dumb shows. But it is also interesting that the term "sennet" occurs almost exclusively in theatrical contexts; it is not found in the theoretical treatises on music or in musical instruction books, nor does it appear in the musical imagery of the poetry. One of the earliest poetic references to the sennet occurs in a dedicatory poem written by Dudley Posthumus Lovelace for John Gamble's *Ayres and Dialogues* (1657). The poem begins, "Enough, Enough, of Orbs and Spheres, / Reach me a Trumpet or a Drum, / To *sound* sharp *Synnets* in your Ears, / And *Beat* a Deep *Encomium*."[18]

It seems probable, at this point, that "sennet" was a specialized theatrical term describing a kind of musical composition used in plays. The term was possibly a recent addition to the playhouse vocabulary and through it to the English language. Naylor has suggested that the word was derived from the Italian *sonare*, noting that the First Folio edition of *Henry V* contains the word "senet," but in a later edition the same direction uses the word "Sonet" as though the first were a misprint. He has also noted that the 1604 edition of Marlowe's *Doctor Faustus* (act 3, scene 1) has the direction "*sound a sonnet*." Naylor has also suggested that the term was derived from the Latin *signum*, or signal.[19] But it is equally probable that, in view of the sennet's use for ceremonious occasions, the word is derived from the Latin *senatus* (senate). The Elizabethan playwrights and prompters were themselves uncertain about the word's origin. A few examples illustrate this uncertainty, reflected both by the various spellings of the word and by the players' customary uses of the sennet.

---

17. See the entry from Brit. Mus. MS Ashmole 857, p. 348, in J. Halliwell, "Scrapbook" 1:1, Folger Shakespeare Library copy.
18. Page 172.
19. *Shakespeare and Music*, p. 174.

In John Marston's *The History of Antonio and Mellida*, Part 1 (1602), *The Cornets sound a Synnet* and *The Cornets sound a Cynet* (act 1, scene 1). In act 2, *The Cornets sound a Synnet, and the Duke goes out in state*. In act 4, *The still Flutes sound a mournful Cynet. Enter a Cofin*. And *Antonio and Mellida*, Part 2 (1602), contains the directions *The Cornets sound a cynet. Enter two mourners in dumb show* (act 2, scene 1) and *The song ended, the Cornets sound a Cynet* (act 5, scene 5). In the anonymous *Look About You* (1600), line 2820, *Enter a Sinet, first two Herraldes. . . .*[20] Here the word apparently refers to a stately procession rather than to the music which accompanied the procession. In Marlowe's *A Larum for London* (1602), line 260, we read *A signet sounded . . . a Drum sounding a dead march*. In this case, the "signet" is used as a signal; the procession is accompanied by a dead march. Dekker's *Satiro-mastix* (1602), page 222, has the direction *Trumpets sound a flourish, and then a sennate: Enter King . . . : whilst the Trumpets sound the King takes his leave of the Bride-groome, and Sir Quintilian, and last of the Bride*. Heywood's *If You Know Not Me*, Part 1 (1605), page 244, has the direction *A sennet. Enter foure Trumpeters: after them Sergeant Trumpeter, with a mace. . . .* Later, page 246, *they sennet about the Stage in order. The Maior of London meets them*. Here the word is used as a verb synonymous with "march."

The difficulty of rigidly defining "sennet" is thus apparent. In close approximation, a sennet is: (1) a musical composition used in the playhouse to accompany lengthy stage business such as processions or dumb shows and usually performed by a "whole consort" of instruments, most often trumpets; (2) a ceremonious march or procession usually accompanied by stately music; (3) as a verb, to march in an orderly or dignified manner.

Since we know of no musical notation for a sennet, we may suspect that the term did not refer to a specific type of music but rather to any kind of march-like music suitable for a particular dramatic incident. The playhouse musicians probably used any music that seemed appropriate. For example, the "De la Tromba Pauin," found in Thomas Morley's *The First Booke of Consort Lessons . . .* (1599), while scored for a broken consort, is written in imitation of a trumpet march (hence the name) and contains a trumpet flourish in its final section. If transcribed for brass instruments, this trumpet

20. These and the following quotations are taken from Malone Society Reprints of the works cited.

pavane could serve for most occasions wherein a sennet is called for. It is important to note that the sennet was not usually a flourish or an extended fanfare; it was most likely a full musical composition of some length, probably including two or three sections, repeated if necessary to conform to the action on the stage. Nor was its performance limited to trumpets; sennets were also played on cornets and recorders. The instruments specified by the playwright in each case depended upon the dramatic mood or atmosphere desired at the moment.

The tucket, like the flourish, was a trumpet signal indicating the "presence" of authority. As Naylor has observed, the tuckets were personalized; that is, a noble family would own an exclusive tucket.[21] In this sense, the tucket was a form of musical heraldry. As the *OED* defines the term, the tucket derives from the French *touchet*, a trumpet signal for cavalry. In Elizabethan plays, the word is used in both personal and military senses. In most cases, a single trumpet sounded the tucket, but occasionally several trumpets were employed, thus differing little from the flourish, the difference being mainly that the tucket was a shorter signal.

All of these military and semimilitary musical forms had one general purpose—to increase the color and pageantry of the actions on the stage. In a different sense, but to much the same effect, we also find music used as a rhetorical device in the histories and tragedies, that is, as an ornamentation or embellishment added to the conventional devices of the orator.

The close association of rhetoric and the art of acting is familiar enough. Not so familiar, perhaps, is the equally close association of music and the dance with rhetoric and acting—at least, in Shakespeare's time.[22] Among those arts which Henry Cornelius Agrippa dispraised in his *Of the Vanitie and vncertaintie of Artes and Sciences* (1569), music, dancing, acting, and rhetoric were denounced almost in the same breath (chapters 17, 18, 20, 21). Their close relationship in Agrippa's mind is evident in his description of stage dancing:

21. *Shakespeare and Music*, p. 174.
22. J. Hollander, *The Untuning of the Sky ... English Poetry, 1500–1700*, pp. 194–206, discusses more fully the relationship between Renaissance music and rhetoric.

The stage plaiers daunsing is the Arte of *Imitation*, and *Demonstration*, expressinge the thinges conceaued in the minde with a seemely gesture: so plainely and liuely repre- sentinge mens manners and affections; that the very be- holder plainly perceaueth him to be a stage player by infinite gestures and mouinges, although he saie nothinge.[23]

And later, "Rhetorisme, or of the Rhetoricall Daunsinge" is the heading of a passage in which he denounced the exaggerated ges- tures and body movements used by orators and preachers.

Francis Bacon also noted the close association, at least in theory, between music and rhetoric. In "The Interpretation of Nature," he observed that

a man should be thought to dally, if he did not note how the figures of rhetoric and music are many of them the same. The repetitions and traductions in speech and the reports and hauntings of sounds in music are the very same things. Now in music it is one of the ordinariest flowers to fall from a discord, or hard tune, upon a sweet accord. The figure that Cicero and the rest commend as one of the best points of elegancy, which is the fine checking of expec- tation, is no less well known to the musicians when they have a special grace in flying the close of cadence.[24]

In "Natural History," he further commented:

There be in music certain figures or tropes, almost agreeing with the figures of rhetoric, and with the affections of the mind, and other senses. First, the division and quavering, which please so much in music, have an agreement with the glittering of light; as the moon-beams playing upon a wave. Again, the falling from a discord to a concord, which maketh great sweetness in music, hath an agreement with the affections, which are reintegrated to the better, after some dislikes; it agreeth also with the taste, which is soon glutted with that which is sweet alone. The sliding from the close or cadence hath an agreement with the figure in

23. Page 32ʳ.
24. *The Works of Francis Bacon, Lord Chancellor of England,* Cent. **VIII**, p. 86.

rhetoric which they call "præter expectatum;" for there is a
pleasure even in being deceived. The reports, and fuges,
have an agreement with the figures in rhetoric of repetition
and traduction. The triplas, and changing of times, have an
agreement with the changes of motions; as when galliard
time, and measure time, are in the medley of one dance.[25]

There is considerable evidence that the stage players practiced
the combination of music and rhetoric, especially in those speeches
whose subject and oratorical style made musical augmentation appropriate. Lorenzo's familiar speech on the music of the spheres in
The Merchant of Venice (act 5, scene 1) comes immediately to
mind, as do Richard's lines on the music of men's lives in *Richard II*
(act 5, scene 5). Likewise, in Rowley's *When You See Me You Know
Me* (Q1613), two consorts—one loud and one soft—are used to
underscore the premises of the prince's speech, "As Musicke, so is
man gouern'd by stops. . . ."[26] When we think of the opportunities
for rhetorical display, and frequently for bombast, given actors by
the Elizabethan playwrights in their histories and tragedies, we should
not be surprised that they would add to other rhetorical devices performed music. They well understood the power of music to move
the emotions and to underscore, by means of "demonstration," the
sentiments of a swelling speech.

Thus, whether the music was military, ceremonious, or rhetorical,
it was clearly an important element of the pageantry that the Elizabethan audience apparently expected to find displayed in histories
and tragedies—and which the playwrights were quite willing to provide. The dramatists, in turn, employed the music for dramatic purposes. In the following chapter we shall see how Shakespeare uses
the types of music previously described, particularly the flourish, in
the three parts of *Henry VI* and in *Richard III*.

25. Ibid., Cent. II, p. 26.
26. J. Long, *Shakespeare's Use of Music . . . Seven Comedies*, pp. 40–41.

TWO

The First Tetralogy

HE ELIZABETHANS NOT ONLY LIKED DRAMA; THEY were individually and collectively dramatic. Life seemed a drama and each person an actor. Shakespeare's audiences expected the stage to imitate and to heighten the drama of everyday life. The playwrights found it difficult to reproduce in the playhouses the magnificent and spectacular state processions, coronations, and other ceremonies that gave drama and color to London life. When the dramatists chose to write plays including scenes of ceremony and stateliness, they were hard put to approach the regal splendor familiar to their spectators. They found it necessary to use all means available to them, and music was a most effective device. Given some trumpets and drums—perhaps the royal trumpeters—and a fife, occasionally augmented by a consort of hautboys, the dramatists could musically imitate most public ceremonies of their time. From long practice they and the players could use their basic musical ensemble to create many theatrical effects and to serve many dramatic purposes. The first tetralogy—the three parts of *Henry VI*, and *Richard III*—reveals many uses of this basic instrumentation, both broad and subtle, and especially the many changes Shakespeare could ring with the ubiquitous flourishes.

The music required by the stage directions in the four plays under consideration is limited almost entirely to the ceremonious and military types described in chapter 1. The instruments employed are those described in chapter 1, with one or two exceptions, which will be discussed later. When we consider the importance of ceremony in these plays and the dramatic ways that music could enhance ritual and pageantry, we might suppose that the musical means available to the actors would be used fully; we realize the extent only after a close examination of each episode employing music—within the contexts of each play and the complete tetralogy. Such an examination enables us to discern three consistent patterns governing musical usage. The obvious one, and perhaps the principal one, involves the use of music to increase the plays' pageantry and color. A secondary pattern emerges from the use of music in the stagecraft required to move large groups of actors on or off the stage or to suggest offstage action. The third, and perhaps most interesting, pattern is the use of music for a particular rhetorical purpose—a kind of dramatic irony in which the feudal and chivalric ideals suggested by the drum roll, the trumpet flourishes, and the solemn processional measures are pointedly in contrast to the plots and treachery of the selfish and proud barons of England, France, and Burgundy, and to an ineffectual Henry VI, whose fate it was to preside over the loss of the English realm in France and the War of the Roses. In short, the funeral of Henry V, which opens *Henry VI*, suggests a major theme woven into the entire tetralogy—the decay of the feudal ideals personified by Henry V and the consequent tragedies, both individual and national, which would continue until some new order ensued.

> [*Dead march. Enter the funeral of* KING HENRY *the
> Fifth, attended on by the* DUKE OF BEDFORD, *Regent
> of France, the* DUKE OF GLOUCESTER, *Protector, the*
> DUKE OF EXETER, *the* EARL OF WARWICK, *the* BISHOP
> OF WINCHESTER, HERALDS, &c.*]

The play begins with the muffled drumbeats which immediately solemnize the scene into which the king's body is borne. The attendance by the great peers, the bier and its several bearers, the state heralds among the attendants, all inform us that this occasion is a state ceremony, and it is the dead march which brings the solemn procession onstage. In keeping with the ritualistic action, the first speeches of Bedford, Gloucester, Essex, and Winchester are rather fulsome eulogies. In ironic contrast to the encomiums on the glorious deeds of Henry V, the ceremony is soon disturbed by the quarrel between Gloucester and the bishop, whose "jars" (discords) quickly introduce the disunity which will provide much dramatic conflict throughout the tetralogy.

In this first example, the funeral march performs the triple function previously described. The drum rolls are appropriate to the ceremony. At the same time, the marchers—including the five peers, probably six pallbearers, at least two heralds, a token guard of honor, and at least two or three drummers—move onto the stage in a dignified, dramatically effective manner. The rhetorical function appears in the ironic contrast between the solemn tone first established by the drums and the disruptive quarrel of Gloucester and Winchester.

The second scene opens with a processional also, but in marked contrast to the first.

> [*Sound a flourish. Enter* CHARLES, ALENÇON, *and*
> REIGNIER, *marching with drum and* SOLDIERS.]

The trumpet flourish completely alters the dramatic mood. In contrast to the dead march which opens the first scene, the flourish immediately evokes those concepts associated with majesty—authority, power, nobility—in short, the "presence" of a king. Charles appears marching against Talbot besieged in Orleans, assuming his primary responsibility as a Renaissance prince—military command. Whereas the flourish announces the kingly nature of Charles, the drum provides the rhythmical march beats and symbolically suggests that the dauphin's army is present, unseen by the audience. The contrast between the English dead march and the flourish announcing the French has the rhetorical effect of antithesis, certainly appropriate to the action. The trumpets sound again at the conclusion of act 1, scene 5, which depicts Talbot's defeat and the recovery of Orleans by La Pucelle. Talbot, attempting to rally his troops concludes:

> Pucelle is entered into Orleans
> In spite of us or aught that we could do.
> Oh, would I were to die with Salisbury!
> The shame hereof will make me hide my head.

The folio stage directions are:

> *Exit Talbot.*
> *Alarum, Retreat, Flourish.*
> *Enter on the Walls, Puzel, Dolphin, Reigneir, Alanson,*
> *and Souldiers.*

Some editors, G. B. Harrison, for example, have placed the scene division of 5 and 6 between the flourish and the entrance of the French on the walls of Orleans, as follows:

> [*Exit* TALBOT. *Alarum; retreat; flourish.*]
> SCENE VI. *The same.*
>
> [*Enter, on the walls,* LA PUCELLE, CHARLES, REIGNIER,
> ALENÇON, *and* SOLDIERS.]

This division is satisfactory only if we overlook the probability that the action was continuous in the original staging. If we assume continuous action, the alarm marks the continuation of the assault on Orleans, the retreat (sounded by trumpets or drums) indicates the defeat of the English forces. The flourish, certainly by trumpets, marks the French victory and probably should be sounded to herald the appearance of Charles and Reignier (one the dauphin; the other, titular king of Naples) on the walls. The flourish therefore seems more appropriate to introduce scene 6 than to conclude scene 5. The distinction may seem overnice, but the dramatic effect is lost if the victorious dauphin and his musical harbinger are separated by a time interval. The flourish must announce the "presence" of the prince just as the flourish at the end of the scene announces his exit and also, incidentally, concludes the first act with a pointed contrast to the funeral march which opened it.

Act 2 opens as French sentinels take their posts on the walls of Orleans. Then, once again we hear the slow roll of muffled drums:

> [*Enter* TALBOT, BEDFORD, BURGUNDY, *and forces, with*
> *scaling ladders, their drums beating a dead march.*]

And now we have a problem.

Why the dead march here? The English forces are supposedly on their way to a surprise assault on the French now occupying Orleans. It seems unlikely that they would announce their approach with the beat of drums, even muffled drums. And yet the surprise of the French is complete and spectacularly successful. H. C. Hart and Hardin Craig, commenting on the question, have suggested that the English "are bringing Salisbury on a funeral procession."[1] This observation has some force when we recall that Talbot considers the projected assault on Orleans revenge for Salisbury's death, and when the city is taken, Talbot commands that Salisbury's body be displayed in the marketplace. The dead march might also echo the funeral march for Henry V, a reminder that one more great English warrior has left the earthly scene. On the other hand, the conversation of Talbot, Bedford, and Burgundy, spoken to the sound of the dead march, is completely unconcerned with Salisbury. Also, why would the French not be warned by the drums? Their sentinels are posted and alert, yet the surprise attack is so successful that Charles,

---

1. Respectively, Shakespeare, *The First Part of King Henry the Sixth;* and Shakespeare, *The Complete Works of Shakespeare.*

Joan, Alençon, and Reignier are barely able to escape half-clothed. Andrew Cairncross, following Dover Wilson, believed the portion of F's stage direction *Their Drummes beating a Dead March* was "obviously intended for the funeral of Salisbury, at II, ii, 6 or 7, just after the entry of the same three characters, Talbot, Bedford, and Burgundy."[2] He therefore moved the dead march to act 2, scene 2, line 6.

I propose another solution that, if not entirely satisfactory, is perhaps as plausible as those previously offered. The action in this scene points to the surprise of the French and their confusion in escaping from the city. This surprise must have been achieved by some stratagem, else why is the alertness of the French early emphasized in their posting sentinels? The stratagem, I think, depends upon the dead march. First, let us envision the setting as the French sentinels describe it. They are on the walls of Orleans; the night is dark, cold, and rainy. Obviously, the visibility is poor. In the distance they hear drumbeats sounding the slow rolls of a march, and perhaps they also hear a large body of troops. Why do they not challenge or sound an alarm? Because they assume that the approaching force is French. As noted in chapter 1, Dekker described the French march as slow, in comparison, presumably, with the English march. Perhaps we are to understand that the sentries, hearing the English funeral march, mistake it for a French march, and it is this error that permits the English stratagem to succeed.

Lest this conjecture seem strained, we should observe that exactly this point—the slow tempo of the French march—is used to indicate the movement of French troops offstage, and also as a subject for wordplay later in act 3, scene 3, lines 28–34, in which La Pucelle describes the offstage march of Talbot and Burgundy toward Paris:

> *[Drum sounds afar off.]*
> Hark! By the sound of drum you may perceive
> Their powers are marching unto Parisward.
> > *[Here sound an English march. Enter, and pass over at a distance,* TALBOT *and his* FORCES.]*
> There goes the Talbot with his colors spread,
> And all the troops of English after him.
> > *[French march. Enter the* DUKE OF BURGUNDY *and* FORCES.]*
> Now in the rearward comes the Duke and his.
> Fortune in favor makes him lag behind.

2. Shakespeare, *The First Part of Henry VI*, ed. Cairncross, p. 138.

John Stevens quoted J. S. Manifold, who wrote that "any march played on muffled drums was called a dead march."[3] It should be noted, however, that the only evidence cited by Manifold is the stage direction in *1 Henry VI* calling for a dead march along with Talbot's scaling ladders at the siege of Orleans.

Act 3 begins with a trumpet flourish, the first accorded the English in the play. The trumpets introduce Henry VI. It is his first appearance in the play, and he enters into Parliament in state, surrounded by English peers. But the flourish is false and empty. In ironic contrast to the aura of kingly dignity and power evoked by the trumpeters, we see a weak and passive young king who stands helplessly aside as Winchester and Gloucester engage in a bitter factional quarrel that soon degenerates into a brawl among servingmen. The quarrel is temporarily patched up, Richard is made Duke of York, and Gloucester announces Henry's forthcoming coronation in France. On this note, some ceremony and dignity is restored to the scene as the king and the noblemen depart to the sound of stately music: [*Sennet. Flourish. Exeunt all but* EXETER].

The direction for the sennet, apparently a formal, ceremonious march, emphasizes the stateliness just concluded. Henry VI has at least acted like a king: he has settled a quarrel, created a new peer, and is setting forth to his coronation and, perhaps, to battle with the French. The sennet now seems appropriate to the occasion as does the flourish with which Henry leaves the stage. But again the flourish rings false. Exeter, remaining onstage, explains the irony:

> Aye, we may march in England or in France,
> Not seeing what is likely to ensue.
> This late dissension grown betwixt the peers
> Burns under feignèd ashes of forged love,
> And will at last break out into a flame.
> As festered members rot but by degree
> Till bones and flesh and sinews fall away,
> So will this base and envious discord breed.

This ironic pattern is repeated in act 3, scene 4. Henry is in Paris for his coronation. He, with Gloucester, York, Suffolk, and others, meets Talbot and his soldiers. This would seem an appropriate occasion for ceremonial music, but no flourish or sennet brings the king and his party onstage, nor is Talbot's entrance marked by music.

3. "Shakespeare and the Music of the Elizabethan Stage," p. 16; and *The Music in English Drama from Shakespeare to Purcell*, p. 30, respectively.

The two parties leave the stage, though, with the following stage directions: [*Sennet. Flourish. Exeunt all but* VERNON *and* BASSET]. If the music is purposefully omitted at the beginning of the scene, why is it required when all the actors but Vernon and Basset exit? The effect repeats the preceding irony. Henry meets Talbot and, after a rhetorical tribute, creates him Earl of Shrewsbury and commands him to attend the coronation. In this ceremonious vein, Henry and Talbot depart to the music of the sennet and the flourish. The music evokes the aura of royal power, but only to contrast sharply with the bitter quarrel between Vernon and Basset that immediately follows.

The flourish sounds but once more in *1 Henry VI*, at the end of act 4, scene 1. Again, the rhetorical pattern is the same. The king and his noblemen are gathered for the coronation. Here, if at any time, we should expect to hear the trumpets' clangor and the processional sennet. But no stage directions call for them. The scene again presents the peers and their quarrels, in the midst of which Sir John Fastolfe is disgraced for his cowardice and Burgundy's defection to the dauphin is discovered. After Henry and his party leave the scene, almost as an echo a flourish sounds, to which Exeter, left alone on the stage, once more croaks his raven warning (4. 1. 187–91):

> But howsoe'er, no simple man that sees
> This jarring discord of nobility,
> This shouldering of each other in the Court,
> This factious bandying of their favorites,
> But that it doth presage some ill event.

It is not mere coincidence that the musical terms "jar" and "discord" so consistently follow the pompous flourishes.

The slow tempo of the French march is put to effective rhetorical, rather than strategic, use in the next scene—act 4, scene 2. The General of Bordeaux, from his walls, taunts the trapped Talbot:

> For ere the glass that now begins to run
> Finish the process of his sandy hour,
> These eyes, that see thee now well colorèd,
> Shall see thee withered, bloody, pale, and dead.
> *[Drum afar off.]*
> Hark! Hark! The Dauphin's drum, a warning bell,
> Sings heavy music to thy timorous soul,
> And mine shall ring thy dire departure out.

The slow, funereal beat of the French march, the distant drum, seems to exhume the funeral marches that marked the deaths of Henry V and Salisbury. For Talbot they are death's harbingers.

Talbot, the last great symbol of chivalry, is gone and, with him, most ceremonious music. A sennet brings King Henry, Gloucester, and Exeter onstage at the beginning of act 5, scene 1, wherein is proposed Henry's marriage to the daughter of the Earl of Armagnac; but the royal flourish is conspicuously absent. In act 5, scene 3, trumpets sound for the meeting of Suffolk and Reignier; but, though Reignier is titular king of Naples, here they probably sound a second parley rather than a flourish. After Reignier descends from the walls and advances to meet Suffolk, the stage direction is [*Trumpets sound. Enter* REIGNIER, *below*]. Probably, the trumpets repeated their call for a parley; the repetition, of course, serves to fill the time while Reignier descends.

The unhappy story continues in *2 Henry VI*, which, once again, opens in a key of high pageantry:

> [*Flourish of trumpets, then hautboys. Enter* THE KING,
>   HUMPHREY, DUKE OF GLOUCESTER, SALISBURY,
>   WARWICK, *and* CARDINAL BEAUFORT, *on the one side,*
>   THE QUEEN, SUFFOLK, YORK, SOMERSET, *and*
>   BUCKINGHAM *on the other.*]

For the first time, hautboys playing a sennet augment the musical resources observed in the first play of the tetralogy. The players probably hired the Waits of London, the municipal musicians, especially for the play production—a practice well established both in public and in university dramatic performances.

The dramatic occasion is the welcome of Queen Margaret by the king and his peers. After the conventional speeches appropriate to the event, the noble subjects kneel shouting "Long live Queen Margaret, England's happiness!" followed by the conventional flourish. So far, so good. But the initial elation is quickly quenched as first Gloucester and then Winchester read the humiliating marriage contract. King Henry finds it acceptable, makes Suffolk a duke, then, accompanied by his queen and Suffolk, departs to the queen's coronation. Another flourish is in order at this exit, but no direction for a flourish or sennet is given in either F or Q. Clearly, this omission is intentional and fits the rhetorical pattern previously found in *1 Henry VI*. In this case, the pomp as part 2 begins, the absence of ceremonial music at the king's departure, and the plotting of Gloucester and others behind the royal back seem to provide a close dramatic and musical paraphrase of a passage in Hall's *Chronicle* (1550):

> the kynges frendes fell from hym, bothe in Englande and in Fraunce, the Lordes of his realme, fell in diuision emongst themselfes, the commons rebelled against their souereigne Lorde, and naturall Prince, feldes wer foughten, many thousandes slain, and this Quene sent home again, with asmuche misery and sorowe, as she was receiued with pompe and triumphe, suche is worldly vnstablenes, and so waueryng is false flattering fortune.[4]

The decay of medieval ideals during the reign of Henry VI is vividly illustrated by the sad parody of trial by combat which the king imposes on the armorer and Peter, his apprentice. Their trial, when contrasted with that of Bolingbroke and Mowbray in *Richard II*, seems especially grotesque. This part of the scene (act 1, scene 3) purports to show how "the commons rebelled against their souereigne Lorde," but the episode also shows Henry, Duke Humphrey, Beaufort, and others entering into a state council. Horner and Peter are brought before Henry, who appoints a time for their trial. When this far-from-kingly action ends, the cue is for a royal flourish; the effect is, again, ironic.

The use of musical instruments in the sixteenth- and seventeenth-century emblem books to symbolize political concord is discussed by John Hollander.[5] A variation of the pattern occurs in the hunting scene and the false miracle at St. Albans (act 2, scene 1). The analogy between the falcons and the ambitious nobles is drawn by the pious king:

> The winds grow high; so do your stomachs, lords.
> How irksome is this music to my heart!
> When such strings jar, what hope of harmony?
> I pray, my lords, let me compound this strife.

At this point comes news of the miracle, which the harassed king takes as a promise of "light in darkness, comfort in despair!" His

---

4. E. Hall, *Chronicle*, as quoted in Shakespeare, *The Second Part of Henry VI*, p. 162.
5. *The Untuning of the Sky*, pp. 47–50.

hope of harmony by divine intervention turns into a mockery. We should expect the point to have a musical emphasis similar to those previously noted. The folio text contains none. But the stage direction for the Mayor and Simpcox to enter in the corrupt version, *The First part of the Contention . . .* (Q1594), states:

> Enter the Maior of Saint Albones and his brethren with
> Musicke, bearing the man that had bene blind,
> betweene two in a chaire.

Which direction should we follow? Q1594 is textually corrupt, but although the speaking lines are corrupt, there is little reason to suppose that this rubric describing easily observed stage business should be inaccurate. Dover Wilson has stuck to the F version, but Andrew Cairncross has accepted the Q text.[6] The two suggested sources for the St. Albans episode provide evidence supporting Q's stage direction. The earliest version appears in Sir Thomas More's *A dyaloge of Sir Thomas More knyghte . . . (1529)*: "But to tell you forth whā the kyng was cume & ye towne full / sodaynly thys blynde man at saint Albonys shryne had hys syght agayne / And a myracle solemply ronge / and Te deū songen / so that nothyng was talked of in all the towne but thys myracle."[7]

If we accept the Q1594 stage direction, our familiar rhetorical pattern is repeated. In this case, though, the irony is directed toward religious faith instead of political loyalty. As medieval chivalry degenerates, so the king's religious faith is severely shaken by the contrast between the pious fraud and the *Te Deum Laudamus*, the long-established expression of gratitude for God's beneficent intercession. Again, if the Q rubric is correct in stating that music should sound at this dramatic point, then we may safely assume that the music was a *Te Deum* as More described. The carol *Te Deum*, no. 95 in *Medieval Carols* (*Musica Britannica* 4:83), should be appropriate for the scene.

Throughout the remainder of the play, the music simply underscores the ebb and flow of Henry's sovereignty. Act 3, scene 1, opens with a sennet, to which the king, queen, and others enter "to

---

6. Respectively, Shakespeare, *The Second Part of King Henry VI* (New Cambridge edition); and Shakespeare, *The Second Part of Henry VI* (Arden edition, 1962).

7. Chapter 43, D.ii.v. The same account, with altered spelling, appears in Foxe's *Actes & Monuments*, p. 705.

the Parliament." On this occasion Gloucester is arrested. Henry objects, but so feebly that his advisers quickly overrule him. In despair he slips away, hardly noticed by his court and certainly not noticed by the royal trumpeters, for no flourish sounds to mark his exit. The king has lost even the show of sovereignty. The musical treatment is identical in the following scene (act 3, scene 2). The trumpets sound for the entrance of king and court, this time for Gloucester's trial at Bury St. Edmund's. Again, the stage is set for a display of majesty. But the king is completely unmanned when he learns of Gloucester's murder. He attempts to control his factious peers and restless commons, then departs (lines 298–99), commanding Warwick to follow: "Come, Warwick, come, good Warwick, go with me. / I have great matters to impart to thee." Again the trumpets are silent as he exits.

The last music in the play sounds when Henry and Queen Margaret arrive to judge the participants in the Cade rebellion. The trumpets sound as Henry and Margaret come onstage; Henry grants amnesty to his subjects, receives word of York's rebellion and return from Ireland, and commands that York's approach be checked. For the moment Henry acts the true sovereign. The trumpets echo the imperial theme; they sound a flourish as the royal pair leave the castle terrace. In act 5, scene 3, a retreat sounds to mark the end of the battle between Henry and York; but, whether a drum or trumpet was used, I cannot say. Also, Warwick commands, "Sound drums and trumpets, and to London all"; but there is no rubric for the actual signals.

In *3 Henry VI* the irony we observed in the preceding plays disappears. Indeed, while the flourishes in part 3 enable us to follow the shifts in sovereignty between Henry, the duke of York, Queen Margaret, and Edward, this function is conventional. The sennet (1. 1. 205) which covers the descent of York and his party from the "state" also is familiar practice by now. The stage direction [*The drum playing and trumpet sounding.*] (4. 3. 27) does not suggest any particular score, but I propose that the musicians sound a "simple cavalquot" (see Appendix I). In five instances, however, the flourishes are so placed as to create an ambiguous effect that poses two minor textual problems. First, let us examine the ambiguities, then we may consider the textual problems.

In act 1, scene 1, line 49, the stage direction is [*Flourish. Enter* KING HENRY, CLIFFORD, NORTHUMBERLAND, WESTMORELAND, EXETER,

and the rest]. This is the conventional fanfare as the king enters
Parliament to take his place in state. Before the king enters, however,
Richard has just placed himself in the seat, and Warwick makes a
ringing proclamation of his claim:

> Neither the King, nor he that loves him best,
> The proudest he that holds up Lancaster,
> Dares stir a wing if Warwick shake his bells.
> I'll plant Plantagenet, root him up who dares.
> Resolve thee, Richard. Claim the English crown.

Immediately, as Warwick speaks the word "crown," the royal flourish
peals—for Henry, yes, but timed to coincide with Warwick's proclamation. Henry is the rightful king, but Richard is on the throne with
powerful support. The trumpets thus ring out for both.

The fanfare indicated between act 1, scenes 1 and 2, perplexes
modern editors attempting to separate the scenes. Henry and Exeter
depart at the end of scene 1; Richard Crookback, Edward, and
Montague enter at the beginning of scene 2, followed, three lines
later, by the duke of York, claimant to the crown. The folio rubric is
printed thus:

> *Henry.* The losse of those three Lords torments my heart:
>   Ile write vnto them, and entreat them faire;
>   Come Cousin, you shall be the Messenger.
> *Exet.* And I, I hope, shall reconcile them all.   *Exit.*
>   *Flourish. Enter Richard, Edward, and Montague.*
> *Richard.* Brother, though I bee youngest, giue mee leaue.
> *Edward.* No, I can better play the Orator.
> *Mount.* But I have reasons strong and forceable.
>   *Enter the Duke of Yorke.*

Conventionally, the flourish should signal the exit of Henry, but he
departs considerably diminished in majesty. A flourish at this point,
perhaps, might be another example of irony. The trumpets would not
raise any clamor, normally, for Richard, Edward, or Montague. The
duke of York, while a powerful contender, is not the rightful king.
And yet the stage direction clearly calls for a flourish at this point.
Either F's direction is in error or the fanfare is made deliberately
ambiguous. If the latter, then it sounds for both Henry's exit and
York's entrance—one who is losing his grip on the scepter, and the
other who is being urged to seize it. If there is no pause in per-

formance between the two scenes, the fanfare would create an ironic elision from one scene to the next.

A deliberate ambiguity might solve the problem that has vexed several modern editors. Neilson and Hill, Hart, and Craig have cut the Gordian knot by omitting the flourish.[8] Wilson and Cairncross have retained it, but moved it to the ending of act 1, scene 1, thus assigning it, at least typographically, to Henry.[9] The crux might have been avoided, if not solved, had these editors placed scene numbers in the margin rather than between the lines of text.

At the beginning of act 3, scene 3, a flourish sounds for the entrance of Louis, the French king, come to give audience to Elizabeth and Warwick. Again, the flourish has its conventional function. But, assuming the performance to have been continuous, that there was no break between this and the preceding scene, the effect is similar to that in act 1, scene 1. Before the fanfare for Louis, Richard Crookback concludes his powerful soliloquy on "how to get the crown" with the words:

> I can add colors to the chameleon,
> Change shapes with Proteus for advantages,
> And set the murderous Machiavel to school.
> Can I do this, and cannot get a crown?
> Tut, were it farther off, I'll pluck it down. [*Exit*]

Immediately the trumpets clamor and we are in Louis' court. But an audience which would automatically associate the word "crown" with the flourish would also link Richard to the fanfare in a musical foreshadowing—a promise that he is not an idle schemer. The ambiguous flourish also permits an interesting *liaison des scènes.* When the flourish begins, the mental association is with Richard and the crown; it ends, sounding for King Louis of France, and the scene is now the French court. It is as simple as that.

The next ambiguity occurs with the fanfare between act 4, scenes 7 and 8, in which two contending kings—Edward and Henry—are shown. The flourish that sounds for the entrance of King Henry at the beginning of scene 8 could equally well have sounded for King

8. Respectively, Shakespeare, *The Complete Plays and Poems of William Shakespeare*, ed. W. Neilson and C. Hill; Shakespeare, *The Third Part of King Henry the Sixth*, ed. H. Hart; and Shakespeare, *The Complete Works.*

9. Shakespeare, *The Third Part of King Henry VI*, ed. J. Wilson; Shakespeare, *The Third Part of Henry VI*, ed. A. Cairncross.

Edward's exit at the end of scene 7, again assuming continuous performance. By sounding for both kings simultaneously, the trumpets
shift the scene of Edward before York to the scene showing Henry
in his London palace, again linking the two scenes by music.

A flourish also links act 5, scenes 3 and 4. As scene 3 ends, the
victorious King Edward leads his forces from the battlefield near
Barnet. A flourish had brought him onto the scene, and we might
expect a fanfare at his exit. Indeed, F's stage direction calls for a
flourish immediately thereafter. But the trumpets apparently should
be associated with Queen Margaret, who enters with a stirring speech
intended to rally her defeated army. In continuous performance,
however, the flourish sounds both for the exit of Edward and the
entrance of Margaret—the two scenes again linked by the trumpet
music.

Here again we see that editors who divide the act into separate
scenes have created a problem. The folio rubric is printed in this
manner:

> *King.* In euery Countie as we goe along,
>   Strike vp the Drumme, cry courage, and away. *Exeunt.*
>   *Flourish. March. Enter the Queene, young Edward,*
>   *Somerset, Oxford, and Souldiers.*
> *Qu.*   Great Lords, wise men ne'r sit and waile their losse,
>   But chearely seeke how to redresse their harmes.

If we separate the scenes at this point, we must assign the flourish
either to the end of one scene or to the beginning of the following. In
the editions of Neilson and Hill and Craig, the flourish is simply
omitted.[10] Hart has placed the fanfare at the end of scene 3, thus assigning it to Edward and typographically denying it to Margaret.[11]
The result, as we now have some reason to believe, may be misleading. Again, future editors might avoid such problems by placing inserted scene numerals in the margins rather than between lines of text.

In *Richard III* there is less music than in the plays comprising
Henry VI. Sennets, flourishes, and a retreat are called for; their use,
however, is largely as conventional as it is infrequent. The ceremonious and military scenes containing most of the music in *Henry VI*
are largely replaced by the plots and slaughters of *Richard III*. The

10. Shakespeare, *The Complete Plays and Poems*; Shakespeare, *The Complete Works*, respectively.
11. Shakespeare, *The Third Part of King Henry the Sixth*.

concentration of this play on the character and acts of Richard also limits the quantity of music employed; as Richard has no music in him, so his tragedy is fit mainly for treasons, spoils, and stratagems.

The fanfare that opens act 2, scene 1, introduces King Edward, briefly seen in his last council, wherein he tries to make peace between the quarreling factions. At the beginning of act 3, scene 1 [*The trumpets sound.*], possibly with a flourish for the young Prince of Wales, but more likely with a sennet to mark the stateliness of the occasion and to bring onto the stage the sizable party accompanying the prince. In act 3, scene 1, line 150, another sennet, this time specified as such, moves the party, excepting Gloucester, Buckingham, and Catesby, from the scene. Not until act 4, scene 2, do we hear music again, when a sennet sounds for Richard, come from his coronation to mount the throne in his palace. Customarily, a flourish precedes the sennet, but in this instance the fanfare is not sounded until Richard actually seats himself on the throne, three lines after the coronation processional has filled the stage. The sennet, of course, furnishes ceremonious music. The absence of the heralding trumpets, though, suggests that the sennet is intended to elide scenes 1 and 2 in the manner observed in *3 Henry VI*.

As we recall, the last sennet (3. 1. 150) before Richard's coronation ushered the two young princes to the Tower. Richard's coronation sennet sounds pat following Queen Elizabeth's address to that grim tower:

> Pity, you ancient stones, those tender babes
> Whom envy hath immured within your walls!
> Rough cradle for such little pretty ones!
> Rude ragged nurse, old sullen playfellow
> For tender Princes, use my babies well!
> So foolish sorrow bids your stones farewell.
>
> [*Exeunt.*]

The sennet played as the queen concludes her lines recalls the earlier sennet associated with the two children. The effect is again an ironic linking of the two scenes by the music—the princes' march to the Tower with Richard's march to the throne. This function of the sennet seems more credible when we note that, when Richard and his court leave the stage, no sennet is called for. The trumpets are silent.

In act 4, scene 4, line 148, Richard commands his trumpeters and drummers to sound "A flourish, trumpets! Strike alarum, drums!" to drown out the duchess of York, his mother, as she rails against him. His turning the royal flourish into a "clamorous report of war" against his own mother is one more mark of his monstrosity in Nature. Another flourish peals as Richard, at the end of act 4, scene 4, departs for the "royal battle" at Salisbury. The final trumpet that sounds for him (act 5, scene 5) blows a retreat signaling his death and his defeat by Richmond. The retreat is echoed by a final fanfare (not included in the Q texts) as the crown is delivered to Richmond and the War of Roses comes to a weary end.

The musical resources required by Shakespeare's first chronicle tetralogy are not great—a few trumpets, a drum or two, and on one occasion a band of hautboys. Yet, considering the type and subject matter of these plays and observing the use of the music in them, these resources seem quite sufficient and effective. Pageantry, rhetoric, sometimes bombast, have their places, and among them the trumpet and drum find congenial fellowship. That Shakespeare linked scenes with trumpet flourishes or other music apparently has not been recognized by editors, and this oversight has created for them several problems where, perhaps, none existed. Some modification in editorial practice might be appropriate in order to indicate these elisions.

THREE

Titus Andronicus

HE STUDY OF THE MUSIC IN *Titus Andronicus* IS COM-
plicated by several textual problems. While recent
editors have designated the Q and F texts as "good"
texts, generally speaking, the musical rubrics in
the Q texts and those in the First Folio differ. These
discrepancies have caused considerable editorial confusion. J. C.
Maxwell has restricted himself to the musical directions found in the
Q1 text, believing they were taken directly from the author's manuscript.[1] H. B. Baildon, Neilson and Hill, and Craig have used
both texts—Q1 and the First Folio.[2] I have chosen to examine the
textual problems posed by the two sets of musical stage directions.
While the Q texts may be closer to the author's manuscript than
F, I will demonstrate that F's directions for music in no way con-
tradict their equivalents in the Q texts. In most cases, F's directions
clarify and augment those in the Q texts.

Sir E. K. Chambers, in discussing the Q1594 text of *The First
part of the Contention . . .* , has suggested that its musical directions
were intended to guide the actors and that the parallel musical
directions in the F version of *2 Henry VI* "might well be the author's,
perhaps expanded by a book-keeper; those of Q an adaptation for
a 'plot.'" He concluded that Q1594 is primarily an acting version,
F a reading version.[3] If his suggestion is correct, it might also apply
to the Q and F versions of *Richard III* and *Titus Andronicus*, for
in each case the differences between the Q and F musical directions
are similar to those discussed by Chambers. In these instances, Q's
directions are more general than their parallels in F. The quarto directions never use the more specialized terms "flourish" or "sennet"; they
state, "Trumpets sound," "Sound trumpets," or "Sound." Nor do direc-

---

1. Shakespeare, *Titus Andronicus*, p. xiv.

2. Shakespeare, *Titus Andronicus*; Shakespeare, *The Complete Plays and
Poems*; and Shakespeare, *The Complete Works,* respectively.

3. *William Shakespeare: A Study of Facts and Problems* 1:283–84. Cairncross stated that the Q text is "a report of *2 Henry VI*—as it is substantially
given in F—by a group of actors who played in it" (*2 Henry VI*, p. xxi).

tions calling for hautboys (waits, shawms) appear in these Q texts—possibly because a band of hautboys was not available to the actors when the plays in question were given their earliest performances.

For these reasons, and considering the additional evidence that follows, I believe that F's directions for music in *Titus Andronicus* are as valid as those in the Q texts and that F supplies a more detailed account of the music as it was actually used in the play's most complete early productions.

The music in *Titus Andronicus* apparently is intended to add to the spectacle. A flourish opens the play as the tribunes and senators enter the senate house "aloft." The quartos omit this flourish, but it is an effective way to gain the audience's attention. It also provides ceremonious music as the Roman statesmen enter. Saturninus and Bassianus then appear, each accompanied by drums and trumpets. There is no direction that these instruments be played; they are merely symbols representing the respective armies of the two contenders and hence indicate the threat of civil war. As Marcus Andronicus concludes his pacifying speech, SATURNINUS *and* BASSIANUS *go up into the Capitol* (line 63). Again, the Q texts are silent here, but the flourish directed by F clearly salutes the reconciliation of the two brothers and fills time while the two go "aloft" to join the tribunes and senators.

Drumbeats and the clangor of trumpets introduce onto the stage Titus Andronicus' victorious entry into Rome (line 69). This is sheer spectacle, an attempt to suggest an ancient Roman triumph. The music performed here was probably a military drum march punctuated by trumpet fanfares. The trumpets sound again (line 149) as the slain sons of Titus are laid into the tomb. And now we must consider another textual problem.

The stage direction in the Q texts is *Sound Trumpets, and lay the Coffin in the Tombe.* The folio direction adds a flourish and at least one more coffin; thus,

> *Flourish. Then Sound Trumpets, and lay the Coffins in the Tombe.*

At first glance, we appear to have duplicate directions; the *Flourish* seems redundant. The plural *Coffins* may be an F revision for a performance in which two coffins—one for each son—were used. But we should keep in mind the ritualistic actions portrayed. After

Alarbus is ceremoniously sacrificed, Lucius states, "Remaineth nought but to inter our brethren, / And with loud 'larums welcome them to Rome." The antecedent of "them" can only be "brethren," and the trumpets sound, surely, the "loud 'larums." No doubt Shakespeare intended to portray a pagan Roman funeral done with high ceremony. The two dead brothers are being returned to the house of the family ancestors and heroes—the tomb of the Andronici—after which they will be worshipped as family gods (*manes*).[4] In this sense, their spirits are welcomed back to Rome; the trumpet flourish salutes them. *Then*, as F's direction states, the trumpets play as the coffins are laid in the tomb. Titus, as *pater familias* and priest, delivers the ritual eulogy. Hence, I infer that the flourish sounds the 'larums to welcome the victorious spirits of the dead, and the trumpets sound a solemn valedictory as the bodies are entombed. If so, it is possible that both salutation and valediction were employed under the single, general direction in the Q texts, and that the *Flourish. Then . . .* was added later to clarify the action on the stage. The customary flourish would do for the salutation; for the valediction, I suggest the "Retraite" shown in Appendix I.

The next direction for a flourish (line 233) also involves us in a textual difficulty. The folio direction follows Marcus' proclamation of Saturninus as emperor:

> *A long Flourish till they come downe.*

This flourish is, of course, a part of the proclamation. But, as the direction makes clear, it also sounds to fill the time required for Saturninus, Bassianus, the tribunes, and the senators to descend from "aloft." This direction, not found in the Q texts, places modern editors in a quandary. The personal address used by Marcus to Titus and his sons (beginning line 169) indicates that Marcus confronts Titus when he offers Titus the palliament (line 182). Some editors have inserted a stage direction at line 168, for Marcus, the tribunes, Saturninus, and Bassianus to descend at that point, apparently leaving the senators above.[5] The folio's *long Flourish* that sounds later would hence sound only for the senators to descend.

I think that the insertion of this stage direction at line 168 is not

4. See F. de Coulanges, *The Ancient City*, bk. 1, chap. 4; bk. 3, chap. 16; and bk. 4, chap. 1.
5. Shakespeare, *The Complete Plays and Poems*, ed. Neilson and Hill; and Shakespeare, *The Complete Works*, ed. Craig.

sufficiently warranted. In the absence of directions describing Marcus' presentation of the palliament to Titus, we do not know that his descent, and that of the others, is either necessary or intended at this point. The folio direction for the long flourish is the only direct textual evidence regarding the time required for their descent, and the adjective "long" suggests strongly that a considerable number of actors—more than the senators—had to move from "aloft" to the main stage. It is probably this practical necessity that explains the long flourish directed at line 233.

The next musical performance occurs in act 1, scene 1, line 275. There seems little doubt that a flourish is sounded here. Saturninus commands (line 275), "Proclaim our honours, lords, with trump and drum." That the flourish also accompanies Saturninus courting Tamora in dumb show, as some editors direct, is a moot question.[6] Although such a direction has no authority from the Q and F texts, one might agree that Saturninus' exchange of Lavinia for Tamora is startlingly sudden. If a courtship, however brief, seems necessary, I suppose that its presentation in pantomime is one way to solve the problem. Elizabethan dramatists conventionally used trumpet music to sustain aural interest during a dumb show.

The stage direction *Flourish* which concludes act 1 appears only in F. As editors have long noted, the direction is misplaced. The trumpets play the conventional flourish for the exit of a ruler, not for Aaron's entrance, which opens act 2.

The hunting scene (act 2, scene 2) provides some variety in instrumentation via the hunting horn. The folio's first stage direction is *Enter Titus Andronicus and his three sonnes, making a noyse with hounds and hornes, and Marcus.* They have come to awaken Saturninus for the hunting party. I do not know what horn peals may have sounded at the entrance of Titus and his sons: the direction might anticipate the Q direction ten lines later, *Here a crie of Hounds, and winde hornes in a peale,* which F includes, as well as a prefatory *Winde Hornes.* The second direction describes, as the context indicates, a "hunts-up" or aubade to rouse the emperor. Fortunately, the notation for Elizabethan hunting peals has been preserved in Turberville's *The Noble Arte of Venerie or Hunting . . . (1575).* The first peal he includes is a hunts-up that he names "The Call for the Companie in the morning" (see Appendix VI).

<hr/>

6. Shakespeare, *The Complete Plays and Poems,* ed. Neilson and Hill; and Shakespeare, *The Complete Works,* ed. Craig.

The hunting horns peal again, according to F, as, during the hunt, Marcus enters a covert and discovers the ravished and mutilated Lavinia. The direction (2. 4. 10) is *Winde Hornes. / Enter Marcus from hunting, to Lauinia.* In this case, Turberville's horn peal "The Straking from Covert to Covert" seems appropriate. We may well believe that the producers of the Elizabethan performances would pay attention to such musical details. The use of various horn peals could suggest the progress of the hunt taking place offstage. Venery was a living art for Shakespeare and his contemporaries; it had its proper forms and vocabulary, including specific horn calls for each stage of the hunt. Turberville said his horn signals "are set downe according to the order which is observed at these dayes in this Realme of Englande. . . ."[7]

Act 5, scene 3, provides the tragic climax, as Titus consummates his revenge in a grisly banquet. The scene is also the climax of the spectacle and the music. As befits a state banquet, trumpets sound a flourish for the entrance of the emperor, empress, tribunes, senators, et al. At line 25, F directs, *Hoboyes. / A Table brought in. Enter Titus like a Cooke*, etc. The quarto texts state here: *Trumpets sounding. Enter Titus like a Cooke*, etc. The disparity between instruments required by each text has caused some editors to include the hautboys, some to omit them; some to include the trumpets, some to omit them.[8] As a matter of fact, both trumpets and hautboys were used in Elizabethan state banquets. The normal procedure was for the trumpets to play a fanfare upon the entrance of royalty, and for the hautboys to play a processional march as the monarch and his train moved into the banqueting hall. The hautboys also played during the banquet, their music punctuated by trumpet fanfares as each course was served. It is possible that only trumpets were available for the performances reported in the Q texts; on a later occasion the trumpets may have been augmented by hautboys as directed in F. If this were the case, this scene provides the first example of Shakespeare's increasing and varying the instrumentation to emphasize a play's climax—a technique that he used frequently in the later comedies.[9]

As for actual performance, I would suppose that the trumpets sound at the entrance of Saturninus and the hautboys play a short

7. G. Turberville, *The Noble Arte of Venerie or Hunting . . . (1575)*.
8. Neilson and Hill included both hautboys and trumpets; Maxwell included trumpets but omitted hautboys; Craig included hautboys but omitted trumpets.
9. J. Long, *Shakespeare's Use of Music: The Final Comedies*, pp. 8–9, 12, 47.

march (beginning at line 25). This march then continues until all the actors are onstage, the table has been brought out, and the company is seated. A trumpet flourish then announces the first course as Titus enters *placing the meat on the Table.* At this point all music ceases.

Figure 1.

For the processional march I suggest "The Lord Souches maske," no. 23 in Morley's *The First Booke of Consort Lessons* ... (1599) (see figure 1). The cantus voice is the treble viol part unchanged. The bassus part is pieced together from Morley's pandora part, since the original bass viol part is unavailable. While Morley scored this march for a broken consort, the parts can be taken by a whole consort of hautboys.

FOUR

Romeo and Juliet

HE LYRIC BEAUTY OF *Romeo and Juliet* IS HAUNTED by a brooding sense of paradox and antithesis in which an exuberant joy in glorious youth is coupled with a poignant awareness of how swift bright things come to confusion. The conflicts between love and hate, youth and age, life and death are all a net in which the universal lovers are tragically entrapped. Shakespeare expressed this bittersweet antithesis, irony, and paradox with extravagant figures of speech, but he also used music to attain the same end. The lovers' first meeting at the Capulet ball provides not only an excellent example of the antithetical quality of the entire play but also includes the first music performed in the play—[*Music plays, and they dance.*] (1. 5. 28). In order to observe the part music plays in the scene, we should attempt to visualize the stage performance suggested by the text.

When old Capulet commands, "Come, musicians, play," the maskers begin to dance. Romeo, we remember, has insisted that he does not wish to dance. When he sees Juliet, however, he says (lines 52–53), "The measure done, I'll watch her place of stand, / And, touching hers, make blessèd my rude hand." Tybalt protests Romeo's presence at the ball and is restrained by Capulet (lines 56–94). Romeo by then has met Juliet and speaks for the first time to her: "If I profane with my unworthiest hand / This holy shrine. . . ." The sonnet lines are spoken as Romeo and Juliet dance, if we may take Juliet's answer to the Nurse literally: "A rhyme I learned even now / Of one I danced withal." The dance probably ends at line 113, where the Nurse speaks to Juliet. One question remains: When did Romeo begin the dance with Juliet?

Shakespeare was careful to keep the hatred of the feud poised against the love of Romeo and Juliet, and he frequently used antitheses to achieve the same effect ("O brawling love, O loving hate"). In keeping with this rhetorical device I think that he had Romeo begin the dance with Juliet during Tybalt's angry words with Capulet. The Elizabethans believed the dance symbolized mating or the union of

(39)

man and woman in marriage, just as musical harmony symbolized
love, both human and divine. The effect achieved is thus a powerful
antithesis—the young couple's love opposed to Tybalt's expression
of hatred. The "rhyme" that Juliet learned from Romeo sums up the
dramatic point:

> My only love sprung from my only hate!
> Too early seen unknown, and known too late!
> Prodigious birth of love it is to me,
> That I must love a loathèd enemy.

Music and dance thus perform a rhetorical and symbolic function
aimed at increasing dramatic irony. Once this effect has been
achieved, the dance ends and the maskers depart.

The musicians probably began playing at Capulet's cue for music
and continued without interruption until the Nurse intervenes (line
113). Either a broken consort or a whole consort of viols, supple-
mented with a tambour or small drum, would be proper here.
Obviously, the music was subdued—loud enough to be heard in the
background but soft enough not to interfere with the actors' lines.
The musicians were perhaps placed in an upper gallery or music
room.

The type of dance music performed poses a problem. Usually, a
ball was opened with a pavane, followed by a galliard, followed by a
coranto or lavolta—a change from a slow, stately rhythm to a quick,
energetic one. Romeo states (line 53), "The measure done, I'll watch
her place. . . ." The late Otto Gombosi presented good evidence that
the term "measure," when applied to a kind of dance, refers to the
"quadro" pavane or, as it was also called, the "passamezzo moderno."[1]
Romeo's remark thus suggests that he waits until the end of the measure
or pavane and then begins his dance with Juliet at the opening of the
galliard, which usually followed the pavane. This would be awkward
for a stage presentation; I doubt that time would permit both a pavane
and a galliard to be staged. Also, the pavane and galliard were normally
danced *en suite*, which might cause some difficulty if Romeo begins the
dance in the middle of the suite. But even if successfully begun, the
lively galliard, which involved leaps into the air, would interfere with
the lines the lovers speak as they dance. For dramatic presentation,
therefore, I suggest that the "measure" continues throughout the scene

1. "Some Musical Aspects of the English Court Masque," pp. 12–18.

and that Romeo began his dance with Juliet with one of the "strains" or repeated portions of the music. For this purpose, I have included the first composition in Morley's *First Booke of Consort Lessons . . .* (1599), which is a quadro pavane. The treble viol part and a pandora bass part are shown in figure 2.

Mercutio's bawdy song "An old hare hoar" is part of the fun he

Figure 2.

has at the Nurse's expense as she accosts Romeo (2. 2. 140). His mind on the earlier lewd conceits of the three young men, Mercutio naturally assumes that the Nurse is a bawd. When he sees her approach Romeo, his solemnity flees; he is delighted and whoops, "A bawd, a bawd, a bawd! So ho!" The hunting cry for sighting a hare prompts Romeo's question, "What hast thou found?" Mercutio answers by bursting into his song with its obvious play on the words "hare" and "hoar":

> An old hare hoar,
> And an old hare hoar,
> Is very good meat in Lent.
> But a hare that is hoar,
> Is too much for a score
> When it hoars ere it be spent.

If Mercutio sings these lines—most editors mark them as sung, though there is no direction to this effect in the Q or F texts—he would, of course, have no instrumental accompaniment. From sheer ebullience he would simply burst into song. The song's tune is unknown; in fact, I know of no other versions. I would guess that the words were set to some raffish ballad tune. I have, therefore, set them to a contemporary popular tune called "Up Tails All." The early texts using this tune are now lost; the text supplied by Chappell is eighteenth-century. The tune appears in *The Fitzwilliam Virginal Book* (c. 1610), and a ballad with this title is mentioned in Sharpham's *Fleire* (1610), Jonson's *Every man out of his humor* (1599), and Beaumont and Fletcher's *The Coxcomb* (1608–1610). Later, the tune appears in Playford's *The Dancing Master* (1651) and D'Urfey's *Pills to purge Melancholy* (1707). As the tune is a little altered in its various printings, I have used the version in W. Chappell's *Popular Music of the Olden Time*[2] shown in figure 3.

As a parting shot at the Nurse, Mercutio speaks or sings a fragment of another popular song—with sarcastic intent, of course: "Farewell, ancient lady, farewell [*Singing*], 'lady, lady, lady.' " The three "lady's" have been described by Kittredge and others as a part of the ballad "Susanna," or "The Constancy of Susanna," as it is titled in W. Chappell's *The Roxburghe Ballads*.[3] Naylor has noticed

2. Chappell, ed., *Popular Music of the Olden Time* 1:196, 2:773.
3. Volume 1, p. 190. See Shakespeare, *Romeo and Juliet*, ed. G. Kittredge, p. 157.

that Sir Toby, in *Twelfth Night* (act 2, scene 3), sings, "There dwelt a man in Babylon," which is the first line of a ballad quoted by Percy:

> There dwelt a man in Babylon
> Of reputation great by fame;
> He took to wife a faire woman,
> Susanna she was callde by name.
> A woman fair and vertuous,
> Lady, lady!
> Why should we not of her learn thus
> To live godly?[4]

This is no doubt the ballad from which Sir Toby sings a fragment; but the "lady, lady, lady," Mercutio sings is, I think, from an older and more popular ballad, probably an amorous ballad of which "The Constancy of Susanna" is a "godlified," and hence later, ballad.

Figure 3.

In the *Heber Collection of Broadsides and Ballads* is a song dated 1559 with the title "The panges of Love & lovers fires." The first verse is as follows:

> Was not good Kyng Salamon
> Ravished in sondry wyse
> With every lively Paragon
> That glistered before his eyes
> If this be true as trewe it was
> Lady lady.
> Why should not I serve you alas
> My deare lady.[5]

This ballad seems more appropriate to Mercutio's character and to the wit he directs at the Nurse than "Susanna," which is a moralistic

4. *Shakespeare and Music*, p. 183; Percy, *Reliques of Ancient English Poetry* . . . 1:200.
5. Huntington Library Copy 18262–348, Heber Collection.

"godly" ballad. Moreover, "The panges of Love" was probably quite familiar to Shakespeare and to his audience, enough so that the fragment would bring to mind at least the subject of the complete ballad. Rollins described this song as "perhaps the most popular ballad written during Queen Elizabeth's reign."[6] The text was registered by William Elderton in 1558–1559.[7] Its tune, "King Solomon," was used for a song in the *History of Horestes* (1567), the same year in which a godlified version appeared in *The Gude and Godlie Ballatis*.[8] An imitation of the ballad was included (no. 10) in *A Handful of Pleasant Delites* (*1584*), a collection John Ward has described as aimed at "the man-in-the-street."[9] The tune "King Solomon" was used for several ballads, including one in *Laugh and lie downe . . .* (1605),

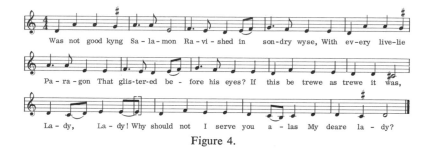

Figure 4.

a set of satirical songs by "T. C." In this case, T. C. includes "a dittie that I have mede to the tune of Lady, Lady, my fair Lady," obviously a reference to "The panges of Love."[10] The probability exists, therefore, that this old, amorous, familiar ballad was the reference that Shakespeare intended and one that his audience caught.

The tune for "The panges of Love" survives as "King Solomon," a cittern piece added about 1570 to *The Mulliner Book*, and as an untitled piece noted by Ward in *The Dublin Virginal Manuscript* copied about the same time and shown in figure 4.[11]

6. H. Rollins, "An Analytical Index to the Ballad Entries . . ." pp. 12, 163. F. Sternfeld ("Music and Ballads," p. 219) believed Mercutio to be quoting a tag found in several ballads and plays.
7. J. Ward, "Music for 'A Handefull of pleasant delites,'" p. 160.
8. E. Reed, *Songs from the British Drama*, p. 16; and A. Mitchell, *A Compendious Book of Godly and Spiritual Songs . . .* p. 213.
9. Page 151.
10. Huntington Library copy of *Laugh and lie downe . . .* sig. E.
11. "Music for 'A Handefull of pleasant delites,'" p. 160. See also *The Dublin Virginal Manuscript*, p. 47.

The proposed wedding between Juliet and Paris is the occasion for the next performance of music (act 4, scenes 4 and 5). Paris appears outside the Capulet palace, which is astir with early morning preparations for Juliet's nuptials. He brings some musicians to awaken her with a morning serenade, or aubade. The cue for the music is given by a stage direction and also by old Capulet: "Good faith, 'tis day. / The County will be here with music straight, / For so he said he would. [*Music within.*] I hear him near."

The music contributes to the festivity and sets the time, that is, early morning. Moreover, as it is Paris who brings the musicians, we see here Shakespeare's first association of the serenade or aubade with the unsuccessful suitor—a pattern he would use throughout his dramatic career. Apparently, Shakespeare thought the use of musicians to forward a love suit suggested some falsity or lack of ardor in the suitor—an artificial, as opposed to a natural, expression of love. The bridal music also elides scenes 4 and 5. In scene 4 we see Capulet and his servants busily preparing the wedding feast. After explaining the purpose of the music heard offstage, Capulet sends the Nurse to awaken Juliet. In the Q and F texts the action is not interrupted as the Nurse exits, presumably on her way to Juliet's chamber, and appears before the chamber door, as scene 5 opens. Capulet exits at the same time as the Nurse, going, as he explains, to chat with Paris. Scene 4 is hence probably placed on the outer stage. At the end of the scene, with the exits of the Nurse and Capulet, the outer stage is momentarily empty. The Nurse then re-enters the outer stage and knocks on a stage door, which then represents the entrance to Juliet's bedchamber. The music, which we assume is sounding continuously and which Capulet has previously associated with Juliet, thus serves as a musical bridge between the outer stage as the lobby or hall of the palace and the outer stage as the hall before Juliet's chamber. It also fills the gap in action while the stage is temporarily vacant.

The most interesting function of the music in this case, as I see it, is its use to create in the audience an emotional effect—a peculiar blend of comedy with tragic irony. Shakespeare, I believe, deliberately introduced the comic element to counter the tragic potentialities of scene 5. After all, a plot in which the happy bridegroom comes to meet his bride and finds her wedded to Death has countless possibilities for tragic irony. Shakespeare was no doubt quite aware of these possibilities. He also knew that he must reserve the full tragic effect for the actual catastrophe and not permit the audience to exhaust its emotions on a feigned catastrophe. Consequently, he wrote this scene as close to a burlesque as he could without turning it into a farce. Now let us see how valid this hypothesis is and, in the process, note how the music fits into the scheme.

Granville-Barker has made the following comment on this scene:

> The text tells us pretty plainly what music is needed. It is a consort of recorders that Paris brings with him to the wedding; and the musicians either enter with him, playing, to be stopped incontinently by the sight of the tragic group around the bed; or (this is, I think, more likely) they stay playing the bridal music without, a tragically ironical accompaniment to the lamenting over Juliet, till they are stopped and come clustering—scared, incongruous figures —into the doorway.
>
> "Faith, we may put up our pipes and be gone," says the leader, when the mourners depart (all but the Nurse, who needs a line or two to speak while she draws the inner-stage curtains) leaving them alone.[12]

This is the way the action is usually staged, and I would agree that Granville-Barker's is the better alternative. But that the effect was intended to be "tragically ironical" I doubt, because I do not think the scene was supposed to create a "tragic" (in the full sense of the word) effect. Nor am I alone in this opinion. As long ago as 1900, Dowden, editing the early Arden edition, quoted Grant White's observation that in act 4, scene 5, "this speech of mock heroic woe" was intended to ridicule the 1581 translation of Seneca's tragedies, as was also the play of Pyramus and Thisbe in *A Midsummer Night's Dream*.[13] More recently, S. L. Bethell, considering the scene in question, has stated that it is a burlesque and should be played so. He has also mentioned a production by Terence Gray in the Festival Theater at Cambridge in which the scene was so played.[14]

Most would agree, I think, that the speeches in this scene, until Friar Lawrence speaks, are notable mainly for high-flown rhetoric. For example:

LADY CAP. Accurst, unhappy, wretched, hateful day! (43)

12. H. Granville-Barker, *Prefaces to Shakespeare* 2:327–28.
13. Shakespeare, *Romeo and Juliet*, ed. E. Dowden, p. 52.
14. *Shakespeare and the Popular Dramatic Tradition*, pp. 110–11.

NURSE. Oh, woe! Oh, woeful, woeful, woeful day! (49)

PAR. Beguiled, divorced, wronged, spited, slain! (55)

CAP. Despised, distressed, hated, martyred, killed! (59)

This can only be an artificial woe for a feigned death. Friar Lawrence puts an end to the clamor: "Peace ho, for shame! Confusion's cure lives not / In these confusions." Once the discovery of Juliet's feigned death is enacted, seriousness returns with the friar's consoling speech.

And how does the music fit into the picture? I believe that the musicians continue to play offstage through the clamorous lamenting until Friar Lawrence ends the burlesque. The combination of merry wedding music, the actors tearing a passion to tatters, and the musicians' later puns and riddles, while not entirely erasing the tragic mood, tempers it and postpones any strong emotional effect on the audience until the death scene in the genuine catastrophe.[15]

Three or four musicians, perhaps the three who carry on the word-play with Peter and the Nurse, could have performed the music. The screnaders were probably two instrumentalists, one of whom doubled as a singer. This is the number Shakespeare usually employed for serenades. Granville-Barker has suggested that the musicians played recorders and, since there is no indication that the singer mentioned by Peter actually sings, which would prevent his piping, I see no reason to disagree. Of course, Q1 mentions fiddlers, and the names "Catling," "Rebicke" (rebec), and "Soundpost" all refer to string instruments or their parts. But these terms may have been used loosely to apply to any instrumentalist. Simon, Hugh, and James are characterized as minstrels or vagabond pipers. Their

15. The lines that Peter sang ("When griping grief the heart would wound, / And doleful dumps the mind oppress, / Then music with her silver sound— / ... With speedy help doth lend redress"), from Richard Edwards' poem "In Commendation of Music" (1576), are Peter's "own comical way of introducing a not so 'sullen dirge.' ... The lamentable fate of the lovers, and to a lesser extent, the grief of Juliet's parents, merited dulcet and refined strains, not the loud merriment of the clown and his consort. ... Instead, they lingered, joked, punned and listened to Peter's song. ... In its oblique way the merry dump became the requisite dirge" (F. Sternfeld, *Music in Shakespearean Tragedy*, pp. 102–4). In his study, pp. 120–21, Sternfeld provided a setting for Edwards' song found in the Brogyntyn Lute Book. R. Ingram ("Musical Pauses and the Vision Scenes in Shakespeare's Last Plays," p. 237) remarked, "Paris' arrival is heralded by cheerful music which adds to the gay bustle in the Capulet household. The noise swells, enhancing the ensuing sudden quiet at the discovery of Juliet's corpse."

characters, plus the fact that they play a wedding aubade and act as clowns, suggest that the music they play is old, popular, and gay. I have therefore chosen an old ballad tune called "The Hunt is Up," which Chappell believed was sung in the reign of Henry VIII, possibly as early as 1537.[16] The notation is given in figure 5.

Figure 5.

In *Romeo and Juliet*, then, we observe music used for its symbolic, rhetorical, and intrinsic values and as a device to establish time and setting. The vocal music, sung only by Mercutio, consists of tags or bits of old songs—the first instance of a practice by Shakespeare that, in his later tragedies, becomes significant in revealing some of his thought about the nature of tragedy.

16. *Popular Music of the Olden Time* 1:60.

FIVE

Ballads in the Histories and Tragedies

EFORE WE CONTINUE OUR EXAMINATION OF THE music in the individual plays, we should digress in this chapter to observe the place occupied by ballads and the ballad tradition in the tragedies and histories. Such a study is overdue. Since Ritson, Percy, and Chappell, there have been many commentaries and short observations by students such as Naylor, Elson, Rollins, Seng, Sternfeld, et al., but these have been either very general treatments or unrelated examinations of specialized problems or of individual ballads. A very broad sketch appears in the first volume of this study. The subject actually requires a book to itself. But one simple and obvious—though overlooked—fact indicates that the ballad has an importance in the histories and tragedies that dictates an inquiry into at least one of its aspects. While the comedies contain many "ayres," which may be defined as art songs written and set to special music by known poets and composers, the songs in the tragedies and histories are, with one or two doubtful exceptions, ballads, ballad fragments, or bits of popular songs anonymous in authorship and apparently belonging to a popular tradition. This almost exclusive use of folk or popular songs in the noncomic plays may be observed in the plays examined in detail in the following chapters.

What affinities existed between the ballad tradition and these dramas that may explain Shakespeare's choosing ballads and excluding the more "artificial" ayres he used in the comedies? A glance at the major affinities between the two may suggest an approach to Shakespeare's reason for associating the ballads so closely with tragedy. At the start I would like to admit two caveats: (1) Shakespeare's practice in selecting the vocal music for these plays may not be unique; the scope of this work prohibits investigation of other dramatists' plays. (2) Since our inquiry will carry us into areas that are both broad and ill-defined, I will not always be able to document my statements, particularly when it comes to dating precisely some of the ballads; therefore, I must appeal to the reader's general literary experience and to his acquaintance with the general processes of oral transmission.

The ballad is a song that tells a story. The story may be tragic or it may be comic, but it contains both characters and actions. Of the two, the action usually receives more development than the characterization, which is sketched in simple and bold strokes. The ballad texts are set to simple melodic tunes usually much older than the texts. The use of old tunes is conventional because the ballad, as folk song, is transmitted orally, and an old, familiar tune simplifies the general populace's learning and broadcasting of the text, which supports and continues the ballad tradition.

The ballads, during the Elizabethan period, were "popular" in the precise sense of the word—that is, "of the whole people." The modern association of the folk ballad with either backwoods denizens and hillbillies or academic collectors loaded with briefcases and tape recorders did not exist in Elizabethan society. In Shakespeare's day king, noble, citizen, and peasant alike sang ballads, because they all shared a common tradition and were interested in the same old stories. Sir Philip Sidney, in his *Defense of Poesy*, paused to tell us how his heart was stirred by the old ballad "Chevy Chace," and the authors of the Tudor interludes and moralities could set their dramatic songs to older ballad tunes confident that the music would please nobility and commoners alike. In their homes, the sophisticated English courtiers sang popular ballads, perhaps, as Dr. Burney noted of the songs in Boccaccio, because "One species of music [carols and ballads] was a plain, simple, popular melody, generally understood and practiced by all persons well educated, on whom nature had bestowed good ears...."[1] The good doctor then mentioned the "elaborate and artificial species of music which professors only ... were able to execute." Yet even the Elizabethan professors used popular music as the basis for many an elaborate canon or division. In the lute books and virginal lessons are many divisions grounded on the old ballad tunes "Fortune my foe," "Go from my window," "Walsingham," "Mall Sims," and others.

Actually, the distinction between art songs and folk songs is often blurred in Shakespearean England. The more accurate picture is one of constant interchange and mutual adaptation. One process was absorption, usually pejorative, of art music by the folk. In Elizabeth's reign and earlier, this process was intensified by the

1. C. Burney, *A General History of Music* 1:642.

continental cultural invasion—chiefly Italian and French—and the religious practices of the Protestants, especially the dissenting sects. Modern musicology has revealed the large debt owed by English popular music to the art of professional composers of Italy and France, and it is common knowledge that many serious compositions by Byrd, Morley, Gibbons, et al., largely imitate the same sources.[2] The popular Elizabethan ballad tunes "Rogero," "Cecilia," and "Lumber me," for example, were earlier "grounds" for Italian lutenists' songs.[3] The dissenting sects, abhorring popery, turned from the sacred and liturgical music of the Roman church and set their hymns and psalms to ballad tunes or popular lute ayres. They not only sang "psalms to hornpipes," but they drew heavily on such performer-composers as John Dowland. In particular, Dowland's tunes were frequently thus used in the Low Countries. As late as 1690, Kamphuyzen's *Stichtelyke Rymen*, a popular hymn and song book, contained hymns set to Dowland's "Frog Galliard," "Can she excuse," and his most popular song, "Lacrimae (O Flow those Tears)."[4]

An intermediary party to this interchange of folk and art music was the drama—the interludes and moralities, the court plays, and the masques. Sometimes the songs in the plays were directed to be sung to popular ballad tunes. The song "Sing care away" in the anonymous *Misogonus* (1560–1577), act 2, scene 2, was intended to be set to the tune "Heart's Ease," the same tune requested by Peter in *Romeo and Juliet*.[5] In Pickering's *The History of Horestes* (1567), the ballad tune "Selengers round" is directed as the setting for the song "Farewell, adieu, that courtly life," as are the ballad tunes "King Solomon" (earlier an art song) and "The Painter" for other songs.[6] On the other hand, some tunes apparently originating as settings for dramatic songs in the early interludes were adapted as tunes for later ballads. The tunes "Queen Dido," "Troy town," and "In Creet [Crete]," I would guess, originally derive from plays written

2. Cf. O. Gombosi, *The Cultural and Folkloristic Background of the Folia*; Ward, "Music for 'A Handefull of pleasant delites' "; A. Byler, *Italian Currents in the Popular Music of England in the Sixteenth Century*.

3. Byler, *Italian Currents*, pp. 15–19; Ward, "Music for 'A Handefull of pleasant delites,' " pp. 150–51, 166–67.

4. D. Kamphuyzen, *Stichtelyke Rymen, Om te lezen of te zingen*, pp. 29, 66–67, 53, respectively.

5. Reed, *Songs from the British Drama*, pp. 12–13.

6. Ibid., pp. 15–17.

about 1560–1575, to judge from their subjects and their early use as ballad settings.[7] "Queen Dido" and "Troy town" may have appeared first in Peele's *Tale of Troy* (1589), but there were several plays based on the same subject on the boards about this time.[8] A lute version of the tune "In Creet" appears in Folger Library MS 448.16 (1559–1571). The ballad tune named "Damon and Pithias" was probably derived from the music for Pithias' song "Awake, ye woful wights" in Edwards' play *Damon and Pithias* (1565).[9] The ballad ayre "Cyclops" seems to be derived from the music used for "My shag hair Cyclops" in Lyly's *Sapho and Phao* (1584), act 4, scene 3.[10] Even the later Stuart masques contributed music to the folk tradition. The tune "Grayes Inn Maske" is a popular version of music originally composed for a great masque performed at court between 1610 and 1614.[11]

7. The only basis I have for this guess is the number of ballads directed to be sung to these tunes. "Queen Dido" was suggested by Deloney ("Strange Histories" [1602], in *The Works of Thomas Deloney*) as a tune for "The Duchess of Suffolk's Calamity" (J. Halliwell, ed., *A Catalogue of an Unique Collection* . . . p. 81). Other ballads set to this tune are "The Wandering Prince of Troy" (Halliwell, ed., *A Catalogue of an Unique Collection* . . . pp. 30, 93), "A Looking Glass for Ladies" (Chappell, ed., *The Roxburghe Ballads* 6:533), "A mirrour . . . for all sinners" (Clark, ed., *The Shirburn Ballads, 1585–1616*, p. 149). "Queen Dido" may have originated as a song in the lost academic play *Dido* by W. Gager, which was performed June 12, 1583 (E. Chambers, *The Elizabethan Stage* 4:374). Ballads directed to be sung to the tune "Troy town" include "The Fair Maid of Dunsmore," "The Londoners Lamentation," and "The Royal Wanderer" (Halliwell, ed., *A Catalogue of an Unique Collection* . . . pp. 42, 62, 109, respectively). Ballads set to the tune "In Creet" include "My minde to me a kingdom is" (H. Rollins, ed., *The Pepys Ballads* 1:229) and "The Dukes daughter of Cornwall" ("Garland of Goodwill" [1631], in *The Works of Thomas Deloney*, p. 311).

8. See the academic and Latin plays listed by Chambers, *The Elizabethan Stage* 4:373–79.

9. Edwards, *The Dramatic Writings*, p. 30. Cf. Ward, "Music for 'A Handefull of pleasant delites,'" pp. 167–69; and Long, "Music for a Song in Edwards' *Damon and Pithias*."

10. Reed, *Songs from the British Drama*, p. 32.

11. The tune probably is a popular version of an instrumental piece originally composed for Beaumont's *The Masque of the Inner Temple and Gray's Inn* (1613). In Brit. Mus. Add. MS 10444, a collection of masque and play instrumental scores (see J. Cutts, "Jacobean Masque and Stage Music"; and A. Sabol, ed., *Songs and Dances for the Stuart Masque* . . .), are six pieces written for a Gray's Inn masque (nos. 91, 99, 101, 103, 133, 134). One of these (no. 99, "Graysinne Masque") appears later as one of the "country dances" in Playford's *The English Dancing Master* (1651), p. 103. Halliwell (*A Catalogue of an Unique Collection* . . . p. 89) also listed a ballad, "A new Mad Tom of Bedlam," to be sung to the tune of "Grayes Inne Mask."

It is hence clear that the dramatic use of ballads had become established long before Shakespeare began to write. When he inserted ballad stanzas or fragments into his plays, he was working well within the limits of conventional practice. But this does not explain why he found the ballads particularly congenial to the tragedies and histories. One explanation may lie in the similar subject matter of the two.

In Elizabethan balladry there were, of course, many subjects—tragic, comic, moralistic, pious, journalistic. Those that persist throughout the folk tradition, however, are the tragic and the moralistic, frequently combined. For proof we need only note that mainly the tragic ballads—"Barbara Allen," "Lord Randall," "Edward," or "Sir Patrick Spens"—have survived and are still popular. Many modern imitations still conclude with some pious or moralistic tag. This is only natural; the poor and the ignorant live intimately with tragedy, and the moralistic stanzas often appended to their ballads are their only answers to the significance of human sorrow, pain, and death.

It is not strange, then, that among the Elizabethan populace, nurtured as it was in the ballad tradition, the playwrights found a ready and popular following for their tragedies. Of special interest to us are the common subjects, linking the tragedies of Shakespeare and the ballad tradition. Ballads with the titles "Titus Andronicus' Complaint," "King Leir and his three daughters," "Troilus and Cressida," and "A jig of Macbeth" appeared, some before and some after, performances of plays on the same subjects.[12] There is little evidence that Shakespeare drew upon these ballads when he composed the plays, but it is certain that the subjects which he chose for dramatic treatment were often part and parcel of a common tradition that both he and his audiences deemed well worn and comfortable.

We find moral lessons in the ballads and in Shakespeare's histories and tragedies. This is not to imply that Shakespeare wrote his plays principally as moral treatises. He wrote to please his audiences as did the balladeers. The fact that many a lugubrious and deadly dull moralistic lesson was set to ballad tunes mainly indicates that these "godly" texts often needed a musical sugarcoating. But underlying many a ballad and pervading Shakespeare's tragedies is a moral

12. Respectively, Chambers, *William Shakespeare* 1:314, 321; Percy, *Reliques of Ancient English Poetry* . . . 1:214–15; C. Robinson et al., *A Handful of Pleasant Delights* (1584), p. 116; J. Playford, *Musick's Delight on the Cithren* . . . p. 65.

system which is the silent partner of all tragedy. This system in Elizabeth's England was still largely medieval, as Tillyard, Lovejoy, and others have described it, though overlaid with Renaissance Neo-platonism.[13] It posited a universe created for the benefit of mankind, in perfect order and balance until original sin turned it into a vast ruin subject to the corruption and mutability that accompanied man's natural sinfulness. The microcosmic conflict between man's attempt to regain his lost paradise and the dictates of his satanic "Rude will," like two opposing kings (as Friar Lawrence muses), provided the tragic conflict that marred the music of men's lives. And always above the conflict brooded pretemporal Chaos waiting to reclaim the ordered cosmos created by God and defended only by His Grace and man's divine faculty, Reason.

Elizabethan tragedy, especially Shakespeare's, shows us the in-exorable process by which all bright things must come to confusion. Of course, we are shown much more than this, but always implicit is the tag so commonly used by the chroniclers and balladeers: "such is worldly unstablenes, and so waveryng is false flattering fortune." The fall of noble men from a high to a low estate is the staple of Elizabethan as well as Greek and medieval tragedy. The peculiar property of Elizabethan tragedy is that this fall could shake a whole cosmos—macrocosm as well as microcosm—and shatter into a thousand fragments both physical balance and that inner order which the Renaissance humanists, preaching balance and the Golden Mean, attempted to create as a brave, new world. In Shakespeare's tragedies the world becomes an unweeded garden; things rank and gross in nature possess it; men and women become wolves and tigers preying upon their proper selves; and man's divine faculty, Reason, becomes like harsh bells jangled out of tune.

Into his tragic (and historic) view of a shattered and fragmented world Shakespeare introduced only popular songs and ballads.[14] They are sung by hero, heroine, villain, and clown; by princes, ladies, topers, and gravediggers. As far as music is concerned, the world of Shakespearean tragedy is also a world of balladry. But in the

13. E. Tillyard, *Shakespeare's History Plays* and *The Elizabethan World Picture*; A. Lovejoy, *The Great Chain of Being*; H. Craig, *The Enchanted Glass*.

14. The doubtful exceptions are Pandarus' song "Love, love, nothing but love," *Troilus and Cressida* (3. 1. 118), and the drinking song "Come, thou monarch of the vine," *Antony and Cleopatra* (2. 7. 111).

histories and tragedies we never hear a complete ballad, seldom even one complete stanza or verse; what we hear are snatches and fragments. One can hardly say, then, that the ballad bits were introduced for their intrinsic musical or textual worth. Rather, their function seems purely dramatic.

In the bardic tradition, excerpts from various lays or sagas were sometimes interpolated into the song-story chanted by the bard. These added excerpts, as some modern students explain, usually point a moral or underscore some wise or unwise action by the characters in the bard's lay. This convention may underlie Shakespeare's use of the ballad fragments and stanzas. By appealing to a common literary, or at least narrative, lore found in the ballads, he could insert ideas, concepts, or comments by power of suggestion. Obviously, he did not select in a vacuum the particular ballads he used; they were probably suggested to him by the characterization, action, or other circumstances at a given point in a play. For example, when Shakespeare has Hamlet quote from the ballad "Jephthah, Judge of Israel," his audience could be expected to associate Polonius' sacrifice of Ophelia on the altar of palace intrigue with Jephthah's sacrifice of his only daughter because of an overhasty oath. Perhaps, when Hamlet exclaims, "Get thee to a nunnery, go!" the Elizabethan audience might recall the ballad's last lines, "So he sent her away, / For to mourn, for to mourn, till her dying day."[15] The ballad would also have suggested the original biblical story, which, in turn, might have suggested Agamemnon's sacrifice of Iphigenia. Thus, Hamlet's quoting a ballad fragment might open a universal and historical view far beyond the literal episode surrounding it, and perhaps also beyond Shakespeare's conscious intent.

We should now consider one specific ballad type which is peculiarly linked to the dramatic tradition inherited by Shakespeare. He often used it as a kind of musical conceit or word play. This type of ballad is the "medley."

Among the many kinds of songs sung by the Elizabethans, perhaps none is more obscure than the medley. To my knowledge, no one has previously recognized the medley, or to be more exact, the ballad medley, as a type of song worth examining or discussing. It is almost unknown even among ballad students and folklorists. Ritson, Percy, and Child ignored it. William Chappell, J. O. Halliwell, and Hyder

15. Percy, *Reliques of Ancient English Poetry* . . . 1:182–84.

Rollins included two medleys each in their respective collections but without comment; Claude Simpson mentioned only the titles of three medley tunes.[16] Perhaps these authorities thought the type insignificant because the ballad medley, while written in the metrical and stanzaic patterns of balladry and usually set to ballad tunes, seldom tells a story except by accident. This neglect may also be explained by the subject matter of the type, which matter mainly is a mixture of nonsense, half-sense, and foolery occasionally laced with a dash of satire. The resulting conglomeration is set to the most common ballad tunes.

Low-born and half-witted as the ballad medley is, it would seem to merit only oblivion under the dust of time. Yet I shall resurrect it here because I believe that it can add much to our understanding of certain scenes in Elizabethan drama, particularly the histories and tragedies with which we are concerned. An examination of the ballad medley and its dramatic history may add considerable interest to the scenes in which ballad fragments are used, for, in writing these scenes, Shakespeare may have been following a dramatic tradition overlooked so far by students of English drama and literature. Let us then define the term "ballad medley" and trace briefly its stage history.

The first definition of the word "medley" in its musical sense listed in the *Oxford English Dictionary* is dated 1811, when the third edition of Busby's *Dictionary of Music* gave this description: "With the moderns, a medley is a humorous hotch-potch assemblage of the detached parts or passages of different well-known songs. . . ." In general, this is an excellent description; but it is strange that the earliest entry in the *OED* should be from a nineteenth-century source, for the ballad medley appeared much earlier on the English scene. Also, as we shall subsequently discover, the subject matter of the ballad medley is not always nonsense, although the type may be considered an example of nonsense literature.

The origin of the ballad medley is obscure. It seems to have appeared during the late medieval period as a form of ballad, but I have no direct evidence on this point. M. J. C. Hodgart has stated that the ballad is derived from the medieval dance-song, or "carole," one type of which produced the ballad stanza characterized by an

16. Respectively, *The Roxburghe Ballads* 1:52, 57; *A Catalogue of an Unique Collection . . .* p. 29; *A Pepysian Garland . . .* p. 451; *The British Broadside Ballad and Its Music*, p. 680.

internal refrain.[17] As an illustration, he quoted the following stanza:

> She laid her back against a thorn
> *Fine flowers in the valley,*
> And there she has her sweet babe born
> *And the green leaves they grow rarely.*[18]

This internal refrain (the second and fourth lines) is, of course, repeated in each stanza, while the first and third lines carry on the story. To quote Hodgart again, "A number of ballads have these irrelevant refrains, which accidentally produce a striking effect: the violence and cruelty of the story is ironically contrasted with the peaceful continuity of Nature."[19]

For the moment, we might notice the irrelevancy of the refrain. It was perhaps inevitable that the carol form using the internal refrain at times evoked a comic response when the irrelevance became absurd or ridiculous. And it seems plausible that some wag would compound the absurdity by stringing together four instead of two irrelevant lines. I have found no examples of this occurrence in the rather superficial search I have been able to make in collections of medieval secular songs; but collectors may not have considered nonsense worth preserving. However, numerous nonsensical songs may be found among the late medieval "sotties," "centoni," and goliardic literature and the musical medley called *quodlibet,* which also antedated the English Renaissance.

The earliest example I have found of what is certainly a ballad medley appears in the interlude *The Four Elements,* printed by John Rastell in 1519. The interlude presents instructive lessons in natural science by means of the usual personifications. As the messenger announces at the beginning,

> But because some folk be a little disposed
> To sadness, but more to mirth and sport,
> This philosophical work is mixed
> With merry conceits, to give men comfort. . . .[20]

Many "merry conceits" are provided by Ignorance, the fool or clown, in his attempts to turn Humanity from serious studies to the lusty life. As the culmination of his folly, Ignorance sings the following

17. In B. Ford, ed., *The Age of Chaucer,* p. 163.
18. Ibid., p. 165.
19. Ibid.
20. R. Dodsley, *A Select Collection of Old English Plays* 1:10.

ballad medley, prefacing it with a taunt at "learned" musicians who could sing pricksong (by notation):

Hu. Then let us some lusty ballad sing.
Ign. Nay, sir, by the Heaven King!
For me thinketh it serveth for nothing,
All such peevish prick-eared song!
Hu. Peace, man, prick-song may not be despised,
For therewith God is well pleased,
Honoured, praised, and served,
In the church ofttime among.
Ign. Is God well pleased, trow'st thou, thereby?
Nay, nay, for there is no reason why,
For is it not as good to say plainly,
Give me a spade,
As give me a spa, ve, va, ve, va, ve, vade?
But if thou wilt have a song that is good,
I have one of Robin Hood,
The best that ever was made.
Hu. Then, a'fellowship, let us hear it.
Ign. But there is a burden, thou must bear it,
Or else it will not be.
Hu. Then begin and care not to . . .
Down, down, down &.
Ign. Robin Hood in Barnsdale stood, [The medley]
And leant him till a maple thistle;
Then came our lady and sweet Saint Andrew.
Sleepest thou, wakest thou, Geffrey Coke?
A hundred winter the water was deep,
I can not tell you how broad.
He took a goose neck in his hand,
And over the water he went.
He start up to a thistle top,
And cut him down a hollen club.
He stroke the wren between the horns,
That fire sprang out of the pig's tail.
Jack boy, is thy bow i-broke?
Or hath any man done the wriguldy wrag?
He plucked muscles out of a willow,
And put them into his satchel!
Wilkin was an archer good,
And well could handle a spade;
He took his bent bow in his hand,

And set him down by the fire.
He took with him sixty bows and ten,
A piece of beef, another of bacon,
Of all the birds in merry England
So merrily pipes the merry bottle![21]

In a note on this passage, William Hazlitt remarked, "This is a very early example of a string of nonsensical incongruities, possessing, however, no further value, except perhaps as affording an insight into what was regarded at that time as *comic effects*." Later commentators, however, have recognized the "incongruities" as a mixture of lines from old popular songs. The most recent student, John Stevens, observed, "But in two plays fools sing a miscellany of popular nonsense obviously quoting popular songs (probably with bits of tunes)...."[22] But, while the song in question may contain a nonsensical combination of song fragments, Ignorance is not all fool; he has a point. He had earlier referred to the musicians who sang pricksong and who could not call a spade a spade but must mix what seemed to him meaningless words or syllables. The practice that Ignorance dislikes is "troping," in which singers of the Mass intercalated nonliturgical texts ("prosa" or "prosula") to match their elaborate melodic ornamentations or melismata.[23] The practice was probably objectionable to laity and clergy alike in 1519; troping was banned by the Council of Trent in 1564. The joke, of course, is that the ballad medley Ignorance sings is no more intelligible than the troping of the learned and literate musicians. The question posed is, which is the more foolish? Humanity can be fooled by both extremes, since he certainly does not hear the promised ballad of Robin Hood.

What both Hazlitt and Stevens did not note is that the ballad medley is a subgenre of the ballad, a subgenre having traditional associations with the early English stage, as I shall demonstrate.

A later example of the ballad medley appears in W. Wager's interlude called *The Longer Thou Livest, The More Fool Thou Art*,

21. Ibid., 1:48–50.
22. J. Stevens, *Music & Poetry in the Early Tudor Court*, p. 255. The plays to which he referred are *The Four Elements* and *The Longer Thou Livest, the More Fool Thou Art*.
23. *Grove's Dictionary of Music and Musicians*, 8:559. The practice of troping has been given closer examination by musicologists in the past several years. See H. Husmann, "Sequenz and Prosa"; P. Evans, "Some Reflections on the Origin of the Trope."

to which Reed assigned the approximate date 1559. In it the following stage direction states:

> Here entereth Moros, counterfeiting a vain gesture and a
> foolish countenance, singing the foot of many songs,
> as fools were wont.[24]

Moros' song is also a true medley comprising the first lines, and
sometimes complete stanzas, of several old ballads including "Broom,
broom on a hill," "Robin lend to me thy bow," "There was a maid
come out of Kent," "Come over the bourn Besse" (also sung by
Lear's Fool), and others. A few lines from the medley provide a taste:

> Broom, broom on a hill,
> The gentle broom on hill, hill:
> Broom, broom on Hive hill,
> The gentle broom on Hive hill,
> The broom stands on Hive Hill a.
> Robin lend to me thy bow, thy bow,
> Robin the bow, Robin lend to me thy bow a.
> There was a maid come out of Kent,
> Dainty love, dainty love,
> There was a maid came out of Kent,
> Fair, proper, small, and gent,
> As ever upon the ground went,
> For so should it be. . . .[25]

The preceding examples show that the ballad medley is an inde-
pendent type, especially significant for two reasons: it is performed
on the stage; it is associated closely with, and seems to be the
peculiar property of, the fool or jester. In both examples, the medley
is sung by a stage fool. It also seems that by about 1559 the connection between the ballad medley and the fool or jester was already
traditional: we note that Moros sings "as fools were wont."

The association of the fool, the stage, and the medley continued
unbroken as Shakespeare began his career as playwright. Richard
Tarleton, the famous clown, was one of Queen Elizabeth's private
jesters. He also became a comedian in the Queen's Men when that
company was formed in 1583.[26] Apparently, Tarleton used the

24. Reed, *Songs from the British Drama*, p. 9.
25. Ibid., pp. 9–10.
26. F. Halliday, *A Shakespeare Companion, 1550–1950*, p. 639.

ballad medley extensively; his name is attached to two, possibly three, tunes to which at least two medleys and several conventional ballads were sung. One tune is called "Tarleton's carroll," the other "Tarleton's Medley."[27] The two titles, however, may refer to the same tune. Both ballads set to these tunes were published around 1615 by Martin Parker, the foremost ballad printer. Parker himself wrote at least one medley and gave it the descriptive title "An Excellent new Medly. / Which you may admire at (without offence), / For every line speakes a contrary sence."[28] The last stanza (part 2) is typical.

> The courtier and the country man,
> Let's live as honest as we can,
> When Arthur first in Court began,
>   his men wore hanging sleeves.
> In May when Grasse and Flowers be green,
> The strangest sight that ere was seene,
> God blesse our gracious King and Queene,
>   from danger. [A]men.

Parker set his medley to the tune "Tarleton's Medley." Again we find the medley an almost inseparable companion of the stage fool Tarleton, who was both court jester and stage clown.

Incidentally, we might note at this point that the terms "medley," "motley," and "patch" were frequently synonymous in the early seventeenth century. All denoted a mixture—"motley," of course, meaning a mixture of colors.[29] According to the *OED*, Hakewell, in his *David's Vow* (1622), act 7, line 252, made the statement "Hee would not haue his family like a motley cloth, or a meddly colour." Likewise, the term "antic," as early as 1564 applied to clowns and jesters (*OED*), has an allied definition—"Grotesque, in composition or shape" (1548). We may also note that the term "patch," in addition to its reference to a scrap or fragment, was applied in 1549 to "fooles, doltes, ideots," and that Cardinal Wolsey's jester was nicknamed "Patch" (*OED*). The medley may thus be linked etymologically with the fool, half-wit, antic, jester, or clown, but most significantly

---

27. Respectively, Chappell, ed., *The Roxburghe Ballads* 1:52; A. Clark, ed., *The Shirburn Ballads 1585–1616*, pp. 334, 351.

28. In Chappell, ed., *The Roxburghe Ballads* 1:52.

29. The colors would seem to have been most frequently mixed in patches despite Hotson's description of them otherwise. See L. Hotson, *Shakespeare's Motley*, pp. 1–15.

with the patch. We may believe, then, that an essential characteristic of the Elizabethan jester, court fool, or "natural" was a fragmentation of wit or personality associated with him and displayed in his motley dress, his antic gestures, and his singing musical medleys. The fool's world is a fragmented world.

During the middle of the seventeenth century, the song medley achieved perhaps its greatest claim to artistic glory. In 1653, no less a composer than Henry Lawes, best known as the composer of the music for Milton's *Comus*, published a medley of his own devising in his *Ayres and Dialogues . . . The First Booke*. But even here the medley's motley shows through. Lawes remarked in his introduction:

> *I neuer lov'd to* Set *or* sing *words which I do not understand; and where I cannot, I desir'd help of others who were able to interpret. But this present Generation is so sated with what's Natiue, that nothing takes their eare but what's sung in a Language which (commonly) they understand as little as they do the Musicke. And to make them a little sensible of this ridiculous humour, I took a* Table *or* Index *of old* Italian *songs (for one, two, and three Voyces) and this* Index *(which read together made a strange medley of Non-sence) I set to a varyed Ayre, and gaue out that it came from Italy, whereby it hath passed for a rare* Italian Song.

One other example will show the ballad medley in a more elaborate form wherein are mixed ballad refrains, first lines and complete ballad stanzas, proverbs, and some pure nonsense. This medley is set for three voices in John Forbes' *Cantus, Songs and Fancies*, the edition of 1666. Here, barely discernible among all the nonsense, is a narration of sorts, made by combining one or two stanzas from several ballads. Apparently, a young man meets a maid at a dance of virgins and falls in love with her. She returns his love, but she is fickle. Before they can wed, she is seduced by a friar. When the next dance of virgins occurs, the girl, now pregnant and forsaken, is excluded and can only appeal to Heaven for aid. The following excerpts give the thread of the story: [30]

30. Later, Percy made a ballad, "The Friar of Orders Gray," by combining scraps of ballads with supplemental stanzas of his own making. But his is not a "true" medley in that it lacks the non sequiturs and nonsense. See his *Reliques of Ancient English Poetry . . .* 1:223–26.

Trip and go, hey: How should I go? How:
It is the guyse of France,
How that ye should sing and play,
With us to stuff our joly dance . . .
Be soft and sober, I pray you,
my Lady will come here away;
Go graith you in your glansand geer,
To meet my Lady pair and pair,
With harps and lutes and guittrons gay,
My Lady will come here away.
Hey troly, loly, love is joly
a while, while it is new:
When it is old, it groweth full cold:
Wo worth the love un-true. . . .
I saw three Ladies fair singing,
Hey and how, upon yon leyland, hey.
I saw three mariners singing,
Rumbelow, upon yon see strand, hey . . .
Three birds on a tree, three and three . . .
The boniest bird come down to me,
The boniest bird came down to me. . . .
So dinckly as her hair was decked,
So lustily she did also both wink & blink, and twinkle too:
So fresily she did ago.
She ran like a Roe, she tript like a Doe:
I would have caught her by the toe:
With that she vanisht, & home did go. . . .
Now here how the Frier had on a coule of red,
He spyed the pretty wench keaming her head.
He prinked he lurked, he lour'd:
To see as he jouked, it was good bourd. . . .
The pretty wench was all alone . . .
Ever alace! for shame alone;
A joly young Frier has raised my womb. . . .
That ever I did it, did it, did it,
Alace! for earthly shame
Betrayed am I uncourteously,
Alone, alone, alone . . .
Meet we your maidens all in array,
with silver pins and virgin lay.
We be all of maiden land,
Maidens ye may see.
Come in our ring then saith Pleasaunce;

Give us your hands, let us go dance: . . .
And can ye dance on a peat,
play lutcock & light the gate
futtikinton sisters, adew; sisters adew.
The heav'n is full of mirth and joy, adew.

In Forbes' medley we find an additional element. The medley's motley here assumes a somber hue tinged with a simple pathos. This pathos is, in turn, related to an intense irony derived from the combination of contrary emotions aroused in us by the weeping jester or the clown whose comic mask is twisted by a tragic, tormented soul. It is this tragic irony that Leoncavallo created in *I Pagliacci* when Canio, the cuckolded clown, driven almost to madness by the laughter and taunts of the village folk, finally slays his wife and her lover. He then sings, heartbroken, the line that is the climax of the opera, "La commedia e finita!" And we also recall the simpleton—God's fool—in Moussorgsky's *Boris Godunov* who with witless innocence questions Boris about the crimes he had committed in obtaining the throne. For idiots and half-wits, unable to dissemble because they are the special wards of God, are prone to speak the truth of God.

There was a long tradition which gave the court fool, whether a "natural" or a sharp-witted jester, a special license for free speech. This license probably originated in the belief that the idiot or half-wit, not having sense enough to lie or deceive, must necessarily tell the truth at all times. When applied to the normal-minded but witty jester, his license permitted much satire at the expense of various members of a court or other institutions. Erasmus used this tradition, we recall, as the basis for his *In Praise of Folly* (1508?). This freedom of speech was not without limits, and the fool might exceed the limits to his own sorrow. As Lear's Fool complains, act 1, scene 4,

> *Fool.* . . . Prithee, Nuncle, keep a schoolmaster that can teach
>   thy fool to lie. I would fain learn to lie.
> *Lear.* An you lie, sirrah, we'll have you whipped.
> *Fool.* I marvel what kin thou and thy daughters are. They'll
>   have me whipped for speaking true, thou'lt have
>   me whipped for lying, and sometimes I am whipped for
>   holding my peace. . . .

The more canny fools no doubt soon learned to make their barbed jests as riddles, puns, or other kinds of indirect speech. By relying on the power of suggestion, they could shift the direct statement from themselves to the object of their sallies. The result usually was that the target swallowed his anger rather than admitting that he had been hurt by the fool's remarks. As one kind of indirection, the fools and later stage clowns employed the ballad fragments for their suggestive force. The close relationship of this use of ballad bits to the conceit we call the pun is worth noting.

The pun is a wordplay suggested by a similarity in sound between words; the similarity in sound leads the thoughts or ideas one associates with the words into strange and accidental combinations. The wit involved is to supply words similar in sound to the initial word, which similar words lead the associated ideas into unusual yet related sequences of thought or imagery. For example, in the opening lines of *Romeo and Juliet*, the puns of Samson and Gregory depend for their wit on the progression suggested by the sequence of the words "coal," "collier," "choler," and "collar." The surprise or extravagance in the pun comes from the unexpected direction into which lines of thought may be shifted, depending upon the almost reflexive thought patterns of both parties. Neither party knows what direction the pattern will take. The resulting combinations of ideas or images might be as fresh and startling as illogical. No wonder that Shakespeare, as poet, delighted in such wordplay.

We observe this same process in the medley, except that in this case the unexpected thought sequence results from combining familiar ballad lines into unexpected combinations rather than from constructing a word sequence. The result may be nonsense, but by suggestion it can supply striking similes or metaphors. Shakespeare described the process when he had the Gentleman in *Hamlet*, act 4, scene 5, describing Ophelia's madness, say that she

> speaks things in doubt
> That carry but half-sense. Her speech is nothing,
> Yet the unshaped use of it doth move
> The hearers to collection. They aim at it,
> And botch the words up fit to their own thoughts,
> Which, as her winks and nods and gestures yield them,
> Indeed would make one think there might be thought,
> Though nothing sure, yet much unhappily.

The medley is a comic song traditionally sung by jesters or stage clowns and comedians. It would therefore seem inappropriate to tragedy. Clowns and fools might also seem inappropriate to serious drama, but as we know, they take important roles in the tragedies and histories of Shakespeare. Indeed, Shakespeare's fools—Touchstone, Feste, Lear's Fool—are the fulcrum of a balance between the comic world and the tragic world. It is they who provide us with the touchstone of sanity in order that we might view both extremes with detachment and balance. As Ernst Cassirer has commented on Shakespeare's humor:

> In the scene from *Much Ado about Nothing* in which Beatrice rudely interrupts a light skirmish of wits with Benedick with the words "Kill Claudio!" we are on the threshold of a new, truly Shakespearean world, where henceforth there is to be no separation between comedy and tragedy. The form of humour now to prevail is not unsuitable to the immediate presence of suffering, or even death . . . humour becomes the touchstone of the true and false, of the genuine and the counterfeit, of the essential and the merely conventional. A new mode of perception, a new science of men and things, thus emerges which finds in humour its own proper and adequate means of expression.[31]

Shakespeare's fools are the epitome of his humor. They seem equally appropriate in that world we describe as normal and in that distraught world Shakespeare shows us in the mad trial of mankind which the insane Lear conducts in a hovel on the storm-shaken heath. Their proper language is the riddle or the pun, their dress motley, their music the unshaped bits of ballads that move us to "collection," but which we interpret, as we would the Delphic oracle, at our own risk. They are the lords of misrule, kin to Chaos himself, and always ready to clap their coxcombs on the heads of those who take an apparently well-ordered world too much for granted. Perhaps in their medleys they reflect the world as the angels observe it. Mersenne described the angels as knowing

> the harmonic order which [God] has hidden in the fabric of the world, and of all its parts. . . . The Angels know [*scavent*] the Music also, and have great satisfaction in the contemplation of the harmony of the heavens, the elements, and of the medley [*melange*] of all the incidents which take

---

31. *The Platonic Renaissance in England*, pp. 178–81.

place in the world; for they see evidently how we discontent ourselves when we think of the fortune of this one, and the disgrace of that one, of sickness, death, doom, etc. . . .[32]

When we turn to specific instances wherein Shakespeare used the ballad fragments in his histories and tragedies, we may call on three possible dramatic practices, or combinations of these, which should aid us in clarifying those passages where the bits of ballads occur. First is the conventional use of ballads as suggestive references; second, the use of ballad bits, following the medley tradition, as a kind of musical conceit; third, the use of song snatches as oracular riddles expressing gnomic pronouncements. With these general rules-of-thumb we are now better prepared to explore that portion of the past opened to us by Shakespeare's balladry—the vocal music of his tragedies and histories.

32. *Traité de l'Harmonie Vniverselle* . . . theorem 4, pp. 19–20 (author's translation).

SIX

The Second Chronicle Tetralogy

HE METAPHOR OF THE DRAW-WELL BUCKETS SHARED by the following quotations provides a striking parallel and exemplifies common themes—the fickleness of Fortune and the fall of princes—shared by many chronicle plays, many tragedies, and many ballads. The upward and downward motion of the buckets aptly figures the fortunes of Bolingbroke and Richard, Prince Hal and Percy Hotspur, the Lord Chief Justice and Falstaff, and hence is a major metaphor controlling the plot structure of the first three plays in Shakespeare's second chronicle tetralogy:

> The worthie Bocas, in his morall buke,
>   The Fall of Princes plainly dois compyle;
> Amangs them all quha euer lykes to luke,
>   Sall finde Dame Fortounis fauour for a quhyle;
> For with the one eye sho [*sic*] can lauch and smyle,
>   And with the vther lurke and play the loun;
> Sum to promotioun, and some to plaine exile,
>   Lyke draw-well bukkets dowkand vp and doun.
>   "Ane Complaint vpon Fortoun" (stanza 2)[1]

> Now is this golden crown like a deep well
> That owes two buckets, filling one another,
> The emptier ever dancing in the air,
> The other down, unseen and full of water.
> That bucket down and full of tears am I,
> Drinking my griefs whilst you mount up on high.
>   *Richard II* (4. 1. 184–89)

Between music and drama, the link provided by balladry expresses the concept of history as "the music of men's lives" that informs Gaunt's dying words and the final soliloquy of the death-marked Richard. *Richard II*, more obviously than other Shakespearean

---

1. J. Halliwell, ed., *A Collection of Seventy-nine Black-Letter Ballads and Broadsides* . . . p. 49.

plays, presents us history as music that, in human lives, is "sweetest at the close."

Richard II

The music in this play is governed by three qualities prominent in the total play—ceremony, symbolism, and rhetoric. The first quality appears as Richard judges Mowbray and Bolingbroke (act 1, scene 3). As a part of the ritualistic and legalistic nature of the entire scene, Richard and his attendants sweep onto the stage to the sound of a trumpet flourish. As the direction states:

> [*The trumpets sound, and the* KING *enters with his nobles,*
> GAUNT, BUSHY, BAGOT, GREEN, *and others. When they are*
> *set, enter* MOWBRAY *in arms, defendant, with a* HERALD.]

The flourish, as F calls the trumpets' sound, speaks the king's majesty, but it also provides a processional piece to which the court party moves, in state, onto the stage. The size of this group suggests a flourish longer in duration than usual, or perhaps a sennet. With the king and his advisers appear guards, heralds, trumpeters, and possibly others. After all assume their proper places, Mowbray enters with a herald. A tucket later sounds for Bolingbroke's appearance (1. 3. 25). The folio direction specifying a tucket at this point can have symbolic significance: as we recall, a tucket is a private trumpet call, usually sounded by a single trumpet, peculiar to an individual or to a noble family. If, in this case, Bolingbroke's family or personal tucket is used, one effect is a musical contrast between the personal tucket and the royal flourish, or between Bolingbroke and the king. In this instance, the flourish, which normally would have announced the first entry of Richard, is reserved for his entrance in this scene. The result states musically the conflict between the two men at the point when Richard is at the top of Fortune's wheel.

Notation for a flourish may be found in Appendix IV.A–E. No notation for the tucket, as defined above, has been found. For production purposes, the trumpet signal shown in the same appendix should be satisfactory.

To signal the onset of the trial by combat between Bolingbroke and Mowbray (1. 3. 117), the Lord Marshall commands, "Sound, trumpets, and set forward, combatants." The direction is [*A charge sounded*]. When the trumpets peal, the Lord Marshall shouts, "Stay, the King hath thrown his warder down." In addition to their ceremonious function in the trial by combat, the use of trumpets also helps stage the scene. It is not likely that the combatants, including their mounts and weapons, were shown on the stage. The beginning of the offstage combat, we assume, was suggested by the trumpets. When the king intervenes, Mowbray and Bolingbroke reappear on the stage as though walking from the lists. The notation for a trumpet charge for cavalry is given in Appendix I.

As the king and his advisors withdraw for a council, Richard states (1. 3. 121), ". . . Withdraw with us, and let the trumpets sound / While we return these Dukes what we decree." The direction is then [*A long flourish*]. The action then pauses for a few moments while the council takes place. It is to fill this awkward pause that the "long flourish" sounds. The flourish, rather than a sennet or some other type of music, suggests that Richard's voice dominates the council— a suggestion that Gaunt's subsequent comments confirm. Later, as Richard exits (1. 3. 248), there is a conventional flourish.

The next two instances of performed music show the music solving stage problems. The first bit (act 3, scene 2) dresses the entrance of Richard and his army before Barkloughly Castle. The direction is [*Drums: flourish and colors. Enter* KING RICHARD, *the* BISHOP OF CARLISLE, AUMERLE, *and Soldiers*]. As I read these rubrics, the drums sound a military march offstage for a few moments before Richard enters; this is to suggest a large movement of troops. Just before Richard enters, there is a trumpet flourish. The two types of music— drums associated with the military, the flourish associated with royalty —combine to set the stage for Richard's appearance as a warrior-king. When he does enter, the drums, trumpets, colors, and a few token soldiers (all of which probably came onstage) are sufficient to suggest an entire army.

The same convention is used when Bolingbroke and his army enter before Flint Castle (act 3, scene 3), though, of course, the royal flourish is absent. In this case, however, the staging must suggest both the exterior of the castle, where Bolingbroke and his forces are situated, and the interior of the castle, occupied by Richard and his followers. This setting "in depth" is achieved first by the trumpet parleys. The rubric describes the technique (3. 3. 61):

[*Parle without, and answer within. Then a flourish. Enter
on the walls,* KING RICHARD, *the* BISHOP OF CARLISLE,
AUMERLE, SCROOP, *and* SALISBURY.]

The trumpet "Parle without" is obviously blown by Bolingbroke's
trumpeter. Another trumpeter answers offstage ("within"). A flourish
is then blown offstage or perhaps is played by trumpeters who precede Richard's entry on the "walls," probably an upper gallery of
the playhouse. This setting seems to be a rather careful preparation
for Richard's symbolic descent to the "base court"; the descent
marks his defeat and his loss of that intangible majesty and "presence" that comprise the aura of kingship.

As act 3, scene 3, ends, Bolingbroke, the victor, and Richard,
shorn of his authority, set off for London. The direction is [*Flourish.
Exeunt*]. The flourish here creates an ironic ambiguity. Does the flourish sound for Richard, who is a king in name only, or for Bolingbroke, who is king in all but name? This question leads to a further
ambiguity. As the trumpet peals die away, the now-empty stage is
entered by Richard's queen as act 3, scene 4, the fulcrum of the
play's structure, opens. It is in this scene, especially in the garden
imagery of old Adam, that the answer to our question appears. The
ambiguous flourish ending scene 3, whether it peals for Richard,
Bolingbroke, or both, elides scenes 3 and 4 by linking the two men
with a flourish, which also, in effect, announces the entrance of
the queen, who will shortly hear of Bolingbroke's triumph over
her husband.

There is no more music in the play until Richard delivers his
final soliloquy (act 5, scene 5). In considering the music here, we
should recall John of Gaunt's dying speech beginning act 2, scene 1,
line 5:

> GAUNT. Oh, but they say the tongues of dying men
> Enforce attention like deep harmony. . . .
> More are men's ends marked than their lives before.
> The setting sun, and music at the close,
> As the last taste of sweets, is sweetest last,
> Writ in remembrance more than things long past.

We are now concerned with the music at the close of Richard's life.

Alone, and shortly to be murdered, he assesses himself and his fate
until his thoughts are momentarily interrupted by music, line 41:

> Music do I hear?　　　　　　　　　　　　　[*Music.*]
> Ha, ha! Keep time. How sour sweet music is
> When time is broke and no proportion kept!
> So is it in the music of men's lives.
> And here have I the daintiness of ear
> To check time broke in a disordered string,
> But for the concord of my state and time
> Had not an ear to hear my true time broke.
> ... This music mads me, let it sound no more,
> For though it have holp madmen to their wits,
> In me it seems it will make wise men mad.
> Yet blessing on his heart that gives it me!
> For 'tis a sign of love, and love to Richard
> Is a strange brooch in this all-hating world.

The music played (we assume by the groom) provides a rhetorical
analogy that Richard seizes and develops as he continues his
soliloquy.[2] His attempt to explain the analogy involves an abbreviated but striking summary of several concepts (macrocosmic and
microcosmic) common in Renaissance *musica speculativa*. He begins with the performed music (*musica practica*) and the necessity
for harmony, order, and proportion (time); this suggests the necessity
for the same elements in men's lives (the microcosm or *musica
humana*); he then makes the analogy to the necessity for harmony in
the affairs of the macrocosm (*musica mundana*). But since he has
wasted (disordered) his time and his kingdom, this disharmony of the
musica mundana, in turn, disorders the music of his life, his *musica
humana*. The curative powers of musical harmony, which "have holp
madmen to their wits," now discordant, serve only to disorder his
mind. *Musica mundana* (the macrocosm) and *musica humana* (the

---

2. Stevens ("Shakespeare and the Music of the Elizabethan Stage ..." p.
18) believed that the music Richard hears is provided by a broken consort or
by a single lutenist playing "within." But Shakespeare almost always indicated
the supposed source of offstage music—in this case, I think, the groom. Provost
("On Justice and the Music in *Richard II* and *King Lear*") also expressed this
belief and contrasted this scene with *King Lear*, act 4, scene 7. T. Greenfield ("Nonvocal Music ... in Five Shakespeare Plays," pp. 107–8) discussed
the episode in detail. She described the use of music to accompany, and to
provide figures of speech for, Richard's soliloquy as a kind of Elizabethan
"moralizing."

microcosm) are now out of tune, and the world is "all-hating." It lacks
the harmony of human love. There remains only that music which "is
a sign of love" and which Richard describes as a "strange brooch."
This "brooch," I think, is a sign of love in the highest form, *musica
divina*.

Of *musica divina*, Mersenne wrote in *Traité de l'Harmonie
Vniverselle* ... (1627):[3]

> But before we begin another discourse, it is necessary to
> note that Music is of God, and with the Angels, for God
> has the knowledge of all things in supreme degree of per-
> fection; and ... the harmonic order which He has hidden
> in the fabric of the world, and of all its parts. ... The
> Angels comprehend (*scavent*) the Music also, and have
> great satisfaction in the contemplation of the harmony of
> the heavens, the elements, and of the medley (*melange*) of
> all the incidents which take place in the world; for they see
> evidently how we discontent ourselves when we think about
> the fortune of this one, and the disgrace of that one, about
> sickness, death, doom, etc.

It is the medley of worldly and personal incidents that Richard tries
but at first fails to comprehend. Only when he considers the music
as a sign of love does he perceive dimly a solution to his puzzle. As he
thinks of this sign of love, the groom appears, personifying that love
which Richard finds so strange in his circumstances. It is that charity,
without which Richard has become as sounding brass, that he finally
recognizes when he addresses the groom, saying, "Thanks, noble
peer. / The cheapest of us is ten groats too dear." It is this recognition,
brought to Richard by the music of the groom, that permits him to
attain an inner harmony before his death—to hear a sweet music
at the close of his life.

It seems reasonable that the groom is also the musician who plays
for Richard. If so, we might suppose that the instrument he plays,
and the music a groom might be expected to perform, would fit into
the popular tradition. For the instrument I would suggest the Welsh
or Celtic harp usually associated, in Elizabeth's time, with folk or
vulgar music. The music played might well be the old song "Heart's
Ease" mentioned in *Romeo and Juliet*. One version, found in Playford's *The English Dancing-Master* (1651), is transcribed by Chap-

3. Theorem 4, pp. 19–20 (author's translation).

Figure 6.

pell.[4] Another version of the tune, perhaps older (Chappell dated it c. 1560) and certainly more appropriate musically to Richard's situation in the play, is in Univ. Cambridge MS D.d.2.11 (page 44). The lute tablature of the MS is transcribed in figure 6. This lute tablature, incidentally, if changed to the key of G, would be within the compass of the Welsh chromatic harp used in Wales and England since the fifteenth century, according to Francis Galpin.[5]

1 Henry IV

When we examine the music performed in *1 Henry IV*, we discover that its use is governed by the conventions found in Shakespeare's comedies rather than by those in the earlier chronicle plays and tragedies. For one thing, Shakespeare focused attention mainly on the music performed before Glendower, Mortimer, and Percy Hotspur

4. *Popular Music of the Olden Time* 1:210.
5. *Old English Instruments of Music: Their History and Character*, p. 15.

in the archdeacon's house at Bangor (act 3, scene 1); the flourishes, retreats, and parleys that sound so frequently in the preceding histories and tragedies are reserved, in this play, for the battle of Shrewsbury. Even then, the military music seems employed quite conventionally. For another thing, the music presented in act 3, scene 1, is introduced for its intrinsic value as well as for dramatic purposes; its performance is staged in a manner that permits two complete pieces to be heard without interruption by dialogue or action. A third point, familiar in Shakespeare's comic techniques, is the topicality of the music used in this scene; the song sung in Welsh by Glendower's daughter seems to be a conscious effort to display the talent of an actor in Shakespeare's company. The music also provides occasion for a historical footnote concerning Glendower's leadership among the Welsh.

The setting for the concert in act 3, scene 1, is a domestic gathering of the Percys and the Glendowers at the archdeacon's house, a pause between completion of the conspiracy against Henry IV and the armed rebellion that culminates in the battle of Shrewsbury. During this calm interlude, familial pleasure and affection form a portrait of human harmony. Glendower, translating his daughter's Welsh for her husband, speaks to Mortimer (line 214):

GLEND. She bids you on the wanton rushes lay you down
        And rest your gentle head upon her lap,
        And she will sing the song that pleaseth you
        And on your eyelids crown the god of sleep,
        Charming your blood with pleasing heaviness. . . .
MORT.   With all my heart I'll sit and hear her sing.
        By that time will our book, I think, be drawn.
GLEND. Do so,
        And those musicians that shall play to you
        Hang in the air a thousand leagues from hence,
        And straight they shall be here. Sit, and attend. . . .
                                        [*The music plays.*]
HOT.   Now I perceive the Devil understands Welsh,
        And 'tis no marvel he is so humorous.
        By'r Lady, he is a good musician.
LADY P. Then should you be nothing but musical, for you are
        altogether governed by humors. Lie still, ye thief,
        and hear the lady sing in Welsh. . . .
                        [*Here* LADY MORTIMER *sings a Welsh song.*]

As Glendower describes it, the purpose of the song is to soothe and calm Mortimer if not actually to put him to sleep. Mortimer says that it will fill the time while the "book," the written articles of the conspiracy, is drawn. But the author's purpose seems to be to insert a musical interlude that would give his audience a treat, perhaps to exploit some topical interest in the Welsh language and history, and perhaps to use the talent of a Welsh singer-actor, possibly Robert Goffe.[6] Welsh harpists and singers were fairly numerous in Elizabeth's London, having followed the Tudors there upon the establishment of the dynasty. A celebrated harpist, Thomas Pritchard, died in London in 1597; most of his fellow harpists eked out a bare existence by playing in taverns and inns.[7]

Some commentators have suggested that Shakespeare also may have intended to use the music to demonstrate Glendower's occult powers, since the Welsh chieftain seems to summon his music from the thin air. Whether Shakespeare believed that Owen was a genuine sorcerer or a charlatan is a moot question; but it is historical fact that Glendower had many Welsh bards under his thumb and that he made them useful in his rebellion. Thomas Percy mentioned an act of Parliament given in the reign of Henry IV which provides that "no 'Master *Rimour*, or *Minstrel*, or other Vagabond, be in "any wise sustained in the Land of Wales, to make COMOITHS or gatherings upon the People ther." ' " Ivor Bowen in *The Statute of Wales* (1908) explained: "This act was probably directed against the bards who were engaged by Owen Glyndwr in rousing the martial spirit of the WELSH, and against the *gwestwyr*, or purveyancers employed also by him to collect money and provisions (*cymortha*) for the insurrection."[8] It is therefore possible that Shakespeare may have been referring to an obscure bit of history.

For our primary purpose, however, we need only note that the playwright had Glendower summon the musicians from a supernatural source, that their music is performed, that Hotspur comments on the excellence of the musicians he has heard, and that the direction says that the music plays—offstage, we may believe. This music is not the accompaniment for the lady's song; it is a separate instrumental piece, played, probably, in its entirety before Hotspur exclaims

6. Chambers, *William Shakespeare* 1:375.
7. Shakespeare, *Supplement to Henry IV, Part 1*, ed. G. Evans, p. 203, note to line 242 (stage direction).
8. *The Percy Letters* 5:72–73, quoted in Bowen, p. 34.

what a good musician the devil is. It strikes me that Shakespeare
here calls for a serenade in order to create a mood of calm and
domestic tranquillity, a brief harmony in human lives, as a dramatic
pause before the action picks up, leading to the climax in the battle
at Shrewsbury. The folio direction calling for "Musicke" is in the

Transcription
incomplete

Figure 7.

center of the column rather than in the margin, where such rubrics
are usually placed. This position implies, I think, that the music
interrupts the dialogue, as do the earlier passages spoken in Welsh
by Lady Mortimer, which are also introduced by directions centered
in the column of type. The instruction for the song is placed in a
similar manner.

The Elizabethan serenade, at least as Shakespeare used it, included
two pieces of music—an instrumental piece played by two or three
musicians, and a vocal piece accompanied by the instrumentalists.
Glendower's musicians play first an instrumental piece; it is this
that Hotspur takes as an example of the devil's skill. Later, Lady
Mortimer sings her song accompanied by the same invisible consort.

Of course, as the play was probably staged, the consort played in a music room or at some other point offstage. As the scene portrays a social gathering, the orchestra was perhaps a broken consort of five or six pieces, the ensemble customarily used for receptions or chamber music in Shakespeare's day.

Finding the type of music that graced this scene is not easy. Since the conversation surrounding the music centers on its Welsh character, we can believe that Welsh music, even that provided by the devil, was used. Satan is not a source that I would willingly turn to; hence I have turned to more mundane possibilities. Very little Elizabethan music that could be called distinctly Welsh is now known. Most of it was still transmitted memorially when *1 Henry IV* was written. There is period music recorded in a special notation for the Welsh harp, but now only the devil knows how to read it. Arnold Dolmetsch attempted some transcriptions, but he expressed dissatisfaction with the results.[9] There is, however, a piece for lute in Univ. Cambridge MS D.d.2.11, page 60, entitled "The Welsh Allmaine," that could serve for the instrumental part of the serenade. A literal transcription of the first three "strains" is shown in figure 7.

Glendower provides the only description of the Welsh song Lady Mortimer sings. To make matters worse, I have been unable to find notation for any Welsh song that could be assigned precisely to the time in which the play was first staged. The nearest I have approached historical accuracy is a love song with a Welsh text set to an instrumental piece not intended for the lyric. The instrumental piece is "La bounette," no. 13 in *The Mulliner Book*,[10] which I have slightly revised. The Welsh lyric I took from John Parry's *The Welsh Harper* . . . (1: 26). The sixteenth-century tune and later Welsh text are given in figure 8.

The remaining music consists of various trumpet signals sounded during the battle at Shrewsbury. The stage direction [*The trumpet sounds a parley*] (4. 3. 29) heralds Blunt's approach before Hotspur and his officers. In act 5, scene 1, line 8, Worcester and Vernon, emissaries of Hotspur, appear before Henry for a last parley. The direction is [*The trumpet sounds. Enter* WORCESTER *and* VERNON]— obviously another parley. At the opening of act 5, scene 2, the stage

9. The harp notation is in Musical Brit. Mus. Add. MS 14905, "Musica neu Beroriaeth." Dolmetsch's transcription is in *The Consort*, no. 3, special number (June 1934).

10. Page 26.

direction is again ambiguous, permitting elision of scenes. As scene 2 ends, Percy is addressing his followers:

> HOT. . . . Now, Esperance! Percy! and set on.
> Sound all the lofty instruments of war,
> And by that music let us all embrace;
> For, heaven to earth, some of us never shall
> A second time do such a courtesy.
> > [*The trumpets sound. They embrace, and exeunt.*]
>
> SCENE III. *Plain between the camps.*
>
> [*The* KING *enters with his power. Alarum to the battle. Then enter* DOUGLAS *and* SIR WALTER BLUNT.]

The folio direction makes no scene division here. It describes the action in this way:

> *They embrace, the Trumpets sound, the King entereth with his power, alarum unto the battell. Then enter Dowglas, and Sir Walter Blunt.*

It is interesting to speculate how this shift of scene was arranged by Shakespeare's company. Some editors have Hotspur and his friends embrace and then leave the stage. The trumpets then sound for the entrance of Henry and his army. This removes the ambiguity and also, I think, the intention behind F's direction; these modern emendations leave Hotspur's preceding command to "Sound all the lofty instruments of war" dangling in a vacuum. Rather, I believe that the trumpets sound, at Percy's command, a call such as the "Bouteselle ad Ephippia" (Boots and Saddles) given in Appendix I, with which Percy and his fellows embrace and leave the stage. This trumpet call is immediately followed by the conventional flourish; then King Henry and his "army" pass across the stage. In this manner, using two musical signals, the musical continuity would smooth the transition from one scene to the other. The battle is indicated, of course, by the "alarum"—probably the clangor of trumpets, the roll of drums, shouts, clashing arms, neighing horses—all produced offstage.

A trumpet call ends the battle (5. 4. 162): [*A retreat is sounded*]. After a brief comment by Falstaff, the scene changes to another part of the field, where Henry IV, his lieutenants, and prisoners enter as trumpets peal (act 5, scene 5). The rubric is not specific here:

[*The trumpets sound. Enter the* KING, PRINCE OF WALES, LORD JOHN OF LANCASTER, EARL OF WESTMORELAND, *with* WORCESTER *and* VERNON *prisoners*]. The trumpets may have played a flourish. More appropriate to the solemnity would be the trumpet call "Le simple cavalkot cantus pomposus," whose notation is given in Appendix I.

Figure 8.

The realistic depiction of battles was seldom done in Elizabethan drama, as Shakespeare acknowledged in the chorus which opens *Henry V*. The actors used all possible suggestive devices; even so, much was perforce left to the auditors' imaginations. We may believe, therefore, that those responsible for staging the original performances of *1 Henry IV* and other similar plays would use their trumpeters and drummers as effectively as possible. By having them sound specific signals or instructions, the actors furnished a musical commentary that aided the audience, no doubt familiar with at least the more common military signals, to follow the course of an offstage conflict.

2 Henry IV

One notable difference between *2 Henry IV* and its predecessor is that in the second play Shakespeare enlarged the comic parts of the plot at the expense of the historical actions, but the technical pattern controlling Shakespeare's use of music in this play is not what we usually observe in the comedies. Here is not the presentation of complete songs or instrumental pieces having intrinsic musical value, but the technique that will become increasingly prominent in his tragedies—the use of song fragments for their dramatic, rather than musical, value.

Music, of a sort, we hear first in act 2, scene 4, during Falstaff's rowdy assignation with Doll Tearsheet in the Boar's Head Tavern. As Sir John enters the scene he is singing (lines 36–37): " 'When Arthur first in court'—Empty the jordan.... [*Singing*] 'And was a worthy king.' How now, Mistress Doll!" The line which he sings, or probably bellows, has been long identified as the first line of the old ballad entered in the Stationers' Register on June 8, 1603, with the title "The noble Actes now newly found of Arthure of the round table." The ballad is printed in Thomas Deloney's "The Garland of good Will" (1631) with the title "The Noble Acts of *Arthur* of the round Table" to the tune of "Flying Fame."[11] Its opening stanza follows:

> When Arthur first in court began,
>   And was approued King:
> By force of armes great victories wan,
>   and conquest home did bring.

The ballad was evidently quite popular at the time *2 Henry IV* was first performed. Chappell noted that its first line also appears in Marston's *The Malcontent* (1604) and in the anonymous *The Little French Lawyer* (before 1616).[12] The same line is also in a ballad

11. *The Works of Thomas Deloney*, p. 8.
12. *Popular Music of the Olden Time* 1:199. See also other uses of this tag line in Sternfeld, "Music and Ballads."

medley which was written by Martin Parker about 1615 (see chapter 5).

Shakespeare selected this particular ballad snatch, Peter Seng has suggested, to point a contrast between knighthood in the person of the low-living, diseased Falstaff and the feudal ideal personified by Arthur and Lancelot.[13]

No notation for the tune "Flying Fame" seems to have survived; however, the title is mentioned as an alternate tune for the ballad "Chevy Chace," which was also sung to another tune, "In Pescod Time," according to Chappell.[14] If so, the tunes assigned these three ballads were interchangeable; hence, any one might also have served as a setting for "The Noble Acts of *Arthur*." The tune shown in figure 9, "In Pescod," was abstracted by Chappell from an art

Figure 9.

setting (the ballad tune used as a subject for variations) by Orlando Gibbons. His "divisions" on the tune were probably composed between 1600 and 1625, the year of his death. Chappell printed a tune for "Chevy Chace," but this tune can be dated no earlier than 1651.[15]

After Falstaff and Doll have completed their meal, they move into another room for music and dalliance. At Sir John's request, a drawer summons fiddlers, Sneak's "Noyse," to play an accompaniment for the old gamester's tender amours.

> I. DRAW. Why, then, cover, and set them down. And see if thou
> canst find out Sneak's noise, Mistress Tearsheet
> would fain hear some music. . . .
> PAGE. The music is come, sir.
> FAL. Let them play. Play, sirs. Sit on my knee, Doll. . . .

Using a bit of external evidence concerning the music actually performed in the early productions of Shakespeare's plays, we can

13. *The Vocal Songs in the Plays of Shakespeare* . . . p. 44. Seng described use of the songs to point up the degeneration of Falstaff's character, in "Songs, Time, and the Rejection of Falstaff."
14. *Popular Music of the Olden Time* 1:198.
15. Ibid., 1:199.

determine the type of music played by Sneak and his men in, probably, the court performance of 1619–1620.[16] Richard Ligon, a Royalist expatriate during the Commonwealth, fled to the Barbados Islands. Upon his return to England after the Restoration, he wrote *A true & exact history of the Island of Barbados*, which was published in 1657 and in 1673. In it is the following allusion:

> Dinner being neere halfe done . . . in comes an old fellow, whose complexion was raised out of red Sack; for neare that colour it was: his head and beard milk white, his countenance bold and Cheerful, a Lute in his hand, and plaide us for a Noueltie, the "passame sares Galiard"; a tune in great esteeme, in Harry the fourths dayes; for when Sir John Falstaff makes his Amours to Mistresse Doll Tearsheet Sneake and his Companie, the admired fidlers of that age, playes this tune, which put a thought into my head, that if time and tune be the Composites of Musicke, what a long time this tune had in sayling from England to this place.

Sir John Hawkins ran across this allusion, but his only comment was to declare, with a fine eighteenth-century huff, that Ligon's supposition that the music was from the time of Henry IV was "very idle and injudicious."[17] The allusion tells us, though, that the music performed in this scene of *2 Henry IV*, in one of the earliest productions, was a passameasure galliard and that it was probably played by a consort of viols. From evidence I have presented elsewhere, it also seems that Sneak and his men were a historical band well known to Shakespeare's audiences.[18]

The passameasure galliard is a type of dance music, not the title of a specific score. Several examples are scattered among collections of lute and virginal music. Two—one by William Byrd and one by Peter Phillips—are in *The Fitzwilliam Virginal Book*.[19] A lute version appears in a commonplace lute book (Folger Shakespeare Library MS 1610.1). The tune in the Folger MS is a rollicking piece quite appropriate to the scene in question. A literal transcription of the lute tablature for the "passinmessers galiard" is shown in figure 10.

16. Chambers 2:346.
17. *History of Music* 3:n383.
18. J. Long, "Sneak's 'Noyse' Heard Again?"
19. Volume 1, pp. 209, 306.

If Richard Ligon actually heard a particular type of dance music played during a performance of *2 Henry IV* and remembered it nearly three decades later, his account is unique. No other such comment has been found about specific instrumental music used in a Shakespearean play before the Restoration. This information supports the opinion that much of the instrumental music performed in Shakespeare's plays was drawn from a body of music so popular that specific scores were not needed by the playhouse musicians.

Figure 10.

To return to Sir John and Doll, Falstaff gives the cue for the fiddlers to play (line 246). There is, though, no such definite cue for them to stop playing: the next reference to the musicians occurs in lines 299–300, when Falstaff says to Doll, "A merry song, come. It grows late, we'll to bed." Later (line 403) he tells his page, "Pay the musicians, sirrah." Apparently, Sneak's band plays from about line 246 to about line 299 (throughout some 53 lines). During this time, Sir John and Doll are clapperclawing each other, "Saturn and Venus in conjunction," under the sarcastic observation of the disguised Prince Hal and Poins. The musicians could exit about line 300, though there is no stage direction concerning their departure.

The music in this instance serves both as an appropriate part of the setting and as a humorous topical allusion. Taverns and bawdy houses were notoriously the haunts of vagabond fiddlers and pipers who were quick to gather around any social event, licit or illicit. We can be sure that the Boar's Head would have provided occasions for their music; and if, as I believe, Sneak's Noise was an actual band familiar to Shakespeare and his contemporaries, its employment on the stage and in the particular circumstances of the play should have added spice and realism to the scene.

Sneak's music may also be considered a parallel to the serenade performed during the domestic scene in *1 Henry IV*. In both cases, music accompanies amatory play before the men leave for battle and possible death. Knight observed that this "analogous use of music occurs in *2 Henry IV*, where the love of Doll Tearsheet for Falstaff rises to lyric beauty before his departure for the wars. . . ."[20] The contrast between the aristocratic setting and marital intimacy of the Mortimer and Percy couples, and the tavern setting and the decrepit pawings of Sir John and his whore, as well as the contrast between Glendower's supernatural musicians and Sneak's band, all might suggest that Knight's comment be taken with a grain of salt.

The next cue for music, like the preceding, is interlinear. In act 4, scene 5, line 3, the dying Henry IV calls for music:

> K. HEN. Let there be no noise made, my gentle friends,
>   Unless some dull and favorable hand
>   Will whisper music to my weary spirit.
> WAR.   Call for the music in the other room.
> K. HEN. Set me the crown upon my pillow here.
> CLA.   His eye is hollow, and he changes much.
> WAR.   Less noise, less noise!
>
> > [*Enter* PRINCE HENRY.]

The weary king seeks from harmonious music that quiet ease and harmony of the spirit that has been denied him throughout his stormy reign. In a brilliant symbolic stroke, Shakespeare has the king call for his crown, the symbol of government and order, almost in the same breath that he calls for music, a symbol of harmony and wise counsel, as we have noted in the previous discussion of *musica speculativa*. At the same moment, Warwick commands, "Less noise, less noise," with double emphasis on the "noise," that is, the disordered element in the music of men's lives. The multiple meanings thus achieved sum up the history of Henry IV and his reign with a rich Elizabethan conceit.

But this is not all. The conceit, as it seems intended to do, carries over to enrich the episode when Prince Hal, left alone with his supposedly dead father, picks up the crown and, after a solemn soliloquy, crowns himself in the full realization that the crown "Derives itself to me." The association of the crown and the music is still present as the prince begins his soliloquy, almost repeating the

20. *The Shakespearian Tempest* . . . p. 57.

line spoken by the king immediately after he has called for music: "Why doth the crown lie there upon his pillow, / Being so troublesome a bedfellow?"

The music's dramatic purpose now becomes clear. It is to underscore the prince's set speech (lines 21–47), as did the music accompanying the last soliloquy of Richard II. We can be fairly certain that music is played while the prince speaks and that it begins upon the prince's entrance three lines after Warwick's cue for the musicians to begin playing "in the other room." Only some thirteen lines are spoken after Prince Henry enters, hardly sufficient time for the consort to have completed the (I assume) solemn piece of music it would have performed on such an occasion. Rather, most of the music would have sounded while the prince soliloquized. The resulting combination of musical harmony, the image of the crown, and Prince Henry's assertion of his lineal right to the crown—all this with the implied absence of any "noise" while he states his claim to the crown—seems surely to foreshadow the healthy and harmonious reign of Henry V.[21]

In practice, the music was probably played offstage by a consort composed of recorders or viols. The specific music used in this instance was no doubt grave, quiet, and lyrical. One program piece of the time seems especially appropriate here. It is an orchestral work called "Last Will and Testament" by Antony Holborne.[22] The cantus and bassus parts appear in figure 11.

Justice Shallow's orchard party (act 5, scene 3) is the occasion for the next rendition of music—several song fragments sung by Master Silence, who, well-gilded by sack, bubbles over with wassail songs. The first (lines 17–23):

> Ah, sirrah! quoth a', we shall   [*Singing*]
>   Do nothing but eat, and make good cheer,
>   And praise God for the merry year,
>   When flesh is cheap and females dear,
>   And lusty lads roam here and there
>   So merrily,
>   And ever among so merrily.

21. Ingram ("Musical Pauses and the Vision Scenes in Shakespeare's Last Plays," p. 238) remarked only that the music is "an agent of restful suspense" which "sets the mood for the scene." The many concepts associated with the word "harmony" are fully treated by L. Spitzer, *Classical and Christian Ideas of World Harmony*.
22. *Pavans, Galliards, Almains, and Other Short Aeirs*, no. 53.

There is no direct evidence that Silence sings this or the subsequent bits of popular songs. There is no stage direction for him to sing at any point in the scene, witness the Q and F texts. Also, both Q and F, which frequently italicize lines from songs, do not do so in any case within this scene. Furthermore, after one song bit (lines 48–50), Falstaff comments, "Well said, Master Silence." Despite this

Figure 11.

negative evidence, both Elizabethan dramatic practice and the weight of scholarly opinion direct the song lines to be sung.

In lines 35–39 Silence picks up some tags of the conversation around him and launches into another stanza:

> Be merry, be merry, my wife has all,
> For women are shrews, both short and tall.
> 'Tis merry in hall when beards wag all,
>   And welcome merry Shrovetide.
> Be merry, be merry.

Both this and the preceding stanza are parts taken from songs, or a song, belonging to a subspecie of the carol, the Shrovetide wassail song. The genre is characterized, as Peter Seng has noted, by four to eight stanzas of three or four lines each, a rhyme scheme aaa, and a chorus or burden of one or more lines rhyming bb.[23] The refrain is frequently "Be merry, be merry." An example of this wassail song is a carol in John Stevens' *Medieval Carols*:[24]

> (Burden) Be merry, be merry, I pray you evrychon.
> (Verse)   A principal point of charity,
>   It is, merry to be
>   in him that is but one; be merry.

The rhyme scheme, however, is best typified by the secular medieval carol "Agincourt," which celebrates the famous victory of Henry V. The last stanza is typical:

> Now gracious God he save our King,
> His people and all his well-willing!
> Give him good life and good ending,
> That we with mirth may safely sing
>   Deo gracias![25]

It is surprisingly difficult to find Shrovetide songs among collections of early ballads and popular songs. The merry drinking songs such as "Back and sides go bare, go bare" or "Three merry men be

---

23. "The Dramatic Function of the Songs in Shakespeare's Plays," pp. 129–30. See also the commentary in Seng, *The Vocal Songs in the Plays of Shakespeare* . . . pp. 47–49.

24. Pages 4–5.

25. E. Routley, *The English Carol*, p. 38.

we" appear in the early years of Elizabeth's reign, but their religious flavor has been largely lost. Perhaps the Puritan morality, always antagonistic to the "pagan" folk customs and festivals frequently associated with religious holidays, was responsible for emptying the wassail songs from the bags of the ballad-sellers, at least in Shakespeare's London.

But the Shrovetide songs would still have been current in the provinces where bibulous countrymen, such as Master Silence, could sing them lustily with no sense of sin. The medieval world still existed in rural England, and so did its music.

Master Silence may well have sung his two stanzas to the tune of "Be merry, be merry." The songs he sings and this song both belong to the carol genre. Several other carols of the same time, roughly, are set to tunes similar in musical phraseology. Greene's *The Early English Carols* contains three Christmas carols—nos. 23, 40, and 62—in which this kinship may be seen.

Do noth-ing but eat, and make good cheer, and praise God
Be mer-ry be mer-ry, my wife has all, For wo-men are

for the mer - ry year, when flesh is cheap and fe - males
shrews both short and tall, 'Tis mer-ry in hall when beards wag

dear, And lus-ty lads roam here and there So mer-ri-ly etc.
all, And wel-come mer - ry shrove-tide Be mer-ry be mer-ry, etc.

Figure 12.

Silence's first two song tags fit the "Be merry, be merry" tune as edited by Stevens; I have therefore set the two stanzas to this tune (see figure 12).

Master Silence then produces two more wassail ballad fragments, apparently also carols:

A cup of wine that's brisk and fine,
And drink unto the leman mine,
    And a merry heart lives long-a.

* * * * * *

Fill the cup, and let it come.
I'll pledge you a mile to the bottom.

Again, the rhyme scheme aa and the tetrameter suggest the genre.
The source of the text is not known, but the lines, like those preceding, may be sung to the tune "Be merry, be merry."

As Falstaff watches Master Silence drain a bumper, he exclaims,
"Why, now you have done me right," an allusion to what must have
been a drinking song very popular when Shakespeare wrote *2 Henry
IV*. In Thomas Nashe's *Summer's last Will and Testament* (1600),
Baccus sings the following lines:

> Mounsieur Mingo for quaffing doth surpasse,
> In Cuppe, in Canne, or glasse.
> God Baccus, doe mee right,
> And dubbe mee knight Domingo.[26]

J. O. Halliwell also noted a parallel in Marston's *Antonio and
Mellida* (1602): "Do me right, and dub me knight Ballurdo."[27]
Master Silence picks up Falstaff's reference and sings a part
of the song: "Do me right, and dub me Knight, Samingo."

A text of this drinking song was published in 1918 by Eleanor
Brougham,[28] following an earlier discovery of the text by G. E. P.
Arkwright. Miss Brougham's source was a Bodleian Music School MS,
"Songs of 3, 4, and 5 parts, English and Latten," by Orlando di
Lasso, fol. 18 (c. 1655–1656). The setting is for four parts.[29] Later,
J. W. Brown published an MS variant of the text, dated c. 1637.[30]
Recently, two musical settings other than the Lasso MS have been
found. Frederick Sternfeld discovered a French love song, "Un jour
vis un foulon," set by Lasso with a marginal notation indicating that
the music supplied a tune to which "Monsieur Mingo" was also
sung.[31] John Cutts has published a setting of the song to a treble
part he found in "Pastoral Ballads, etc.," National Library of Scotland Adv. MS 5.2.14, fol. 25 (c. 1639).[32] Since the setting found by
Sternfeld is in a collection of songs by Lasso, *In Recveil du Mellange
de Lassus* (1570), it would seem that the version found by Cutts is

26. *The Works of Thomas Nashe* 3:264 (lines 968–71).
27. Quoted by Seng in "The Dramatic Function of the Songs in Shakespeare's Plays," p. 137.
28. *Corn from Olde Fields*, pp. 279–80.
29. Shakespeare, *The Second Part of Henry the Fourth*, p. 206, notes to
lines 72, 74.
30. "Some Elizabethan Lyrics."
31. "Lasso's Music for Shakespeare's 'Samingo.' "
32. "The Original Music of a Song in *2 Henry IV*."

an MS copy made from the earlier printed score. The text, as collected by Cutts, and Lasso's music, as published by Sternfeld, are shown in figure 13.

Figure 13.

As Pistol bursts into the company to announce his tidings of "lucky joys / And golden times and happy news of price," Falstaff begs him to "Let King Cophetua know the truth thereof." Silence again picks up what he thinks is a cue and sings one line from an old Robin Hood ballad, "And Robin Hood, Scarlet, and John." The line is from the ballad "Robin Hood and the Pinder of Wakefield" as found in the Percy manuscript (Brit. Mus. Add. MS 27,879, fol. 6), with versions in many other collections. The Child version gives the line in this stanza:

> All this beheard three wighty yeomen,
> 'Twas Robin Hood, Scarlet and John;
> 'Twas Robin Hood, Scarlet and John;
> With that they espy'd the jolly pinder,
> As he sat under a thorn.[33]

The version of the ballad (1557–1558) printed in *The Roxburghe Ballads*[34] directs it to be sung to the tune, or tunes, "Wakefield on a Green" and "The Bailiff's Daughter of Islington." The latter ballad was included in collections by Joseph Ritson, William Percy, Francis Douce, and others. In *The Roxburghe Ballads*[35] the tune to which "The Bailiff's Daughter . . ." is sung is called "I have a good old mother at home"; there are also variant titles: "I have a good old woman at home" and "I have a good wife at home." Edward Rimbault found a tune with the title "The jolly Pinder" in a lute MS.[36] The stanza from Child's version is set to Chappell's transcription of the lute tune (melody line only) in figure 14.

Figure 14.

The Robin Hood fragment is the last line sung by Master Silence. Upon the news of Henry IV's death, he slides under the table and into silence.

The merry party in Shallow's orchard—the half-senile Shallow, the diseased and unscrupulous Falstaff, the dim-witted and drunken Silence with his wassail songs—all seem to be presented by Shakespeare in pointed contrast to the approaching coronation scene that will contain the dramatic rejection of Falstaff by Henry V. The new king is Henry V of England, no longer Prince Hal of the Eastcheap taverns. Silence's bibulous songs are drowned out by the trumpets pealing for the coronation.

Act 5, scene 5, opens with two grooms strewing rushes in prepara-

33. J. Child, ed., *English and Scottish Ballads* 5:205.
34. Chappell, ed., *The Roxburghe Ballads* 8:530.
35. Ibid., 2:457.
36. Chappell, ed., *Popular Music of the Olden Time* 1:203.

tion for the entrance of Henry V. The trumpets bray a flourish (the third of the conventional three fanfares) as Henry enters the scene (line 43): [*Shouts within, and the trumpets sound*]. Falstaff is banished; the play is ended.

2 Henry IV needs no epilogue, but one is provided, to be spoken by a dancer who, before beginning his footwork, announces a forthcoming play, *Henry V*. The practice of concluding plays, both

Figure 15.

comedies and tragedies, with a jig performed by dancing and singing comedians was evidently well established at the end of the sixteenth century. The practice, however, was not universally admired. Thomas Dekker in his *Strange Horse-Race* (1613) complained:

> I haue often seene, after the finishing of some worthy tragedy or catastrophe in the open theaters, that the sceane after the Epilogue hath beene more blacke (about a nasty bawdy jiggc) then the most horrid sceane in the play was.[37]

37. *The Non-Dramatic Works* 3:340.

Dekker referred, apparently, to the dialogue song-dances such as those described by Charles Baskervill in his *The Elizabethan Jig and Related Song Drama*. The dance following the epilogue of *2 Henry IV* is not of this sort; it is a solo act, just a dance. The dancer was most likely Will Kemp, who was admired as a dancer and comedian. The music to several of "Kemp's jigs" exists in various collections. The "Kemps Gigge" shown in figure 15 is a transcription of the lute tablature in Univ. Library Cambridge MS D.d.2.11, fol. 92 (c. 1588). There is also a "Kemps Jegg," no. 25 in Playford's *The English Dancing Master* (1651), but it is not the same tune as the first I mentioned. No doubt the music for the epilogue dance was played by a musician on a pipe and tabor. In 1600, between February 11 and March 11, Kemp danced from London to Norwich, an event which he described in his *Kemps nine daies wonder* (1600). The title page of his account is illustrated with a woodcut portraying Kemp dancing a morris. He is accompanied by a musician playing simultaneously a pipe and tabor.

Henry V

The major theme of *Henry V* is the emergence of Prince Hal as the ideal Christian king—pious, just, wise, and valiant. The swelling scene is laid in royal councils and battlefields, the proper setting for kingly actions. The music is hence appropriate for the majestic theme. The tavern tunes, drinking songs, and the social music of the two preceding plays are replaced by ceremonious and military music. In the prologues to the first three acts, Shakespeare was interested in evoking by sheer poetic effort the "vasty fields of France" and "the very casques that did affright the air at Agincourt." In his attempts to overcome the limitations of his wooden O, Shakespeare combined magnificent descriptive poetry with trumpet flourishes which, as they were intended to do, suggest the pomp and presence of the royal Henry.

There is no rubric calling for a trumpet fanfare to introduce the prologue to act 1, though we may be rather certain that the trumpets sounded. No such direction was probably thought necessary since the openings of plays in the public playhouses were conventionally signaled by three trumpet calls. Considering the dramatic tone clearly established in the first prologue, surely the players would have used as many trumpeters as they could afford in order to produce a flourish royal enough to suggest "A kingdom for a stage, princes to act / And monarchs to behold the swelling scene!"

Likewise, the prologue to act 2 is introduced by a flourish. Here the trumpet music is not only appropriate to the description given by the Chorus, but it also links, in continuous performance, the end of act 1 with the beginning of act 2. It is an exclamation point for the exit of Henry and also introduces the Chorus. The folio text has it this way:

> *King.* ... Wee'le chide this *Dolphin* at his fathers doore.
> Therefore let euery man now take his thought,
> That this faire Action may on foot be brought.
>
> > *Exeunt.*
> > *Flourish. Enter Chorus.*
>
> Now all the Youth of England are on fire,
> And silken Dalliance in the Wardrobe lyes: ...

The same technique governs the flourish preceding the prologue to act 3. Keeping in mind that F seems written for continuous performance even though there is an act division at this point, we observe that act 2 (act 1 in the F text) ends with a statement by the French king. A flourish is then directed, and the Chorus speaks the prologue to act 3, thus:

> FR. KING. You shall be soon dispatched with fair conditions.
> A night is but small breath and little pause
> To answer matters of this consequence.
>
> > [*Flourish. Exeunt.*]

Act III

PROLOGUE

> [*Enter* CHORUS.]

Since the French king's entrance to his audience with the English ambassadors (act 2, scene 4) is marked by a royal flourish, we might assume that his exit would also occasion a fanfare. Actually, we must account for two flourishes—one which sounds six lines before the king exits and that which sounds for the entrance of the Chorus. The explanation for the apparently premature fanfare (2. 4. 140), I think, involves some theatrical "business" that would have delighted the patriotic spirit of Shakespeare's audience.

At line 140 the French king concludes his meeting with the emissaries, saying "Tomorrow shall you know our mind at full." The trumpets signal the end of the audience as the king rises to leave the council chamber. He and his councillors are already moving off the stage when Essex, breaking protocol, halts the regal procession with his dramatic announcement, "Dispatch us with all speed, lest that our King / Come here himself to question our delay, / For he is footed in this land already." The French court pauses in confusion, the king replies to Essex, then all move off the stage as the second flourish sounds. The Chorus then enters and describes King Henry's expedition sailing to lay siege to Harfleur.

The prologue to act 4 (act 3 in F) is spoken by the Chorus without introductory trumpets. The omission in this instance substantiates our earlier observation that the flourishes are used primarily to suggest the pomp and presence of kingly sway. The mood of act 4, though, as created by the Chorus, is a quiet pause, a pensive interlude:

> Now entertain conjecture of a time
> When creeping murmur and the poring dark
> Fills the wide vessel of the universe.

King Henry, in contrast to his decisive actions earlier portrayed, is presented in a philosophic mood, questioning the meaning of wars and kingly responsibilities when weighed against the superficial ceremony that clothes a king. Obviously this pensive mood would not have been suggested by braying brass instruments. For the same reason, the flourish is absent when the prologue to act 5 is presented. Although the Chorus describes the tumultuous welcome Henry receives from his subjects upon his return to England, the point of the Chorus is the king's pious humility:

> . . . So swift a pace hath thought that even now
> You may imagine him upon Blackheath,
> Where that his lords desire him to have borne
> His bruisèd helmet and his bended sword
> Before him through the city. He forbids it,
> Being free from vainness and self-glorious pride,
> Giving full trophy, signal, and ostent
> Quite from himself to God. . . .

The royal (and ostentatious) flourish would be out of place in this depiction of an ideal Christian king.[38]

This nice discrimination in the use of the trumpet is discernible elsewhere in the play. Although King Henry enters the stage early in the play (act 1, scene 2), no flourish is directed at this point. Henry is, in this case, described as a modest young man listening with respectful attention to the counsel of Gloucester, Bedford, the bishops, and other elders. There is no fanfare until Henry dismisses the French ambassadors as described above. In act 2, scene 2, line 11, the direction is [*Trumpets sound. Enter* KING HENRY. . . .] for his judgment of Scroop, Cambridge, and Grey—clearly a matter of state. Conventionally the trumpeters exclaim when he leaves at scene's end, but the music also amplifies Henry's ringing words as he exits, "Cheerly to sea. The signs of war advance. / No King of England if not King of France." The folio text calls for a flourish here; G. B. Harrison, for no obvious reason, omits it in his edition. Later on (3. 3. 58), a trumpet salute is directed as Henry and his army enter victoriously the gates of Harfleur and, again, when Henry claims Katherine as his queen (5. 2. 386). The king of France is assigned only one flourish (act 2, scene 4) as he enters to discuss the defense of his realm with the Constable and others. Shakespeare apparently did not intend to have the light of his hero-king dimmed by more than grudging attention to another monarch.

A parley (3. 2. 149) and two tuckets (3. 6. 120 and 4. 3. 78) complete the military music in the play. Their functions are obvious and need no comment. The sennet which concludes the play proper is, of course, a solemn and stately processional march. Its practical purpose is to aid in clearing the stage. Esthetically, the sennet ends the play on a lofty note appropriate to the dramatic theme, and its harmony symbolizes the political harmony between England and France promised by the union of King Henry and Katherine.

38. Shakespeare probably found his source for this passage in Holinshed, who wrote (*Chronicles* 3:84): "The king like a graue and sober personage, and as one remembring from whome all victories are sent, seemed little to regard such vaine pompe and shewes as were in triumphant sort deuised for his welcomming home from so prosperous a iournie, in so much that he would not suffer his helmet to be carried with him, whereby might haue appeared to the people the blowes and dints that were seene in the same; neither would he suffer any ditties to be made and soong by minstrels of his glorious victorie, for that he would wholie haue the praise and thanks altogither giuen to God."

SEVEN

Julius Caesar

T FIRST GLANCE *Julius Caesar* SEEMS TO CALL FOR little music, but, as usual, the quantity and dramatic possibilities of the music therein are greater than first impressions suggest. There is, of course, ceremonious music such as Shakespeare used in *Titus Andronicus*, but in *Julius Caesar* this public music is also used to make some telling comments on the characters of Caesar, Cassius, and Antony. Later, private [*Music, and a song.*] in Brutus' tent adds a fine stroke to the characterization of Brutus; it augments a piece of stagecraft and presents an example of forceful musical symbolism. As was also true of *Titus Andronicus* the directions for music in this play have resulted in some editorial confusion that our examination may alleviate.

Caesar enters the celebration of the Lupercalia (act 1, scene 2) to processional music—in triumph. There is no direction to this effect, but Caesar's remark (lines 16 and 17) about the music, "I hear a tongue, / shriller than all the music, / Cry 'Caesar' " seems clear evidence that music is playing at this point. The circumstantial nature of the evidence, however, has caused some editorial disagreements. T. S. Dorsch followed F without comment; Hardin Craig inserted the direction [*Flourish.*] before the entrance of Caesar and his train; J. Dover Wilson agreed that the entrance was accompanied by music; Neilson and Hill added no directions concerning the music; Kittredge inserted the rubric [*Music.*], but did not specify what kind of music he believed was called for.[1] Thus, some clarification should be attempted.

Kittredge's edition, I think, most closely approximates the way in which the music was used. He had Caesar and his train enter to the strains of music. When Casca shouts, "Peace, ho! Caesar speaks" (line 2), Kittredge inserted the direction [*Music ceases*]. Later, when Caesar commands, "Set on, and leave no ceremony out" (line 11),

---

1. Respectively, Shakespeare, *Julius Caesar* (Arden edition); Shakespeare, *The Complete Works*; Shakespeare, *Julius Caesar* (New Cambridge edition); Shakespeare, *The Complete Plays and Poems*; Shakespeare, *The Tragedy of Julius Caesar*, ed. G. Kittredge.

Kittredge's instruction is [*Music*]. The Soothsayer calls, and Casca again shouts (line 14), "Bid every noise be still—peace yet again!" Here Kittredge inserted the direction [*Music ceases*]. Caesar converses with the Soothsayer and concludes (line 24), "He is a dreamer. Let us leave him—pass." At this point, F's direction is *Sennet. Exeunt. Manet Brut. & Cass.*

From our previous observations on the sennet and its use in the playhouse, we can muster considerable argument supporting Kittredge's inserted directions for the performance of music in act 4, scene 3. The sennet was habitually used for two purposes—to bring in or usher off the stage large groups of actors and to add solemnity and ceremony. The folio direction for the exit of Caesar and his followers clearly calls for them to move off to the music of a sennet. Also conventionally, Caesar's train would have entered to the music of a sennet. Moreover, the occasion was such that a sennet would have been appropriate; Plutarch, describing Caesar's attendance at the Lupercalia, did not mention music specifically, but wrote of "triumphs" and "ancient customs." The procession with which Caesar enters is indeed a triumphal one: he has returned to Rome from his victory over Pompey. Dover Wilson envisioned a procession of priests and courtiers, Caesar on a litter and surrounded by oriental pomp amid a vast crowd of spectators.[2] Shakespeare would certainly use all the means at his disposal, including music, to suggest a Roman triumph. In any event, the crowded stage and the ceremonious scene both imply that Caesar enters, and also departs, to the stately tempo of a sennet, played, I suppose, by a choir of wind instruments— trumpets, sackbuts, or cornets. Music suitable for the sennet may be found in Appendix IV.

The sennets also serve another purpose; there is a psychological effect to be considered. The music suggests that Caesar is, in effect if not in name, a king, and a victorious warrior-king at that. Remembering the concepts of order, harmony, and stability that Shakespeare seems to have associated with monarchy, we may infer that the sennets characterize Caesar as a strong ruler, politically if not physically, on whose life depend the strength and order of the Roman state. Certain it is that the flourish which rings out each time Caesar refuses the crown (lines 78 and 131) would have connoted royalty to the Elizabethan auditors as the first flourish and the shouts of the populace suggest it to Brutus, who asks (lines 79–80), "What

2. Shakespeare, *Julius Caesar*, p. xxix.

means this shouting? I do fear the people / Choose Caesar for their king."

As Caesar and his friends return from the games (line 177), the direction for music is absent—intentionally so in this case, I believe. The Caesar who returns from the games is not the same haughty man who had been heralded to the games by the preceding sennet and for whom the two flourishes sounded. The whole train of followers is shaken. Brutus notes (lines 183–88):

> The angry spot doth glow on Caesar's brow,
> And all the rest look like a chidden train.
> Calpurnia's cheek is pale, and Cicero
> Looks with such ferret and such fiery eyes
> As we have seen him in the Capitol,
> Being crossed in conference by some Senators.

Caesar is, for the moment, a frightened colossus. Upon the third offer of the crown, Casca reports (lines 254–55), "He fell down in the market place and foamed at mouth and was speechless." Caesar's "falling sickness"—probably epilepsy—can only have been taken as an ill omen by his followers and by the great man himself. For a few moments the warrior-king falters, voicing publicly his fear of Cassius. In these circumstances, ceremony is interrupted. There is no place for a sennet; hence none is directed. It is not until Caesar recovers his composure that he can offer the rather lame excuse (lines 211–12), "I rather tell thee what is to be feared / Than what I fear, for always I am Caesar." With this vaunting statement, the pomp and pride of the occasion is restored, and once more the procession moves off the stage in majesty.

We can be fairly sure that Shakespeare had in mind the association of musical harmony with the political harmony of the state as personified by Caesar. He had Caesar remark, in explaining why Cassius is dangerous (lines 203–4), "He loves no plays / As thou dost, Antony; he hears no music." That is, Cassius is fit only for spoils and stratagems because his temperament is dissonant and incompatible with the harmony of music. He is politically dangerous because he is a discordant note in the harmony of the state. Likewise, when Caesar is physically and mentally shaken by his falling sickness, his *musica humana* is untuned. To indicate this loss of personal temper, no music sounds as his procession returns from the Lupercalian games. Perhaps Shakespeare considered Caesar's physical disabilities as much a danger to the state as Cassius' lean and hungry look.

Music is completely absent from the play as the conspirators develop their plan to assassinate Caesar: where political harmony is lacking, again music is lacking. It is only when Caesar, again with a following, approaches the Capitol (act 3, scene 1) that a direction calls for a flourish. The beginning of act 3 is designed to parallel the first appearance of Caesar in act 1, scene 2. Again Caesar meets the Soothsayer, but in this case there is no interlinear reference to music being played after the dialogue begins. Evidently, the fanfare was all the music Shakespeare thought necessary here, possibly because this scene does not attempt to suggest a Roman triumph as did act 1, scene 2. Moreover, the tempo of the action has accelerated. The murder of Caesar is too near to have the dramatic pace slowed by an excess of ceremony.

With the death of Julius Caesar, the ceremonious music associated with him is heard no more. When music is performed again, it is for an entirely different purpose and is associated this time with Brutus, but also indirectly with the Ghost of Caesar. In act 4, scene 3, line 265, a direction states that Brutus' boy, Lucius, sings a song to the lute just before the visit of the Ghost. Brutus requests the music (lines 255–57), saying, "Bear with me, good boy, I am much forgetful. / Canst thou hold up thy heavy eyes awhile, / And touch thy instrument a strain or two?" After a few lines, F's direction is *Musicke, and a Song.* Lucius then falls asleep, perhaps before the completion of the music. Brutus then comments (lines 267–72),

> This is a sleepy tune. O murderous slumber,
> Lay'st thou thy leaden mace upon my boy,
> That plays thee music? Gentle knave, good night.
> I will not do thee so much wrong to wake thee.
> If thou dost nod, thou break'st thy instrument,
> I'll take it from thee, and, good boy, good night.

The music played by Lucius is a revealing brushstroke in Shakespeare's creation of Brutus' character. Brutus, unlike Cassius, shares Antony's love of music. He possesses an inner harmony that explains his charismatic power over Cassius. As Antony eulogizes him at the conclusion of the play, "His life was gentle, and the elements / So mixed [harmonized] in him that Nature might stand up / And say to all the world, 'This was a man . . . ,' " Brutus displays his gentleness in his treatment of Lucius.[3]

Lucius' music also helps Shakespeare's preparation for the appearance of Caesar's Ghost. In keeping with his practice when presenting specters, the poet suspended the action and introduced some calm or lyrical digression amidst which a ghost appears in startling contrast. The first presentation of King Hamlet's Ghost midst a description of the calm and holy Christmas season is a case in point.[4]

Brutus describes the mood of the music supplied by Lucius as a "sleepy tune"—something quiet, sweet, and slow. It is also clear that Lucius plays a lute, one of the anachronisms in the play. The folio stage direction plainly states that there is both *Musicke, and a Song.* But this raises a question. Did Lucius actually sing a song? Or, if he did, was he following the intention of Shakespeare? I have the impression that Shakespeare did not intend for a song to be performed here—that what he wanted was instrumental music only.

Brutus asks Lucius to "touch thy instrument a strain or two," but he says nothing about a song. When the music ends, Brutus comments, "This is a sleepy tune," but again says nothing to indicate that a song has been sung. Furthermore, this is one of the very exceptional cases wherein a rubric calls for a song in a Shakespeare play, and no text is provided. The casual nature of the direction is foreign to Shakespeare's customary practice; in almost all cases, he supplied the lyrics for the songs in his plays. In fact, the use of the indefinite article "a" suggests that no specific song was written for Lucius and that any song that satisfied the general requirements of the scene was acceptable to the writer of the rubric. Then there is the question of acting technique. How would Lucius fall asleep in the middle of a song? It would be easier for the singing boy to manage this while simply playing a lute. In deference to authority, however, I bow to the F text and to subsequent editors, none of whom questioned that portion of the stage direction which calls for a song.

But now another question arises. What song was selected for performance in the original production of the play? There is no clue that would provide an answer. I shall therefore follow the direction and choose "a" song that would meet the dramatic requirements.

3. Cf. Ingram, "Musical Pauses and the Vision Scenes in Shakespeare's Last Plays," pp. 239–40.
4. Cf. T. Herbert, "Shakespeare Announces a Ghost."

If we assume that the lyric of the song would be a "good night" piece with a languorous and sweet musical setting, may we narrow the choice? Perhaps; the fact that the song is to be sung by a boy actor able to accompany himself on a lute suggests that the song was a lutenist's ayre written for a trained musician, possibly with the skill that an apprentice actor, late from one of the choirboy groups, might

Figure 16.

be expected to have. Dover Wilson remarked that "Orpheus with his lute" from *Henry VIII*, act 3, scene 1, is traditionally used in modern productions.[5] This practice supplies an early text, but no pre-Restoration musical setting for this lyric is now known.

A song meeting the dramatic requirements and having an early musical setting is "Care Charming Sleep" (figure 16). Its text appears in John Fletcher's *Valentinian* (1647), act 5, scene 2, where it is sung to the dying emperor. An anonymous musical setting with Fletcher's text (and a few slight variants) is in Bodleian Library MS Don. c. 57, page 36. The MS song is among other songs by Robert Johnson, John Wilson, Robert Ramsey, and some musical settings for sonnets by Sir John Suckling.

Our examination of the performed music in *Julius Caesar* reveals two distinct types of music—public and private. The public, ceremonious music is associated with Caesar; the intimate lute music and song (if Shakespeare really called for a song) is associated with Brutus. The former is intended to provide a measure of pomp; the latter, a relaxation of the psychological tension both in Brutus and in the audience before the sudden visitation by Caesar's Ghost. This functional dualism of the music is not new in Shakespeare's practice, but in *Julius Caesar* it could imply that Shakespeare saw the death of Caesar as a public, or state, tragedy; and the fate of Brutus as a private, or inner, tragedy. The critical potentialities of this dualistic point of view, however, do not come within the province of this study.

5. Shakespeare, *Julius Caesar*, p. 182, note to line 264. Sternfeld (*Music in Shakespearean Tragedy*, pp. 81, 93) suggested that John Dowland's "Weep you no more sad fountains" be sung by Lucius.

EIGHT

Hamlet

*amlet* PRESENTS MANY CRITICAL PROBLEMS, BUT the dramatic use of the music is not one of them. Quite clearly the performed music is aimed primarily at characterization and, to a lesser extent, at setting. This dual function is, in turn, supported by a division of the music into two elementary classes, vocal music and instrumental music. This simple division is obvious, of course, but it must be stated, because upon it hinge the uses of the music, and from it we may derive several analogies that relate the performed music to larger elements of the play. The songs and singing in the play are assigned to characters who are either clowns and fools or who feign madness; that is, the songs are given to Hamlet, Ophelia, and the First Gravedigger. The instrumental music is placed in scenes in which Claudius plays a prominent part. We may thus see the relationship: Claudius and instrumental music; Hamlet, Ophelia, and the Gravedigger and vocal music.[1] The instrumental music, excepting that which accompanies the dumb show, is all ceremonious in type and use, and it suggests the majesty of temporal power. The vocal music, in contrast, is popular in origin, sung only in intimate circumstances, and (most important) is fragmentary and incoherent and therefore an outward sign of the inward character of the singers.

The instrumental music and its relationship to Claudius first claim our attention. The initial instance is the flourish (act 1, scene 2) which announces the entrance of Claudius and his court into the audience chamber of Elsinore—clearly an occasion of state and

1. R. Ingram (*"Hamlet, Othello,* and *King Lear*: Music and Tragedy," pp. 162–65) found a dualism in the kinds of music performed in the play. He has insisted that the music associated with Hamlet, which is quiet like "the recorder, which 'could discourse eloquent music,' " and the "quiet and pathetic" singing of Ophelia each contrast with the "ostentatious and vulgar" trumpets, kettledrums, and ordnance associated with Claudius and, by inference, with his court. I prefer to describe the music assigned to Hamlet and Ophelia as "private" and that assigned to Claudius as "public." After all, while Claudius' cannon salutes might seem a bit ostentatious, his "court" music was no more vulgar than that of any Renaissance court, including the court of Queen Elizabeth.

ceremony, as witness the fulsome dignity of the king's opening address to the court. When the royal council ends (1. 2. 128), another flourish sounds as Claudius and court leave the chamber. So far we see only the conventional practice. But Hamlet remains on the stage, and he is posed in poignant, lonely grief against the brassy clamor of the trumpets. Claudius has purported to be pleased with his announcement making Hamlet his "most immediate to the throne," and he makes his exit with a statement that rings as hollow as his haughty salute to the heavens:

> This gentle and unforced accord of Hamlet
> Sits smiling to my heart. In grace whereof,
> No jocund health that Denmark drinks today
> But the great cannon to the clouds shall tell,
> And the King's rouse the Heaven shall bruit again,
> Respeaking earthly thunder. Come away.

But Hamlet's reaction is quite different:

> Fie on't, ah, fie! 'Tis an unweeded garden,
> That grows to seed, things rank and gross in nature
> Possess it merely. That it should come to this!
> But two months dead!

The king and Gertrude are at home in the natural world. The death of King Hamlet was to them the common lot. But the death is special to Hamlet; the obsequious shows of mourning "are actions that a man might play" as actors play a part on the stage. Claudius' world is one of show, of appearances. The natural world of Hamlet is "that within which passeth show." Claudius, at least when the play begins, is quite content with the world and is well equipped to act his part; Hamlet, refusing to act, insists upon the reality of the nature which he sees—an evil world in which he cannot be at ease in Zion.

The ostentatious [*A flourish of trumpets, and ordnance shot off within.*] (1. 4. 6) signals the king's carouse while Hamlet and Horatio await the appearance of the Ghost. To Hamlet, the trumpets and ordnance represent the swaggering upstart whose wassail is capable of poisoning the whole state. He does not know at this time, of course, that Claudius has already poisoned the state in the person of King Hamlet, but he comments on men who have "some vicious mole of nature in them / . . . Oft breaking down the pales and forts of reason."

The royal fanfare that, normally, would suggest the majesty and dignity of a sovereign implies to Hamlet an intemperance which overthrows reason and strikes him as ironic since Reason is the sovereign power of the microcosmic state.

As King Claudius enters at the beginning of act 2, scene 2, he is acting in the hypocritical sense of the word. As the preceding flourish saluted the health which he outwardly drank to the accord which he knew did not exist between himself and Hamlet, so the flourish that opens this scene serves to introduce Claudius, Rosencrantz, and Guildenstern, who outwardly plan to seek the cause of the prince's madness but who are actually interested in his political ambitions. Setting the two schoolfellows to spy on Hamlet is a step by the king in the shadowboxing already in progress between the royal antagonists. The trumpets again are part of the "persona" of Claudius, part of his public mask.

The next trumpet call (2. 2. 385) sounds for the entrance of the players as they arrive at Elsinore, but it is indirectly associated with Claudius also. The fanfare follows immediately Hamlet's comments on the boy players. He compares their success to that of Claudius in seizing the throne of Denmark (lines 380–85):

> It is not very strange, for my uncle is King of Denmark, and
> those that would make mows at him while my father lived give
> twenty, forty, fifty, a hundred ducats apiece for his
> picture in little. 'Sblood, there is something in this more than
> natural, if philosophy could find it out.

Hamlet, I think, means that it is unreasonable that people should equate success with superficial novelty, or a king's quality with the outward garb and ceremonies of the kingship. Then the trumpets sound as though, with their signal for a royal entrance, the king himself is approaching. Instead, in comes a company of wandering players. It seems odd that the players should be announced by a royal flourish; usually the trumpets sound before a performance, but not for the players outside their playhouses. We might expect two or three blasts blown by one of the players for advertisement, but the royal flourish is out of place unless the word is used very loosely. As a matter of fact, when the trumpets announce the beginning of the play-within-the-play, the Q2 direction is *The Trumpets sounds* [*sic*], whereas the Q2 direction for all previous trumpet music is *Flourish*. Not to unbearably belabor the point, it seems that this flourish is closely allied both with the hypocrisy of the king—hence the royal flourish—and with the professional hypocrites, the players—hence the advertisement.

The instrumental music next heard follows the same pattern but on a more extravagant scale, for this is the performance of the "Danish March"—the processional music which moves Claudius, Gertrude, Polonius, Ophelia, courtiers, *Trumpets and Kettledrums*, and soldiers with torches into the castle hall for the production of "The Murder of Gonzago" (3. 2. 94). This episode is the turning point of the play, and for it Shakespeare pulled out all the stops, including the musical resources available and appropriate to the scene. The "Danish March" marshals Claudius to the revelation of his secret guilt, hidden until this occasion. The formal processional entry of king and court is contrived to form a dramatic contrast with the swirling confusion of king and court as Claudius interrupts the play and stumbles off the stage to the music of Hamlet's wild song snatches.

After the spectators have settled themselves for the play, the trumpets sound and the dumb show enters. While the actors present their pantomime, hautboys provide a musical background as is customary. The music, of course, accompanies the plot summary given by the player-king, his queen, and his murderer. The player-king is a reflection of Claudius, and we may be sure that Claudius begins to writhe as the pantomime unfolds. As Kittredge has remarked, the dumb show is a form of torture, the first turn of the screw.[2]

After Claudius gives away his secret to Hamlet and Horatio, the mighty opposites recognize each other as opponents condemned to mortal combat. The grim battle is, with growing lack of success, hidden from the populace and the courtiers while its destructive power claims the lives of Polonius, Rosencrantz and Guildenstern, and Ophelia. As the action moves to its catastrophe, the atmosphere of the play becomes charged with the smell of death: the circle of existence that began its cycle in the audience chamber in act 1 has almost completed its circuit. The gap is closed in act 5, scene 2, when for the first time since the presentation of "The Murder of Gonzago" the king, queen, and all the court are assembled as spectators of another show, "The Murder of Hamlet." This time the script is written by Claudius, and he attempts also to direct the play.

As the swordplay between Hamlet and Laertes begins, Claudius speaks some lines (278–89) that ring familiarly in our ears:

2. Shakespeare, *Hamlet*, ed. G. Kittredge, p. 223.

Let all the battlements their ordnance fire.
... And let the kettle to the trumpet speak,
The trumpet to the cannoneer without,
The cannon to the Heavens, the Heaven to earth,
"Now the King drinks to Hamlet."

The drums speak to the trumpet, the trumpet to the cannoneer, the cannon to the heavens, and within minutes the brassy voice of Claudius is stilled, Hamlet ends his weary ministry, Laertes achieves his revenge—and death. The perturbed spirit can rest. The play has ended; there remains only to clear away the bodies from the great stage of Elsinore. A march afar off signals the beginning of a new play, as Fortinbras, the new king, approaches from the wings. Then a dead march of muffled drums speaks to the cannoneers, the cannon speak to the heavens; but no trumpets sound as the bodies of Hamlet, Claudius, Gertrude, and Laertes are borne off in solemn procession.

Thus the instrumental music expresses a temporal world of appearances, of ceremony. It is theatrical. It accompanies King Claudius from his first appearance on the stage; through each climactic episode, it sounds in the background; and its dead march moves him off the stage at the end of the play. The music of Hamlet's life is quite different.

When we turn to Hamlet and the vocal music in the play, we must concern ourselves with the songs as they help to characterize Hamlet and Ophelia. As the nonvocal music was related to the surface world, so the songs, or fragments of songs, partially reflect the inner world of the spirit. The instrumental music, which in Renaissance thought was a mechanical reproduction of the human voice, is "artificial" and, in one sense of the word, false; the vocal music is a natural expression of human thought and emotion and therefore more true to nature. Like Perdita's "gillyvors," vocal music is subject to art, but the art itself derives from nature. Hence, Claudius' music is the music of a sensory world and is artificial in the same way that the music of Spenser's Bower of Acrasia is false and therefore evil. Neither of them reflects nature completely; while they include *musica mundana* and *musica humana*, they fail to include *musica divina*; that is, both reflect a beautiful, naturalistic view of the universe, but they fail to reflect a divinely supernatural view.

Hamlet, on the other hand, cannot fail to observe the supernatural world, divine or otherwise; nor can the audience of the play. The

communication between Hamlet and the Ghost is, I think, the central
fact of the drama. Once he has talked with the Ghost, he knows much
that no other character in the play can know, excepting the stoical
Horatio, who has no call to act on his knowledge. And what he learns
determines the songs he sings. As he questions the Ghost, he asks:

> What may this mean,
> That thou, dead corse, again, in complete steel,
> Revisit'st thus the glimpses of the moon,
> Making night hideous, and we fools of nature
> So horridly to shake our disposition
> With thoughts beyond the reaches of our souls?

Hamlet, by his expression "we fools of nature," implies, I think,
that mankind, unable to grasp the entire scheme of things, is, in the
eyes of higher intelligences—God and His angels—like the half-wits
or "naturals" in the human scale. The fool has thoughts beyond the
reaches of his mind; likewise, men have thoughts beyond the reaches
of their souls. To both, the scheme of things is unknowable; therefore,
the men who perceive only a "natural" comprehensible order in the
universe are fools, for they claim to know that which, as mortal men,
they cannot know. Hamlet, like Plato's philosopher, has ascended from
the cave and has attained a glimpse of the supernatural world. When
he returns to the cave and attempts to converse with Horatio and
Marcellus, he acts like a fool; he speaks wild and whirling words.
Mersenne has told us that God and the angels understand all things
and events, and that they enjoy great content by observing men's
efforts to comprehend the incoherent medley of events that seem to
mock human understanding.

   Therefore, when Hamlet returns to the "normal" world of Elsinore,
he sees it as a stage on which is to be played a drama. His role has
been assigned; indeed, he really has no choice. He speaks of his
part with despair but also with fatalism. He has earlier referred to
himself as a fool of nature; it is, then, not surprising that he decides
to play the part of the fool or jester on the stage that awaits his
entrance.[3] He instructs Marcellus and Horatio (lines 169–79):

3. The belief that Hamlet at times plays the court jester has been stated by
many students since G. Murray's essay "Oedipus and Hamlet." A recent argument in support has been offered by H. Levin, "The Antic Disposition."

Here, as before, never, so help you mercy,
How strange or odd soe'er I bear myself,
As I perchance hereafter shall think meet
To put an antic disposition on,
That you, at such times seeing me, never shall,
With arms encumbered thus, or this headshake,
Or by pronouncing of some doubtful phrase,

* * * * * * * * * * *

Or such ambiguous giving out, to note
That you know aught of me.

The word "antic" is used by Hamlet in its two most common Elizabethan senses, as an adjectival form of the noun meaning a fool or a lackwit, or (contemptuously) an actor or a farcical play. Polonius and Gertrude, with their dull perception, and the lovelorn Ophelia will call this antic disposition madness, but the crafty king is never so persuaded. It is an act which the prince foregoes only when he addresses Horatio and Gertrude, or when he soliloquizes. Moreover, from his point of view, the role of fool or jester is appealing. In his melancholy mood he conceives the world to be filled with things rank and gross in nature. The melancholy Jaques in *As You Like It*, we recall, finds his greatest pleasure in the company of Touchstone, and he himself desires to be a fool. We note the fitness of Jaques' lines (2. 7. 36–61) to the character of Hamlet:

> JAQ. Oh, worthy fool! One that hath been a courtier,
>   And says if ladies be but young and fair,
>   They have the gift to know it. And in his brain,
>   Which is as dry as the remainder biscuit
>   After a voyage, he hath strange places crammed
>   With observation, the which he vents
>   In mangled forms. Oh, that I were a fool!
>   I am ambitious for a motley coat.
>   . . . It is my only suit,
>   Provided that you weed your better judgments
>   Of all opinion that grows rank in them
>   That I am wise. I must have liberty
>   Withal, as large a charter as the wind
>   To blow on whom I please. For so fools have,
>   And they that are most gallèd with my folly,

They most must laugh. And why, sir, must they so?
The "why" is plain as way to parish church.
He that a fool doth very wisely hit
Doth very foolishly, although he smart,
Not to seem senseless of the bob. If not,
The wise man's folly is anatomized
Even by the squandering glances of the fool.
Invest me in my motley, give me leave
To speak my mind, and I will through and through
Cleanse the foul body of the infected world,
If they will patiently receive my medicine.

The player-fool, or clown, thus has his part in achieving the whole purpose of playing, which is to show virtue (or vice) her own feature; scorn, her own image; and the very body of the time, his form and pressure. The time, as Hamlet knows, is out of joint; it is the cue for the fool to cleanse the foul body of an infected Denmark. Only with the license of the fool can Hamlet proceed with his ministry, or, if we prefer, his minstrelsy.

In assuming his antic disposition, Hamlet also assumes many of the traditional characteristics of the stage fool. He has already mentioned two of them: the foolish gestures and the doubtful phrase. The doubtful phrase, of course, refers to the bawdy conceits, riddles, old twisted proverbs, paradoxes, non sequiturs—the mixture of wit, half-sense, and nonsense behind which the fool launches the stinging shafts that make fools of those who rest too securely in their assumed wisdom. Another property of the fool is his disorder. It is his business to unsettle a world that, putting too much trust in its presumed knowledge, is inclined to take itself too seriously. He is the enemy of convention and habit, tradition and dogma. In a word, he is the destructive agency necessary to the life and growth of human natures. In setting the time back to rights, Hamlet must of necessity destroy the time that is out of joint, the world of Claudius. He operates by using his mockery, innuendos, and ambiguous phrases as a mirror held up to the face of Denmark. Indeed, Hamlet in several instances is quite explicit about his part as court jester–actor. When Ophelia comments on his foolery (3. 2. 129), "You are merry, my lord," he answers, "O God, your only jig-maker." He refers to himself as the interpreter of a puppet show (lines 256–57); he says (line 288) that his success with the "Mousetrap" should get him a fellowship in a cry of players. When Polonius humors him regarding the shape of the clouds (lines 400–401), he remarks in an aside, "They fool me to the top of my bent," that is, they treat him as the fool he is trying so hard to play. Finally, we remember that the only glimpse Shakespeare gave us of Hamlet's childhood is his affection for, and his intimacy with, Yorick, the king's jester, whose gibes, gambols, songs, and flashes of merriment were wont to set the table on a roar.

What has all this to do with *Hamlet*'s music? We have earlier observed that a peculiar property of the stage fool is his practice of singing bits of songs. In the early interludes, apparently, the song fragments were strung together to form a comic medley of half-sense and nonsense intrinsically humorous. With the growth of psychological characterization in the later Elizabethan drama, especially in Shakespeare's works, the ballad medley as a self-contained comic device is altered as the stage jester's role becomes more sophisticated. The song bits are retained, but they are separated and distributed according to the needs of dramatic characterization, which technique enables them to serve as satiric, ironic, or gnomic auxiliaries. In this manner the song snatches provide a musical form of indirect comment; Hamlet's singing, like his doubtful phrases, is a method in madness or foolery.

A part of Hamlet's antic act is his use of ballad tags, usually when he is acting the fool to the top of his bent. But his songs are in themselves rational enough; they are simply fragmentary scraps, for the most part, of old, familiar, popular songs like those sung and spoken by Lear's Fool. When Polonius comes to tell Hamlet about the arrival of the players (2. 2. 425–39), Hamlet replies with a scrap of an old ballad, "Jep[ht]ha, Judge of Israel." He quotes a line from another old song "For O, for O, the hobby-horse is forgot!" as an example of the brevity of human grief (3. 2. 144–45). After the play-within-the-play ends, he bursts into what seems to be a song stanza, "Why, let the strucken deer go weep"—a reference to Claudius' discomfiture—closely followed by what seems to be a song about Damon and Pythias. This, too, refers to Claudius.

The question necessarily arises, since we are concerned with the performed music in the play, whether or not Hamlet is supposed to sing these snatches of songs. There are no stage directions in the Q2 text or in the First Folio to the effect that he should sing any of them; however, actors playing Hamlet sometimes sing or chant one or more of these bits. If Hamlet is acting the court jester, as I believe he is, it would be in character for him to sing.

Ophelia, torn between her love for Hamlet and her duty to Polonius, permits herself to be drawn into the court intrigue in the belief that she may help to cure her lover's madness. When Hamlet murders her father and disappears from Elsinore, she is unable to cope with her double grief and withdraws into madness. Her inner world becomes a realm of childhood, of old, simple ballads sung by the spinners in the sun, of wildflowers and brooks. Chanting her old lays and decking herself with virginal garlands, she slips into a stream and contentedly sinks to a watery death.

Ophelia is a pathetic figure, but even those familiar with the play find her entrance in the first mad scene (act 4, scene 5) comic: the reaction of those seeing their first performance of the play is usually a snicker. Perhaps we expect a continuation of Hamlet's antics. If so, we are mistaken, but not entirely so. In many ways, Ophelia's lunacy closely resembles Hamlet's when he is acting especially droll. But Hamlet knows that he is acting; Ophelia does not, and that is the essential difference. She may be one of the fools of nature, driven to insanity by thoughts beyond the reaches of her soul, but she does not act the sophisticated court jester as does Hamlet. Rather, she becomes a "natural" fool, a half-wit incapable of "acting" or of hypocrisy. We thus view her with a poignant mixture of emotions—superiority, amusement, and pity. The marks of her lunacy are much the same as those assumed by Hamlet, and they are equally the traditional properties of the stage fool—the foolish gestures, doubtful phrases, snatches of ballads. Also, her innocent, witless speech, songs, and actions, like Hamlet's foolery, serve to hold a mirror up to nature; but, whereas the prince's mirror reflects the outward signs of corruption in the world of Elsinore, Ophelia's glass seems to reflect the inner thoughts of those persons exposed to her attention. But let Shakespeare describe this quality of her distraught mind and speech (4. 5. 4–13):

> She speaks much of her father, says she hears
> There's tricks i' the world, and hems and beats her heart,
> Spurns enviously at straws, speaks things in doubt
> That carry but half-sense. Her speech is nothing,
> Yet the unshaped use of it doth move
> The hearers to collection. They aim at it,
> And botch the words up fit to their own thoughts,
> Which, as her winks and nods and gestures yield them,
> Indeed would make one think there might be thought,
> Though nothing sure, yet much unhappily.

Her speech, like a mirror, is nothing in itself; it serves only to reflect the thoughts which the hearers fit to it. Thus, as the "Mouse-trap" play, by Hamlet's contriving, reveals Claudius' guilt, so Ophelia's speech and song lines may add the torture of self-revelation to Claudius and Gertrude—Ophelia's madness or "naturalness" picking up where Hamlet's "art" leaves off. For example, the question in the first line sung by Ophelia, "How should I your true-love know" is apparently addressed to the queen. Most students of the play, following Samuel Coleridge, believe that Ophelia is with this stanza making a distracted reference to Hamlet. This is quite possible. But, if the song is to reflect the thoughts of the hearer, as Shakespeare invited us to believe, Gertrude could very well see in this stanza—as well as in the following two, respectively, "He is dead and gone, lady" (line 29) and "White his shroud as the mountain snow" (line 35)—not Hamlet or Polonius alone, but also the dead King Hamlet, who also "to the grave did not go / With true-love showers" even though Gertrude wept like Niobe.

Likewise, Ophelia's four stanzas beginning with "Tomorrow is Saint Valentine's day" (line 48) seem to be sung to Claudius. In this old lay relating the betrayal of a love-tryst, we may see an allusion to the forsaken love between Hamlet and Ophelia, but to Claudius' guilty conscience it may suggest his deceitful and, according to church law, incestuous marriage to Gertrude—a kind of betrayal. May we then consider these ballad snatches as several more turns of the thumbscrew for Claudius and Gertrude?

Later, when Ophelia makes her second entrance (line 153), Laertes speaks to her. In reply, apparently turning toward her brother, she sings the bit of ballad beginning "They bore him bare-faced on the bier" (line 164). Laertes takes this as a demented recollection of Polonius' death and, for him, a persuasion to revenge —a clear reflection of the thought already uppermost in his mind.

So far, if I am correct, we have seen Ophelia singing her songs to specific hearers—Gertrude, Claudius, and Laertes. Her singing thus parallels her distribution of real or imaginary flowers (beginning line 175) and her naming each flower with its symbolic equivalent as she turns to Claudius, Gertrude, and Laertes. The parallel is firmly established by her next ballad fragment (line 187), "For bonny sweet Robin is all my joy." The association occurs in the old Whitsuntide or morris folk plays. Two of the main characters in these plays are Robin Hood and Maid Marian. Marian, the "leman" of Robin, is usually a merry and wanton wench given to bawdy jokes and coarse language. The title of several lute tunes in a popular style is "Robin Hood is to the greenwood gone" or, in one case, simply "Robin Hoode." Ophelia's line seems to be a refrain, possibly from the same song for which the lute tune was a setting. The text of the song itself is unknown. As a part of her act, Maid Marian sings songs and carries a bouquet of flowers and, possibly, distributes them as does Perdita in the "Whitsun pastoral" of *The Winter's Tale*.[4] It would appear, then, that in her clouded mind Ophelia may at times assume the role of Maid Marian in the folk plays.

The concluding stanzas sung by Ophelia, beginning "And will a' not come again?" (line 190), are apparently allusions to Polonius. Then, with her exit line, "God be wi' you," she slips away to the brook, where, chanting her song tags, she tries to hang her flower garland on a willow tree as do the forsaken lovers in the ballads. Should we be surprised that Shakespeare buried this pathetic clown, with her winks, nods, gestures, her unshaped speech and patches of ballads, in the grave of Yorick the jester?

As the First Gravedigger, another clown, empties Yorick's grave to receive the body of Ophelia, he sings at his task (5. 1. 69). But his song is a grim jest in itself. He begins, "In youth, when I did love, did love." The lyrics then trace the lover as he ages, dies, and is buried. The third stanza concludes with the statement, "Oh, a pit of clay for to be made / For such a guest is meet." The point, of course, is that golden lads and lasses must, as chimney sweepers, come to dust. The stanzas are mangled excerpts (stanzas 1, 3, 8, 13) of a song attributed to Lord Vaux by George Gascoigne.[5] The MS title is "A dyttye or sonet made by the lord Vaus, in the time of the noble quene Marye, representing the image of Death."[6]

The song presents the image of Death in more ways than one if its performance be considered within the circumstances of the play. Harley Granville-Barker noted that "It is Ophelia's grave that is digging, the Clown's song is a counterpart to hers."[7] Peter Seng saw

4. An anti-Martin pamphlet written by Thomas Nashe on the Martin Marprelate controversy used the traditional May game or Whitsun play, for satiric purposes. Nashe compared Martin to the Maid Marian of the folk play, saying, "Martin himselfe is the Mayd-marian, trimlie drest vppe in a cast Gowne, and a Kercher of Dame *Lawsons*, his face handsomlie muffled with a Diaper-napkin to couer his beard, and a great Nosegay in his hands, of the principalest flowers I could gather out of all hys works." See Chambers, *The Elizabethan Stage* 4:231.

5. Shakespeare, *Hamlet*, ed. H. Furness, nn59–62.

6. Ibid.

7. *Prefaces to Shakespeare* 1:35.

the confusion of the song by the Clown as a commentary on the disordered moral universe of the entire play, and he recalled the hasty funeral of King Hamlet, the hugger-mugger of Polonius' obsequies, and the maimed rites accorded Ophelia.[8] Suffice it for us to observe that the Gravedigger's song is a proper part of the atmosphere—the smell of death—that permeates the scene, and that, like a grinning skull, it tunes its music to the skull of Yorick that "had a tongue in it, and could sing once" even as the Clown sings, and to whose favor the gentle face of Ophelia must come. Truly the scene presents us with a convocation of clowns—Yorick's bones thrown unceremoniously out to make room for those of Ophelia, while the Gravedigger sings at his work, and Hamlet the jester makes macabre jokes on the old theme *Contemptu mundi.*

Not all the sources of the ballads used in *Hamlet* have been identified. William Percy discovered texts for "Jephtha, Judge of Israel" and "Walsingham," of which latter ballad Ophelia's first stanza beginning "How should I your true-love know" seems to be a fragmentary version. As we have seen, there is some evidence that the line "For bonny sweet Robin is all my joy" is part of the song "Robin Hood is to the greenwood gone." I revert to these latter two ballads because they provide an interesting coincidence that again suggests a connection between *Hamlet* and the traditional singing of ballad medleys by stage fools. It is possible that one of Shakespeare's contemporaries, noting the dramatic use of the ballad fragments in the play, saw a family resemblance to the ballad medleys made popular by the late Richard Tarleton. Perhaps, hoping to capitalize on the popularity of both *Hamlet* and the ballad medleys, he took the titles of songs in the play and, with them and others, constructed a ballad medley for public sale. However it came about, on September 3, 1604, the same year in which the Q2 edition of *Hamlet* was published, the following entry was made to one Symon Stafford in the Stationers' Register: "Symon Stafford. Entred for his copie vnder the handes of the Wardens A Ballad called *Tytles of Ballades or A newe medley beginning* 'ROBIN *is to the grene gone*' '*as I went to Walsingham.*'...."[9] Unfortunately, the medley text is unknown.

Although we have examined the dramatic possibilities of the per-

8. "The Dramatic Function of the Songs in Shakespeare's Plays," p. 419.
9. *A Transcript of the Registers of the Company of Stationers* 3:113b. H. Wooldridge (*Old English Popular Music* 1:154) erroneously transcribed this entry to read "Tythes of Ballads," etc.

formed music in *Hamlet*, we have yet to consider the music and its performance. Let us begin with the instrumental music.

We need only to treat the music of the "Danish March" and the music played during the dumb show. The flourishes and the dead march pose no problems. The fact that the "Danish March" is the only instance where Shakespeare calls for an instrumental work by

Figure 17.

a specific title might imply that this particular march had some topical interest for him and for his audiences beyond its appropriateness to the stage court of Denmark. Moreover, the Q2 stage direction speci-fies that this march be played by trumpeters and a kettledrummer. The topical interest could have originated in the coronation proces-sion of King James and Queen Anne of Denmark through London on March 15, 1603. Thomas Dekker, in his description of the oc-casion, published in 1604 (probably quite early in the year), reported that "to delight the Queene with her owne country Musicke, nine Trumpets, and a Kettle Drum, did very sprightly & actiuely sound the *Danish march.* . . ."[10] Since the royal trumpeters sometimes augmented their incomes by performing in the playhouses, the King's Men could easily have requested them to duplicate the march for some early productions of the play.[11]

The notation of the "Danish March" is no longer known: the trumpeters transmitted their music memorially and probably did not record the music. The sennet shown in Appendix IV is an arrangement of the trumpet march "De la Tromba Pauin" in Thomas Morley's *First Booke of Consort Lessons* (1599 and 1611). It is not the "Danish March," but it may satisfy the practical requirements of stage production.

Although the instrumentation, a consort of hautboys, is given for the music played during the dumb show, there is no hint of the musical score or scores used by the hautboists. I would guess that two contrasting pieces were used—one during the scene presenting the player-king and his queen, the other during the pantomimed murder of the king. From a collection of popular instrumental pieces, Antony Holborne's *Pavans, Galliards, Almains, and Other Short Æirs* (1599), I have selected two program compositions which should be appropriate: no. 28, the anonymous "Ecce quam bonum," for the first half of the dumb show, and no. 31, "The funerals," by Holborne, for the second half (see figures 17 and 18). Only the cantus and bassus parts are available, but the inner voices can be realized without much difficulty.

The song snatches chanted or spoken by Hamlet are, of course, unaccompanied. The first fragment is a dramatic paraphrase of a ballad, "Jepha, Judge of Israel," as Steevens first noticed.[12] It belongs to the class of scriptural ballads usually heavily didactic in matter. It was entered in the Stationers' Register in 1567 or 1568 and then was re-entered in 1624.[13] The text has been published in *The Roxburghe Ballads* (3:201), and in *The Shirburn Ballads* (page 175), from the manuscript copy of about 1600. Here is the first stanza:

> I read that, many yeares ago,
>> When *Jepha*, Judge of *Israel*,
> Had one faire Daughter, and no moe,
>> Whom he beloued passinge well,

10. *The Magnificent Entertainment* . . . pp. E2–E2^v.
11. See chap. 1, *n*15.
12. Shakespeare, *Hamlet*, ed. Kittredge, p. 195, note to line 421.
13. Ibid.

And as by lot, God wot
It came to passe, most like it was,
Great warres there should be,
And who should be chiefe but he, but he.

The continuation of the ballad relates the biblical story (Judges 11)
and ends as Jephtha sends his daughter away to be sacrificed.

Figure 18.

The tune for this ballad is unknown; I have therefore set the text
to a tune known in its earlier usage as "Well-a-day" and later by
several other titles, including "Essex's last Good-night," "O hone,
O hone," "Sir Walter Rauleigh his Lamentation," "Murther un-
masked," and others suggesting equally lugubrious matter.[14] The

14. Chappell, ed., *Popular Music of the Olden Time* 1:176.

tune is one of those, such as "Fortune my foe," frequently used as settings for doleful ballads. The setting is shown in figure 19.

In act 3, scene 2, lines 144–45, Hamlet quotes what appears to be the refrain of an old song, "For O, for O, the hobby-horse is forgot!" There is a song including a line much like Hamlet's, "The hobby horse was quite forgot, when Kempe did dance alone a," no. 20 in Thomas Weelkes' *Ayres or phantasticke spirites . . .* (1608).[15] Weelkes' song has some interesting allusions to Robin Hood, Maid Marian, and Little John, and also to Kemp's visit to France and Italy in 1600, but no apparent connection with Hamlet's line (see Appendix VII).

As noted previously, the stanza beginning "For thou dost know, O Damon dear" (lines 292–95) is sometimes chanted by actors

Figure 19.

playing Hamlet. No song or music has been found that can be connected directly with these four lines. They contain a reference to Damon, which suggests the famous friends Damon and Pythias. There is an old play by Richard Edwards called *Damon and Pithias* (1565).[16] There is also an old song, "A Newe Ballade of a Louer / Extollinge his Ladye. To the tune of Damon and Pithias" (1568), printed in a broadside including both tune and text.[17] John Ward has published the tune, but it does not fit Hamlet's stanza. The tune, however, does fit a song from Edwards' play, "Awake, ye woful wights," suggesting that the ballad tune may earlier have been the music for

15. New York Public Library MS Drexel 4300. The song is reproduced and discussed by Ringler, "The Hobby Horse is Forgot."

16. Chambers, *The Elizabethan Stage* 4:81, 143, 193.

17. Ward, "Music for 'A Handefull of pleasant delites,'" p. 167.

Edwards' song.[18] Another ballad, entitled "A Louer in the praise of his lady," of roughly the same date as "A Louer / Extollinge his Ladye," is directed to be sung to the popular tune "Calen O Custure me."[19] This tune fits Hamlet's lines with ease. Both ballad tunes were probably well known by the time *Hamlet* was staged. The music for "Calen O Custure me" may be found in several collections: *The Fitzwilliam Virginal Book* (c. 1600) contains an arrangement by William Byrd, later printed by William Chappell in his *Popular Music of the Olden Time* (2:793). The music I have used in setting Hamlet's lines (figure 20) is that recently published by John Ward, who reproduced a lute version from Trinity College, Dublin, MS D.1.21 (the William Ballet lute book).[20]

Figure 20.

The first ballad fragment sung by the distraught Ophelia, "How should I your true-love know," was early identified by Thomas Percy, who found a close resemblance between it and one of the "Walsingham" ballads. These "Walsingham" songs, as Percy and others have noted, are variants on the story of a lover who meets a pilgrim returning from a journey to the shrine of Our Lady of Walsingham. The lover asks the pilgrim if he has seen his mistress, who had gone on the same pilgrimage. The pilgrim, after some questions and answers that identify the mistress, answers that she is dead, far away. The lover then grieves over her distant death.

Peter Seng quoted an example of the "Walsingham" type (Brit. Mus. Add. MS 27,879, the Percy Folio MS, fols. 251a, b):

18. Long, "Music for a Song in Edwards' *Damon and Pithias*."
19. Ward, "Music for 'A Handefull of pleasant delites,' " pp. 161–62.
20. Ibid., p. 85.

As yee came fr: the Holye
AS: yee came ffrom the holy Land
of Walsingham
mett you not wth my true loue
by the way as you came
how should I know yor true loue
yt haue mett many a one
as I ame ffrom the holy Land
yt haue come yt haue gone

She is neither white nor browne
but as the heauens ffaire
there is none hathe their fforme diuine
on the earth or the ayre
such a one did I meete good Sr:
wth and angellike fface
who like a nimph like a queene did appeare
in her gate in her grace

Shee hath left me heere alone
all alone as unknowne
who sometime loued me as her liffe
& called me her owne
what is the cause shee hath left thee alone
& a new way doth take
yt sometime did loue thee as her selfe
& her ioy did thee make

I haue loued her all my youth
but now am old as you see
loue liketh not the ffalling ffruite
nor the withered tree
for loue is like a carlesse child
& fforgets promise past
he is blind he is deaffe when he list
& infaith neuer ffast.[21]

(Two final stanzas omitted.)

As was sometimes his practice, Shakespeare has reversed the sexes of the lovers in Ophelia's version of the ballad.

The following fragment, beginning "He is dead and gone, lady"

21. As quoted by Seng, "The Dramatic Function of the Songs in Shakespeare's Plays," pp. 357–59. The various musical settings for Ophelia's songs are fully discussed and reproduced in Sternfeld, *Music in Shakespearean Tragedy*, pp. 61–75.

(line 29), is not a part of the "Walsingham" ballad quoted above, nor is the next quatrain, beginning "White his shroud as the mountain snow" (line 35). Indeed, the two quatrains have not been identified as parts of any known ballad. They may be segments of some Walsingham ballad now lost, or may be lines borrowed from other ballads now disappeared. Line 38, "Which bewept to the grave did not go," was regularized by Alexander Pope and other early editors who removed the "not" from the line. This was done with no textual authority; the "not" appears in all F and Q texts and is therefore

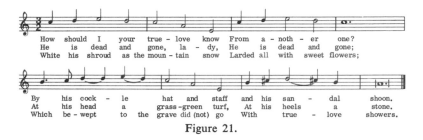

Figure 21.

retained in most modern editions. Kittredge suggested that the word should be considered an interpolation by Ophelia to make the ballad line fit the circumstances of her father's funeral.[22] And, we may also note, the insertion makes the line applicable to the funeral of King Hamlet, whose widow wept like Niobe but whose love was hardly constant.

The music for the "Walsingham" ballad is well known, and all three of the quatrains sung by Ophelia may be set to it (see figure 21). It was also quite popular in Shakespeare's day; as Naylor observed, there are two arrangements of the tune—one by John Bull and the other by William Byrd (in *The Fitzwilliam Virginal Book*) and other versions in Antony Holborne's *The Cittharn Schoole* (1597).[23] Modern editions include those of Chappell, Wooldridge, Naylor, Gibbon, and Sternfeld.[24] The version shown in figure 21 appears in *Old English Popular Music*.[25]

22. Shakespeare, *Hamlet*, p. 257, notes to lines 37 and 38.

23. *Shakespeare and Music*, pp. 59, 190. See also V. Duckles, "The English Musical Elegy in the Late Renaissance," p. 149.

24. *Popular Music of the Olden Time; Old English Popular Music; Shakespeare and Music*; J. Gibbon, *Melody and the Lyric from Chaucer to the Cavaliers*. A collation of the Walsingham texts and a musical setting are in F. Sternfeld, "Ophelia's Version of the Walsingham Song," p. 111.

25. Volume 1, p. 69.

The next series of quatrains, beginning "Tomorrow is Saint Valentine's day" (line 48), belongs to a ballad completely distinct from the "Walsingham" group. This song seems to be one of a type usually called an aubade or "hunts-up," and it belongs, as Charles Baskervill has stated, to a group of songs associated with an ancient folk custom whereby a young lover was permitted to spend the night with his betrothed before marriage.[26] Baskervill related three types of songs to this custom: "Open the door (or window)" songs, which describe

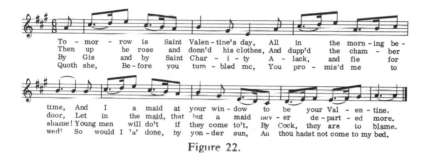

Figure 22.

the lover as he seeks admission to his mistress' house; "Go from my window" songs in which the mistress states the conventional protest against her lover's intentions; and the aubades of several kinds which warn away the lover before the sun rises.

In Ophelia's version of the Saint Valentine ballad, the mistress is betrayed by the lover—a possible allusion to the betrayal of Ophelia feared by Polonius and Laertes, as Peter Seng suggested.[27] In it also, as Seng noted, there is a reversal of the sexes: it is the mistress who comes to the house of the lover, not vice versa as in the traditional ballads of this folk group.

The tune to which Ophelia's Saint Valentine song has been traditionally sung since Drury Lane is one of two tunes having the titles "Who list to lead a soldier's life" and "Lord Thomas and Fair Ellinor."[28] The former title is given as a ballad tune in George Peele's *Edward I* (1593).[29] The tune which Chappell provided is from Playford's *The English Dancing Master* (1651), with the title "Soldier's Life."[30] Ophelia's song is set to this tune in figure 22.

26. "English Songs on the Night Visit," pp. 565–614.
27. "The Dramatic Function of the Songs in Shakespeare's Plays," p. 388.
28. Chappell, ed., *Popular Music of the Olden Time* 1:144.
29. Ibid.
30. Ibid., 1:65.

The three-line fragment offered by Ophelia in act 4, scene 5, "They bore him bare-fac'd on the bier," can be sung to the "Walsingham" tune discussed previously, as Naylor long ago observed.[31] He felt that the second line, usually a merry or bawdy refrain, is a stage corruption characteristic of Ophelia's plaintive and wanton medley.[32]

The single line "For bonny sweet Robin is all my joy" comes from an old song whose text has not been recovered. Probably it refers to Robin Hood and was sung by Maid Marian in the old Whitsuntide folk play, as we noted earlier. The probable music for the song survives in several collections contemporary with Shakespeare. In Trinity College, Dublin, MS D.1.21 (William Ballet's lute book) are two slightly different versions of the tune, "Bonny Sweet Robin" and "Robin Hood is to the greenwood gone."[33] Another variant of the tune, "Robin is to the Greene wood Gonn," also for lute, is in the

My Ro - bin is to the green - wood gone

For bon - ny sweet Ro - bin is all my joy.

Figure 23.

Folger Shakespeare Library MS 1610.1, fol. 16[v]. Other arrangements of the tune may be found in *The Fitzwilliam Virginal Book*, nos. 15 and 128, in Antony Holborne's *The Cittharn Schoole* (1597), and in Thomas Robinson's *Schoole of Musicke* (1603).[34] The tune has been reproduced by Chappell, who used a heavily edited version of "Bonny Sweet Robin" above.[35] In figure 23 Ophelia's line is set to the same tune, but I have used the melody line of the original lute tablature. There exists another tune, also for lute, called "Robin Hoode," in the Folger Shakespeare Library MS 448.16, fol. 4[r] (c. 1576). This tune is quite different from the variants described above, and Ophelia's line cannot be set to it.

Some readers see in Ophelia's reference to "bonny sweet Robin"

31. *Shakespeare and Music*, p. 169.
32. Ibid.
33. Pages 27 and 113, respectively. See Seng, "The Dramatic Function of the Songs in Shakespeare's Plays," p. 398.
34. Seng, "The Dramatic Function of the Songs in Shakespeare's Plays," p. 398.
35. *Popular Music of the Olden Time* 1:234.

a phallic allusion, and in her line "Hey non nony, nony, hey nony" an equally bawdy reference.[36] If, as we have observed, Ophelia may have assumed at times the role of Maid Marian in the Whitsun play, and if this role called for wanton speech and gestures, these readers may be correct concerning the nature of her madness—that she suffered from sexual frustration. But it is equally plausible that, as an "antike," she is simply doing what the appellation suggests: she is drawing on the ancient folk songs, folk plays, and remnants of pagan customs as a part of her "act." These, being old-fashioned, no doubt seemed rustic and ludicrous to thc Elizabethan of London and, having been taken over by the folk, would have included language and behavior that seemed coarse to later audiences.

The final two stanzas given Ophelia, beginning "And will 'a not come again?" (lines 190–99), cannot be identified as parts of any known ballad, nor is there any known musical setting for them con-

Figure 24.

temporary with Shakespeare. Chappell printed a variant of a tune discussed earlier to which he gave the title "Lord Thomas and Fair Ellinor" and remarked, "It is, evidently, the air of *Who list to lead a soldier's life?* adapted for words of a somewhat different measure."[37] As it happens, this adaptation fits exactly Ophelia's last song stanzas. I have therefore used "Lord Thomas and Fair Ellinor" as a tune for "And will 'a not come again?" (see figure 24).

An early musical setting for Lord Vaux's song, "I loathe that I did love" (5. 1. 69), has been known for some time. It is in Brit. Mus. Add. MS 4900, fols. 62ᵛ and 63 and has been published in several studies.[38] Even though Shakespeare's version of the song is garbled,

36. See H. Morris, "Ophelia's 'Bonny Sweet Robin' "; J. Patrick, "The Problem of Ophelia"; Seng, "The Dramatic Function of the Songs in Shakespeare's Plays," p. 148.

37. *Popular Music of the Olden Time* 1:145.

38. Seng, "The Dramatic Function of the Song in Shakespeare's Plays," pp. 410–11. See also Sternfeld, *Music in Shakespearean Tragedy*, pp. 151–55.

in keeping with the Gravedigger's character, it still fits the musical setting snugly. The first stanza of Lord Vaux's text, and the stanzas in *Hamlet*, are set to the manuscript notation in figure 25.

To summarize the performed music in *Hamlet*, the instrumental music requires a rather large array of instruments—several trumpets, at least one kettledrum, several military drums, and a consort of hautboys. There is no evidence that the recorder Hamlet uses to illustrate his lecture to Rosencrantz and Guildenstern (3. 3. 360)

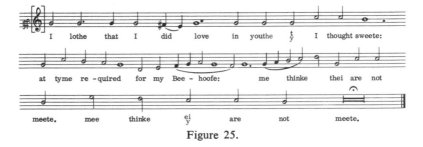

Figure 25.

is actually played upon, other than in words. Nor is there any indication in the later texts that Ophelia plays a lute in her mad scenes as the Q1 direction requires.[39] The instrumental music, excepting the music played during the dumb show for the purpose of sustaining aural interest, is entirely ceremonious in function and closely associated with Claudius and his court.

The songs require no trained singers for adequate performance since the vocal music is popular in taste and simple in form. Most of the ballads used by Shakespeare in *Hamlet* seem to be quite old, old even in his day. It is as though the playwright intended them to suggest an "antike" characterization in the actors who sang them. The ancient nature of the ballads, their performance in fragments, the foolery that frequently accompanies each performance, all assert that Shakespeare's technique governing the use of songs in this play was derived from the practices traditionally used by stage fools in their performance of ballad medleys. Since none of the songs are sung in circumstances which would make their rendition musically valuable, we may conclude that their function is purely dramatic and

39. Granville-Barker (*Prefaces to Shakespeare* 1:120n4) accepted the Q1 stage direction "Enter Ofelia playing on a Lute, and her haire downe singing" and remarked, "The dramatic point of the lute is that you must stand—or better, sit still—if you are to attempt to play it. Modern Ophelias have an ineffective habit of drifting vaguely about the stage. A lute is at least an admirable anchor."

aimed specifically at characterization and, in the broad sense of the word, setting.

The instrumental music is related closely to the superficial pomp and ceremony in which Claudius and his court exist. In contrast, the vocal music which Shakespeare assigns to Hamlet, Ophelia, and the Gravedigger, and the incoherent quality of their song snatches, reflect an inability to reconcile their inner spirits with an outer world which to them seems false, rotten, and bewildering. Death, and a pit of clay, the Gravedigger-clown sings with grim humor, is the final resolution of the spiritual conflict which marks the medley of men's lives. But Horatio may be speaking the final words when he refers to other music in his farewell to Hamlet:

> Now cracks a noble heart. Good night, sweet Prince,
> And flights of angels sing thee to thy rest!

NINE

Troilus and Cressida

HAKESPEARE'S DRAMATIZATION OF THE MEDIEVAL VER-
sion of an episode in the classical Greek-Trojan
war has puzzled critics to this day. It presents many
problems; classification and philosophical point of
view are but two. Its pervading atmosphere is a
strange one, an overripe odor, a sweetness gone sour, an excessive
idealism turned to a cynicism so profound that it has earned the play
the descriptive term "bitter." Unlike *Hamlet*, this play presents no
characters with whom we may long sympathize, from whom we may
hear noble sentiments, or in whom we may discern lofty and noble
actions. The most powerful voice in the play is that of the bastard-
clown Thersites, and he speaks only invectives, emptying his soul
like a very drab in paroxysms of frustration.

It is little wonder that the popularity of *Troilus and Cressida* has
never been great, that there is some question that it was even staged
in Shakespeare's lifetime. Certainly he made in this drama few
concessions to the popular tastes of his time, or perhaps any other
time. His "book" was read, apparently, for there was an edition published in 1609, before it appeared in the First Folio. The subject
had been used for moralization long before Chaucer wrote his
romance; hence, the drama no doubt found a prepared audience.

Before considering the music in the play, a word about the problem
of its classification. We have observed from time to time that Shakespeare used different techniques with the music in the comedies and
with that in the histories and tragedies. In particular, we note that he
frequently employed complete songs—usually ayres—of intrinsic
musical value in his comedies, whereas in the histories and tragedies
he used fragments of songs—generally ballads or popular songs, with
few exceptions. *Troilus and Cressida* is one exception if we call the
play a tragedy. If we call it a comedy, the complete ayre sung by
Pandarus is not an exception but follows the general rule. Lawrence
called the play a "bitter comedy";[1] Chambers, noting the lack of

1. W. Lawrence, *Shakespeare's Problem Comedies.*

humor in the drama and the unhappy ending, called it a tragedy.[2]

A study of the music in the play has been presented by Frederick Sternfeld, whose interest has centered mainly on music used as an ethical device and as a means of characterization.[3] He has also found Shakespeare's use of music in the play evidence of the playwright's revulsion from a degenerate "Italianate-English aristocracy." While I find this latter point exaggerated, my conclusions follow his in the main; I think it necessary, however, to qualify some of his statements.

In general, the music in *Troilus and Cressida* is related to the traditional concepts and practices of chivalry and courtly love—a reminder that the actions and setting of the play are derived from a medieval romance, not a classical epic. The part played by music in the chivalric tradition was still known and practiced in Elizabethan England by many who maintained the forms long after the spirit was dead. The trumpet music in the play supplies several cases in point.

What might be the first musical notes heard in the play sound in the three alarums toward the close of act 1, scene 1, lines 91, 107, and 116. Normally, the term "alarum" signifies a battle or onslaught and includes clashes of weapons, drumbeats, trumpet blasts, shouts— anything to make a tumult. These particular alarums introduce the battle being waged outside the walls of Troy which provides the occasion for Troilus to comment on the inanity of war waged over a woman, Helen. Following the first alarum, he remarks, "Peace, you ungracious clamors! Peace, rude sounds! / Fools on both sides! Helen must needs be fair / When with your blood you daily paint her thus." The second alarum accompanies Æneas' entrance as he comes from the fray. He reports that Paris has been wounded, to which Troilus replies, "Let Paris bleed. 'Tis but a scar to scorn. / Paris is gored with Menelaus' horn." The third alarum sounds the cue for Æneas to comment chivalrously, "Hark, what good sport is out of town today!" In contrast, Troilus, burning with his desire for Cressida, answers, "Better at home if 'would I might' were 'may.' " To Æneas the alarum suggests chivalric combat; to Troilus it suggests a purposeless war which interferes with the delights of courtly love. Both men treat the war that will topple Troy as an insignificant matter. If trumpets were used in these alarums, no specific calls seem necessary: a few distant blasts should suffice.

2. *William Shakespeare* 1:438–49.
3. *"Troilus and Cressida*: Music for the Play," pp. 107–37. See also his discussion in *Music in Shakespearean Tragedy*, pp. 131–42.

A retreat (1. 2. 191) ends the day's battle and sets the stage for the Trojan knights' return to the city. It is on this occasion that Pandarus slyly calls Cressida's attention to Troilus, marching into the town. The notation for a trumpet "retraite" may be found in Appendix I. Retreats were sounded by both drums and trumpets—drums for the infantry and trumpets for the cavalry, or in this case the chivalry. Although there are infantrymen shown on the stage, there is no direction calling for drums.

The military signals used so far establish the background of the war. As Shakespeare created it, this conflict is strangely lacking in heroic actions. There is much talk of great deeds and honor, but the action reveals precious little of either. With the possible exceptions of Hector and Ulysses, "haute noblesse" is conspicuously missing. The flourish, with its suggestion of royal "presence," is sometimes absent on occasions when it might be expected. When the flourish is called for, its use seems to be more for processional purposes than an evocation of majesty. For example, consider the opening of act 1, scene 3.

To open the scene, F reads, *Senet. Enter Agamemnon, Nestor, Vllyses, Diomedes, Menelaus, with others*, truly an impressive collection of kings led by their arch-king, Agamemnon, general of the Greek host. The sennet, normally used for processional entrances into state councils, moves this group onto the stage, where they open a council of war. But there is something missing. Where is the flourish that ushers in kings in other plays of Shakespeare? The sennet has its place here, for it moves a rather large group of actors onstage. The fact that it is not preceded by the royal flourish might imply that there are no genuinely royal persons in the assembly, that majesty and magnanimity are absent from the Greek chivalry. Without a true king, the hierarchy of medieval political and social structure collapses. As Ulysses' well-known musical metaphor puts it, "Take but degree away, untune that string, / And hark, what discord follows! Each thing meets / In mere oppugnancy." (Music for a sennet is shown in Appendix IV.)

Later in the same scene (line 211), a stage direction calls for a tucket to be sounded:

[*Tucket.*]

AGAM. What trumpet? Look, Menelaus.
MEN.   From Troy.

[*Enter* ÆNEAS.]

AGAM. What would you 'fore our tent?

ÆNE. Is this great Agamemnon's tent, I pray you?

AGAM. Even this.

ÆNE. May one that is a herald and a prince
Do a fair message to his kingly ears?

Æneas has come to deliver a challenge from Hector for single combat with any champion of the Greek host. In what seems to be strict conformity to the code of chivalry, Æneas is announced not by a royal flourish, to which he is entitled, but by a tucket that signifies his special office on this occasion. In his words, he comes first as a herald, and as a prince only because he represents a royal challenger. After several lines of courtly conversation, Æneas turns to his trumpeter.

ÆNE.   Trumpet, blow loud,
Send thy brass voice through all these lazy tents,
And every Greek of mettle, let him know
What Troy means fairly shall be spoke aloud.
                              [*Trumpet sounds.*]

Æneas then formally delivers his challenge to the Greeks.

The first trumpet call, although it is called a tucket in F, probably is not intended to be a personal musical signature in this instance. None of the Greeks identify it as belonging to Æneas. The appropriate call to announce a herald would be a "parle" (see Appendix I). The second trumpet call should be performed, like the first, by a single trumpet. The folio direction *The Trumpets sound* is perhaps quite general. The direction in Q1609 is merely *Sound trumpet*, as Æneas' lines would require, rather than a tucket. The particular call used in this case was probably a "troop" (Assembly), since Æneas' challenge is directed to the full Greek chivalry. For the notation of a "troop," see Appendix I.

The direction *Sound a retreat* in act 3, scene 1, line 160, reminds Paris and Helen, in the midst of their dalliance, of the war outside the walls of the city. In his frequent coupling of Mars and Venus—military signals and amorous encounters—in the play, Shakespeare not only kept poised the concepts of chivalry and courtly love, but also reminded playgoers of the human paradox sung by bards since the time of Homer and before.

Opening act 3, scene 3, the stage direction is:

[*Flourish. Enter* AGAMEMNON, ULYSSES, DIOMEDES,
NESTOR, AJAX, MENELAUS, *and* CALCHAS.]

This flourish bridges a change of scene from that which concludes as Troilus takes Cressida to bed to that which opens with Calchas requesting the Greek leaders to obtain his daughter in exchange for a Trojan prisoner, Antenor. The trumpet voice is a dramatic contrast to the sweet seduction carried on in the preceding scene and serves to emphasize the ironic fact that almost as soon as Troilus gains Cressida, destiny decrees that he lose her. Before, a joy proposed; behind, a dream.

The position of the word *Flourish* in F's stage direction suggests that it is not intended solely to bridge a change of scene or to proclaim the royalty of the assembled kings, even though they are giving audience to Calchas. Rather, its primary purpose is to move the Greeks onstage. For large groups, as we noticed at the beginning of act 1, scene 3, a sennet is often used. In this case, only seven characters enter; the flourish—shorter than a sennet—serves also as a brief processional.

As Troilus, Cressida, and Diomedes prepare to leave Troy for the Greek camp (act 4, scene 4), the stage direction (line 141) is [*A trumpet sounds*]. Paris then remarks, "Hark! Hector's trumpet." The call reminds Paris and Æneas of the forthcoming battle between Hector and Ajax. Since Paris recognizes the call as the personal property of Hector, there can be little doubt that the trumpet should sound a tucket. After a few lines the Trojans *exeunt*, and scene 5 begins with the entry of the Greek kings, a trumpeter, and attendants into the lists where Hector and Ajax are to do battle. Ordinarily, we might expect a sennet to usher in such a large troop; however, the scene presents not a state occasion, but combat between two champions. Ajax is, for the moment, the center of attention. Agamemnon tells Ajax (scene 5, line 3):

> Give with thy trumpet a loud note to Troy,
> Thou dreadful Ajax, that the appallèd air
> May pierce the head of the great combatant
> And hale him hither.
>
> AJAX.   Thou, trumpet, there's my purse.
> Now crack thy lungs, and split thy brazen pipe.

Blow, villain, till thy spherèd bias cheek
Outswell the colic of puffed Aquilon.
Come, stretch thy chest, and let thy eyes spout blood.
Thou blow'st for Hector.   [*Trumpet sounds.*]

Francis Markham wrote that in the proper conduct of military affairs "he [the drummer] may upon tolleration from the Generall, carrie Challenges and Defiances from one enemie to another, and either for Honour or Ladies loves make composition for single Encounters, provided it bee upon foot . . . but if it be upon Horseback, then it is the office of the *Trumpet*, and the Drumme hath no interest in it."[4] Hector and Ajax, as mounted chivalry, of course employ trumpets to make their "Defiances." In recompense for his service, the trumpeter or drummer may "challenge" a fee. For example, Markham stated that "any man dying (above the degree of a common Souldier) the *Drum* performing the last dutie, may for his fee challenge the Sword of the deceased. . . ."[5]

Shakespeare used the trumpets in this episode as a part of the formality and ceremony with which he invested the preparations for the combat. This is one way he can suggest, on the Elizabethan stage, the full panoply of overblown chivalry. He is thus preparing us for an ironically comic contest. In answer to Ajax' brazen defiance, not Hector but Cressida and Diomedes appear, and the battle—that is, a prolonged kissing game—ensues. The behavior of Cressida and the Greek chieftains not only mocks the ideals of chivalry and courtly love, but leads Ulysses to characterize Cressida (lines 58–63):

Oh, these encounters, so glib of tongue,
That give accosting welcome ere it comes,
And wide unclasp the tables of their thoughts
To every ticklish reader! Set them down
For sluttish spoils of opportunity,
And daughters of the game.   [*Trumpet within.*]

ALL.   The Trojans' trumpet.

AGAM.   Yonder comes the troop.
     [*Flourish. Enter* HECTOR, *armed;* ÆNEAS, TROILUS, *and*
      other TROJANS, *with* ATTENDANTS.]

4. *Fiue Decades of Epistles of Warre*, pp. 59–60.
5. Ibid., p. 59.

The flourish here again has a dual function: it announces royalty, and it furnishes processional music to bring the numerous Trojans onstage. The Greeks describe it as "The Trojans' trumpet," but this may be a collective term for several trumpets. After observing the courtly amenities, the assemblage turns its attention to the combat. Ajax and Hector enter the lists, probably going offstage. From this time to the end of the encounter, the combat is described by an *alarum*—probably the offstage clashing of swords, beating of drums, shouts, and trumpet blasts—and by the comments of the Greeks and Trojans remaining on the stage. Æneas and Diomedes (lines 117–18) then stop the conflict. At this point the stage direction is [*Trumpets cease*]. Hector and Ajax then rejoin the group onstage, and there follows what is almost a love feast between the enemy parties. At its conclusion, Agamemnon invites Hector to stay the night as an honored guest (lines 271–76):

> AGAM. First, all of you peers of Greece, go to my tent,
> There in the full convive we. Afterward,
> As Hector's leisure and your bounties shall
> Concur together, severally entreat him.
> Beat loud the tabourines, let the trumpets blow,
> That this great soldier may his welcome know.

There is no stage direction calling for drums and trumpets to sound as Agamemnon commands, but a processional of some sort seems required here. The lines indicate that all the Greeks and Trojans, excepting Ulysses and Troilus, go out together—an awkward situation unless the exit is smoothed in some way. Since the trumpets would have been available and also, probably, some military drums, a sounding of a "retreat," perhaps repeated, would have served the purpose.

The drama concludes with the final battle, in which Hector, the noblest Trojan of them all, is murdered by Achilles and his Myrmidons. Two "retreats"—Trojan and Greek—signal the end of the battle (5. 8. 14 and 5. 9. 1), and the sorry spectacle comes to a close.

The instrumental music we have observed is a part of the chivalric, or masculine, actions of the play, consisting as it does of military signals and ceremonious marches. The most important performance of music in the drama, however, is associated with the more feminine qualities of the characters and actions, especially the practices of courtly love. Our ears must now be attuned not to the martial clamor of brass instruments and drums but to the ingratiating strains of strings and woodwinds and the lisping lyrics of a dulcet song symbolic of the sweetness and harmony of human relationships. In this case, the harmony is too close, the sweetness becomes saccharine, and warm affection becomes the heat of lust.

The central performance of music in *Troilus and Cressida* is the presentation of Pandarus' song in act 3, scene 1. Not only did Shakespeare place this music in the structural center of the play, but he used it to express the luxurious, hothouse atmosphere of the Trojan court, where the red roses in the Court of Love grow monstrous and fill the air with a cloying perfume. Within this sensuous world move Helen, Paris, and Pandarus, the first two whose hot love engendered the Trojan War and the third whose impotent lust will pander to the unhealthy decay of a tradition—courtly love—that festers like the lilies which smell worse than weeds. Although Shakespeare earlier had made fleeting allusions to the evil effects of music, especially music associated with erotic love, he did not make a point of these effects until he wrote the scene in question. The music performed therein provides a focal point for the entire scene; in order to observe the several functions of the music, then, we must quote rather extensively.

At the end of the preceding scene, laid in the Greek camp, the stage direction in F is *Exeunt. Musicke sounds within*. The consort music "within" is used as a bridge to shift, musically, the setting from the Greek camp to the Trojan court. Those editors, such as G. B. Harrison, who move the direction for the music to a point seventeen lines later in the scene are thus balking the clear intent of Shakespeare, who knew what he was doing. While the consort plays, Pandarus and a servant enter. After some badinage with the servant, Pandarus calls attention to the music.

> PAN.   What music is this?
> SERV. I do but partly know, sir. It is music in parts.
> PAN. Know you the musicians?
> SERV. Wholly, sir.
> PAN. Who play they to?
> SERV. To the hearers, sir.

After more wordplay about the music, Pandarus elicits the information that the musicians are playing at the command of Paris for

Helen's pleasure. These two then enter and are greeted by Pandarus.

PAN.   Fair be to you, my lord, and to all this fair company!
Fair desires, in all fair measure, fairly guide them!
Especially to you, fair Queen! Fair thoughts be your
fair pillow!

HELEN. Dear lord, you are full of fair words.

PAN.   You speak your fair pleasure, sweet Queen. Fair
Prince, here is good broken music.

PAR.   You have broke it, Cousin. And, by my life, you shall
make it whole again, you shall piece it out with a piece
of your performance. Nell, he is full of harmony.

*   *   *   *   *   *   *   *

PAN.   Come, come, I'll hear no more of this. I'll sing you a
song now.

*   *   *   *   *   *   *   *

HELEN. Let thy song be love. This love will undo us all. O'
Cupid, Cupid, Cupid!

PAN.   Love! Aye, that it shall, i'faith.

PAR.   Aye, good now, love, love, nothing but love.

PAN.   In good troth, it begins so.   [*Sings.*]
"Love, love, nothing but love, still more![6]
For, oh, love's bow
Shoots buck and doe.
The shaft confounds,
Not that it wounds,
But tickles still the sore.
These lovers cry 'Oh! oh!' they die.
Yet that which seems the wound to kill,
Doth turn oh! oh! to ha! ha! he!
So dying love lives still.
Oh! oh! a while, but ha! ha! ha!
Oh! oh! groans out for ha! ha! ha!"
Heigh-ho!

HELEN. In love, i'faith, to the very tip of the nose.

PAR.   He eats nothing but doves, love, and that breeds hot
blood, and hot blood begets hot thoughts, and hot
thoughts beget hot deeds, and hot deeds is love.

PAN.   Is this the generation of love? Hot blood, hot
thoughts, and hot deeds? Why, they are vipers. Is
love a generation of vipers? . . .

6. The Rosenbach-Wally Quarto of 1609, in the Folger Shakespeare Library,
prints this line, "Love, love, nothing but love, still love, still more."

Sternfeld, in explicating this passage, has observed that the music which opens the scene is a performance by a "broken" consort, that is, one composed of instruments of different choirs or families such as strings, both plucked and bowed, and woodwinds.[7] The mixed composition of the consort provides the springboard for the puns about "music in parts" and Pandarus' having "broke it," that is, having interrupted the sweet music Paris and Helen were amorously making together before the old pander makes a crowd by becoming the third in the company.

Sternfeld also made the point that the broken consort is the instrumental ensemble used in Shakespeare's time for chamber music, receptions, and other social occasions. It, hence, is associated with the aristocracy and court. By extension, the broken consort becomes a symbol of an Italianate and decadent English nobility, its music a part of excessive luxury and the frayed remnants of courtly love. All this is credible; but we may find a more direct explanation of Shakespeare's purposes if we recall the attitude toward music and erotic love that he expressed in other works. Then we shall see that Shakespeare, while perhaps commenting on the English aristocracy of his day, was also restating a belief found in other plays; what is true in the Trojan court is also true in Illyria and elsewhere.

The first act of *Twelfth Night* opens in much the same manner as the third act of *Troilus and Cressida*. To the sound of consort music from within, Duke Orsino and other lords enter, and the duke speaks his opening lines.

> DUKE. If music be the food of love, play on.
>   Give me excess of it, that, surfeiting,
>   The appetite may sicken, and so die.
>   That strain again! It had a dying fall.

Two of the statements made by Duke Orsino are particularly pertinent: that music is the food of love, and that a surfeit may sicken and eventually kill the appetite. It follows then that, if music is the food of love and if love becomes excessive, then the appetite craves an excess of music. But, according to the Golden Mean, excess is an evil. The love of Paris and Helen, being excessive, becomes lust; and Pandarus, in feeding their lust with music, is as much a pander to them as when he fans the fire of love in Troilus and

---

7. *"Troilus and Cressida*: Music for the Play," p. 132.

Cressida. Moreover, the music used for such a purpose—in feeding excessively—becomes evil in itself. Sir Francis Bacon made a similar observation when he commented, "yet generally music feedeth that disposition of the spirits, which it findeth."[8] In *Measure for Measure*, the duke, who appears as Mariana is feeding her melancholy with the song "Take, oh Take Those Lips Away," remarks, " 'Tis good, though music oft hath such a charm / To make bad good, and good provoke to harm."[9] If music is a food for the spirits—melancholy, in this case—excessive music can "provoke to harm."

The lines spoken by Pandarus, Helen, and Paris in the scene in question are obviously designed to suggest a sweetness so pronounced as to be nauseous. The words "fair," "sweet," and "love" are repeated again and again. Pandarus' song is a musical counterpart to the lines which introduce it. Clearly, we are to understand that it is the excessive love, excessive courtesy, excessive music, that compose this bouquet of the flowers of evil.

We may also note that the music performed in this scene is offered by Paris to Helen as food for her love. When Pandarus adds his song to the music played by the broken consort, there emerges another example of what I have called "the Shakespearean serenade" —a suite of two musical pieces, the first instrumental, the second vocal. We may recollect also that Shakespeare usually associated this form of serenade with male lovers who are more lecherous than loving, or who otherwise fail as "true" lovers. Thurio's serenade to Sylvia in *The Two Gentlemen of Verona* and Cloten's serenade to Imogen in *Cymbeline* are two examples.

Once Shakespeare had announced his theme regarding the music of excessive erotic love, he was free to develop variations on it. In applying his variations, he turned to Troilus and Cressida, thus linking the lust of Paris and Helen with their amour. When Troilus and Cressida meet in Pandarus' garden (act 3, scene 2), Troilus kisses Cressida for the first time—at Cressida's urging.

CRES.		Sweet, bid me hold my tongue,
		For in this rapture I shall surely speak
		The thing I shall repent. See, see, your silence,
		Cunning in dumbness, from my weakness draws
		My very soul of counsel! Stop my mouth.
TRO.	And shall, albeit sweet music issues thence.
PAN.	Pretty, i'faith.

8. "Natural History," *The Works of Francis Bacon*, Cent. II, p. 26.
9. Long, *Shakespeare's Use of Music: The Final Comedies*, pp. 20–21.

Troilus likens Cressida to a musical instrument discoursing sweet music; and so she is. But a musical instrument will produce music at the touch of any musician; " 'tis as easy as lying." And this leads us to Shakespeare's second variation.

As Ulysses and the anguished Troilus watch Cressida whispering her faint denials to Diomedes (act 5, scene 2)—obviously a parallel to her first meeting with Troilus in Pandarus' orchard—she speaks (line 8):

CRES.   Now, my sweet guardian! Hark, a word with you.
TRO.   Yea, so familiar!
ULYSS. She will sing any man at first sight.
THER.   And any man may sing her, if he can take her cliff [clef]. She's noted.

Here Ulysses compares Cressida to a song that any man may sing (seduce) on sight. Thersites obliquely paraphrases the authors of books on courtesy and music instruction, who claim that every gentleman should have enough musical skill to find the clef or key of a song and to sing the notes of a prick-song on sight.[10] He thus calls Cressida, with obvious ribaldry, a prick-song. A somewhat similar metaphor appears in *Pericles* where Pericles, aware of the incestuous love between King Antiochus and his daughter, refers to her as "a fair viol, and your sense the strings . . . Hell only danceth at so harsh a chime."[11]

The music in act 3, scene 1, therefore, serves to bridge a change of scene, to provide a vehicle for puns and conceits in the spoken lines, to characterize Paris, Helen, and Pandarus as voluptuaries, to underline what is perhaps the major theme of the play—chivalry and courtly love choked by luxuriant growth gone to seed—or, as Thersites says, "Nothing but lechery! All incontinent varlets!"

Apart from their dramatic uses, the consort music and Pandarus' song could have been intrinsically valuable. In performance, Sternfeld suggested for the consort piece Giles Farnaby's arrangement of an old folk dance and ballad tune, "Mall Sims," found in *The Fitzwilliam Virginal Book*. While Farnaby's version of the tune is sophisticated, I offer as an alternative a consort piece marked, I think, by more

10. Naylor (*Shakespeare and Music*, p. 13) stated, "We find that it was the merest qualification that an Elizabethan bishop should be able to sing well: and that young University gentlemen of birth thought it nothing out of the way to learn all the mysteries of both prick-song (a *written* part) and descant (an *extempore* counterpart). . . ."

11. Cf. Long, *Shakespeare's Use of Music: The Final Comedies*, p. 37.

Notes in brackets are my corrections of apparent errors in the original score. In the second part, measures 3, 5, 6 of the bassus line were omitted in the original.

Figure 26.

sweetness, in keeping with the dialogue which accompanies the music. The piece "Wanton" was scored for consort by Antony Holborne and is no. 61 in his *Pavans, Galliards, Almains, and Other Short Aeirs* (1599).[12] Only the cantus and bassus parts have survived. They are transcribed in modern notation in figure 26.

As the stage direction opening act 3, scene 1, states, the consort plays offstage, thus providing a subdued musical background for the spoken lines. The consort music should end a few lines before Pandarus' song, perhaps when he requests Helen to give him "an

12. Holborne's composition should not be confused with another by Robert Johnson, "Witty Wanton."

instrument." Sternfeld has interpreted Pandarus' request as a cue for her to give him a lute with which he will play the accompaniment for his song.[13] The song is certainly written, probably by Shakespeare, in the form of a lutenist's ayre, and some skill in playing the lute should be expected of an accomplished courtier. Assuming that a lute is brought to Pandarus, what music was set to the song text? The

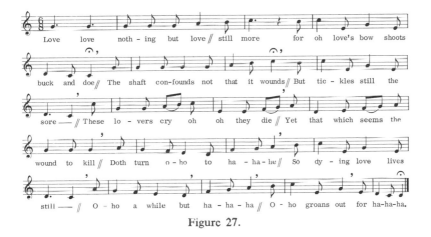

Figure 27.

original score is missing, but Sternfeld has supplied a setting by adapting a tune, "In sad and ashy weeds," found in Chappell's *Popular Music of the Olden Time*.[14] The tune was used for several ballads, as Chappell has noted, most of them laments or elegies. Providing alternate musical settings for most lutenist's ayres is a difficult task; in this case Sternfeld's setting is quite appropriate and practical (see figure 27).

As Cressida takes leave of Troilus and Pandarus (4. 4. 15–25), Pandarus quotes four phrases from a song or poem, lines which Sternfeld has set to music from Thomas Morley's canzonet "Hold out, my heart":[15]

> PAN. What a pair of spectacles is here! Let me embrace too. "O heart," as the goodly saying is,

13. *"Troilus and Cressida*: Music for the Play," p. 133.
14. Ibid., p. 132.
15. Ibid., p. 136. Sternfeld listed as the source of Morley's music Bruce Pattison, *Poetry and Music of the English Renaissance*, p. 195.

> "Oh heart, heavy heart,
> Why sigh'st thou without breaking?"
> where he answers again,
> "Because thou canst not ease thy smart
> By friendship nor by speaking."
> There was never a truer rhyme. Let us cast away
> nothing, for we may live to have need of such a verse. . . .

Referring to this quotation, Sternfeld stated, "in *Troilus* the only other instance of song in the drama occurs in Act IV, where Pandarus performs fragments of another air." While the remark "Let us cast away nothing" may be intended as a pun on "noting," or singing notes, Sternfeld's assertion is of dubious validity. I doubt that Pandarus sings the lines in question. While modern editions italicize or otherwise set off the lines from their context, indicating that they are quotations, neither the First Folio nor Q1609 does so. Moreover, Pandarus refers to the lines as "the goodly saying," a "rhyme," a "verse," but not as a song. He probably speaks the quotations.

To conclude, *Troilus and Cressida* is without doubt a powerful drama considered either as tragedy or comedy. But it is not an attractive play. It is cathartic, but the purgation leaves the reader a bit sickened rather than with the sense of health that Aristotle thought should be bestowed by great tragedy. The music, in its context, adds a bitter note to a chivalry gone sour and a tradition of courtly love become overripe. Pandarus, appropriately, sums up the matter with one of his ubiquitous rhymes (5. 10. 42–45):

> "Full merrily the humblebee doth sing
> Till he hath lost his honey and his sting,
> And being once subdued in armèd tail,
> Sweet honey and sweet notes together fail."

TEN

Othello

ENERALLY CONSIDERED ONE OF THE BEST CON-
structed of Shakespeare's plays, *The Tragedy of Othello, the Moor of Venice*, is well defined in its plot and characterization. The music used therein is also conformable, in its dramatic functions, to that employed in the histories and tragedies that precede *Troilus and Cressida*. In fact, the music in *Othello* is quite reminiscent of *Hamlet*; we see a return to the pattern in which instrumental music is associated with the world of action and appearance, and vocal music —fragments of old ballads only—portrays the inner world of character.

The instrumental music in the play includes three trumpet calls interspersed throughout the play and an aubade (morning serenade) performed probably by a consort of hautboys. The first trumpet signal (2. 1. 179) announces the arrival of Othello in Cyprus, thus suggesting action going on offstage. Since the Moor is not royalty, the trumpet call is his personal tucket; Iago states (line 180), "The Moor! I know his trumpet." The second (4. 1. 225) announces Lodovico's arrival in Cyprus from Venice. Since Lodovico comes as an emissary of the doge, he would doubtless be entitled to a call more elaborate than a tucket—perhaps a "parle" or a flourish. As Frederick Sternfeld has commented, this ceremonious music helps to establish the diplomatic climate so rudely disrupted when Othello publicly strikes Desdemona.[1] The third trumpet piece (4. 2. 165) serves both a dramatic and a ceremonious purpose. Desdemona, almost frantic, questions Iago in a futile attempt to discover the cause of Othello's anger toward her. Iago finally answers:

> IAGO. I pray you be content, 'tis but his humor,
> The business of the state does him offense,
> And he does chide with you.
> DES. If 'twere no other——

1. "The Dramatic and Allegorical Function of Music in Shakespeare's Tragedies," p. 266. See also his *Music in Shakespearean Tragedy*, pp. 142–50.

IAGO. 'Tis but so, I warrant.   [*Trumpets within.*]
Hark how these instruments summon to supper!
The messengers of Venice stay the meat.
Go in, and weep not, all things shall be well.

The trumpets in this instance tell us that the supper is a state occasion, given with full ceremony. Iago, of course, is not invited: he uses the interim to plot with Roderigo. Othello and Desdemona dine with Lodovico and the other emissaries. How hollow must this pomp sound to Othello, whose occupation is gone, whose commission has

Figure 28.

been revoked, and who is resolved to do away with his wife as soon as the banquet concludes! To Desdemona, perhaps, the trumpet music gives hope, suggesting to her those affairs of state which Iago has just said might be the cause of her husband's distemper.

The sounding of trumpets during state banquets was customary in Elizabeth's reign. The practice was for the trumpets to sound as each course was being brought to the table. Peter Hentzner's *Itinerarium* reports that "Elizabeth used to be regaled during dinner with twelve trumpets and two kettle-drums; which, together with fifes, cornets, and side-drums, made the hall ring for half an hour together."[2]

The trumpet music played for official dinners was probably not the same as the usual flourishes and military signals, whose notation is given in the appendices. No English trumpet music is known that was used for state banquets in Elizabeth's reign. The music of ceremony, however, was international in flavor. In Girolamo Fantini's *Modo per imparare a sonare di tromba . . . Francoforte 1638,*[3] there is a trumpet "Entrata" that should be appropriate for performance in the play. Its modern notation is provided in figure 28.

2. Page 53, as quoted by L. Elson, *Shakespeare in Music*, p. 201.
3. Pages 17–18.

The instrumental serenade occurs at the beginning of act 3, scene 1, where musicians, hired by Cassio, perform under Othello and Desdemona's window. The episode involving the serenade is frequently cut in modern stage productions, but, as we shall see, with a loss in characterization, dramatic foreshadowing, and symbolism:[4]

[*Enter* CASSIO *and some* MUSICIANS.]

CAS. Masters, play here, I will content your pains—
Something that's brief, and bid "Good morrow, General."
[*Music.*]
[*Enter* CLOWN.]

CLO. Why, masters, have your instruments been in Naples,
that they speak i' the nose thus?

I. MUS. How, sir, how?

CLO. Are these, I pray you, wind instruments?

I. MUS. Aye, marry are they, sir.

CLO. Oh, thereby hangs a tail.

I. MUS. Whereby hangs a tale, sir?

CLO. Marry, sir, by many a wind instrument that I know.
But, masters, here's money for you. And the General
so likes your music that he desires you, for love's
sake, to make no more noise with it.

I. MUS. Well, sir, we will not.

CLO. If you have any music that may not be heard, to 't
again. But, as they say, to hear music the General
does not greatly care.

I. MUS. We have none such, sir.

CLO. Then put up your pipes in your bag, for I'll away. Go,
vanish into air, away!

Of this passage Harley Granville-Barker has remarked, "For relaxation before the tense main business of the tragedy begins we next have Cassio in the early morning bringing musicians to play beneath Othello's window (a pleasant custom, and here what delicate amends!), to this being added the grosser conventional japes of the Clown."[5] By implication, the time of the action is also established—an important point according to J. Dover Wilson.[6] But these students miss what I believe are the more important allusions in the scene,

4. The symbolic value of the scene is ably treated by L. Ross, "Shakespeare's 'Dull Clown' and Symbolic Music."
5. *Prefaces to Shakespeare* 2:23.
6. Shakespeare, *Othello*, p. xxxiii.

one to Cassio, who provides the music, and the other to Othello, to whom the music is directed.

We remember that one of Shakespeare's usual practices is to have undesirable lovers or unsuccessful petitioners provide serenades. When we see Cassio bringing on the stage musicians who are to serenade Othello, we have a sure foreboding of Cassio's (and Desdemona's) failure to regain his lieutenancy. One reason that he fails and that Desdemona fails is the fact that the Moor does not like music—a bit of information the Clown mentions twice to be sure that we notice it. Shakespeare apparently wished his audience to recall that a distaste for music is an index to character. We need only refer to Lorenzo's familiar words in *The Merchant of Venice* (5. 1. 83–88):

> The man that hath no music in himself,
> Nor is not moved with concord of sweet sounds,
> Is fit for treasons, stratagems, and spoils.
> The motions of his spirit are dull as night,
> And his affections dark as Erebus.
> Let no such man be trusted. . . .

This bit of musical lore was a common derivation from contemporary and classical literature. In Joseph Barnes' *The Praise of Musick* (1586), John Case quoted and then translated Polydore Virgil: "When I made man I gave him a soule either harmony itselfe, or at least harmonicall. Nay besides this, *Non est harmonica compositus qui Musica non delectur.* If I made any one which cannot brook or fancy Musicke, surely I erred and made a monster." Elsewhere in the same work,[7] Case quoted Pindar, "Al those things that *Jupiter* doth not love, do only contemne the songs of the Muses."

While Othello is no monster, his dislike of music, Shakespeare implied, should warn us that there are dark depths in his character, that being wrought, perplexed in the extreme, he is capable of dark and bloody deeds. The fact that the poet placed this information about the Moor's lack of musical appreciation during the consummation of the marriage (apparently interrupted by Othello's hasty dispatch to Cyprus) may not have been unintentional on his part.[8]

The aubade was probably played by three or four hautboists, as

---

7. Pages 73–74 and 52–53, respectively.
8. Shakespeare, *Othello*, ed. H. Furness, p. 154n3. As Ross remarked

Joseph Ritson has surmised, although Lawrence Ross assumed that the musicians played bagpipes.[9] The musicians could have been the municipal waits of Cyprus hired by Cassio for the occasion. For the music of the aubade, or hunts-up, I suggest the first sixteen measures of an anonymous work called "the honsok [hunts-up]," the sixth complete composition in Folger Shakespeare Library MS 1610.1 (1588–1609?). The aubade, written in lute tablature in the MS, I have given a literal transcription in figure 29.

Figure 29.

("Shakespeare's 'Dull Clown' and Symbolic Music," p. 113), "The disturbance of these lovers' music, thus foreshadowed, immediately begins in the scene at the end of Act II where the peace of their wedding night is broken by the riot and Othello's 'blood begins [his] safer Guides to rule' (iii.205). The discord Iago's malice promises to effect is unmutely sounded at the end of the Temptation Scene when Othello displaces the love which should rule his soul by commanding it to yield its 'Crowne, and hearted Throne' to 'tyrannous Hate' (III.iii.448–449). The interlude of the Clown and Cassio's morning music . . . initiates the transition between these actions, linking the two, and preparing for the second by ironically commenting on the situation from which it will develope."

9. Ross, "Shakespeare's 'Dull Clown' and Symbolic Music," p. 113. Ross

The first vocal music in the play occurs in act 2, scene 3, during the drinking party. Iago sings parts of two songs as his contribution to the jollity and also, perhaps, to cover up the fact that he is not drinking as much as the others. Cassio has already had a rouse when Iago first sings (line 70–77):

IAGO. Some wine, ho!   *[Sings.]*
        "And let me the cannikin clink, clink,
        And let me the cannikin clink.
          A soldier's a man,
          A life's but a span.
        Why, then let a soldier drink."
      Some wine, boys!
CAS. 'Fore God, an excellent song.

A few lines later, Iago offers another song (lines 91–101):

IAGO. O sweet England!   *[Sings.]*
        "King Stephen was a worthy peer,
          His breeches cost him but a crown.
        He held them sixpence all too dear,
          With that he called the tailor lown.

        "He was a wight of high renown,
          And thou art but of low degree.
        'Tis pride that pulls the country down.
          Then take thine auld cloak about thee."
      Some wine, ho!
CAS. Why, this is a more exquisite song than the other.

---

built an interesting and almost persuasive study of the musical symbolism of this scene largely on the assumption that the "Pipes" refer to bagpipes. Other than the line "Then put up your pipes in your bag . . ." there is no direct evidence that bagpipes are played by the stage musicians. The description "wind instruments" that "speak i'th' nose"—"pipes"—could have described hautboys, as Ritson supposed. Moreover, while we find hautboys frequently called for in Shakespeare's plays, in none are bagpipes called for by name. This instance, of course, may have been an exception, but we also note that the stage direction calls for "Musicians," and I know of no example, during the Renaissance, of bagpipes played in consort, or in groups, on the stage. Of course, Ross wrote (p. 117), "these wind instruments probably were, at least predominantly, bagpipes. . . ." Still, I do not know any instance of bagpipes being played in consort with other instruments; indeed, the illustrations of Renaissance bagpipes and pipers I have seen, including those provided by Ross (figs. 2, 3, 5; plates 3, 5, 6, 7), show always a *single* bagpipe or bagpiper.

Peter Seng has explained, I think, the dramatic functions of Iago's two songs—they establish an atmosphere of drunken wassail and also create an illusion of the passage of time. Hence, Cassio's drunkenness—which overcomes him actually in the course of forty-five lines—will not seem too sudden.[10] Music creating this particular illusion is especially prominent in *The Tempest*.[11] Shakespeare even suggested the progress of Cassio's inebriation by the comments Cassio makes on each song. At the end of the first, Cassio exclaims "an excellent song!" This is a passable piece of musical criticism if, in this case, we understand "excellent" to mean "appropriate" or "mirthful"; we have no reason to expect excellent singing from Iago under the circumstances, and certainly this drinking song is not a noble work of art. Hence, when at the end of the second song Cassio judges it "a more exquisite song than the other," we may be sure that his critical faculties are considerably less keen than before.

The source of the text and the original music for Iago's first drinking song are both unknown. Chappell set the text to an old ballad tune called "Wigmore's Galliard," which appears in Thomas Deloney's "Strange Histories" (1602).[12] His setting is shown in figure 30.

Iago's second song is a fragmentary version, as Percy early noticed, of a ballad, "Bell my Wiffe," found in Brit. Mus. Add. MS 27,879. The complete ballad is printed in Percy's *Reliques*. . . . Iago sings stanza seven, which follows, in the version given by Percy:

> King Harry was a verry good king,
> I trow his hose cost but a crowne,
> He thought them 12d. over to deere,
> Therefore he calld the taylor clowne,
> He was a king and wore the crowne,
> And thouse but of low degree:
> Itt's pride that putts this country downe,
> Man, take thine old cloake about thee.[13]

No known musical setting of this song is contemporary with Shakespeare. Chappell believed the tune was a variant of "Green-

10. Seng, "The Dramatic Function of the Songs in Shakespeare's Plays," p. 474.

11. See Long, *Shakespeare's Use of Music: The Final Comedies*, pp. 101 ff.

12. *Popular Music of the Olden Time* 1:242.

13. *Reliques of Ancient English Poetry* . . . 1:190.

sleaves."[14] The old Scotch tune in James Johnson's *The Scotish National Museum* (1839),[15] entitled "Tak your auld cloak about ye," was chosen by Louis Elson and Peter Seng as the best possible setting, and I see no reason to disagree with them.[16] The Scotch setting appears in figure 31.

Figure 30.

Figure 31.

14. *Popular Music of the Olden Time* 1:201–2.
15. Volume 3, pp. 258 ff. (quoted in Chappell, ed., *Popular Music of the Olden Time* 1:n14).
16. Seng, "The Dramatic Function of the Songs in Shakespeare's Plays," p. 481; Elson, *Shakespeare in Music*, pp. 202–3.

The climax of the music in *Othello* is, without doubt, Desdemona, singing a few stanzas from an old ballad called "A Lover's complaint," which has since become known as "The Willow Song." The dramatic situation in which she sings it is poignant. Preparing to retire, as the Moor has commanded her to do, she is aware that she is the object of Othello's anger and that the matter, whatever it is, will be resolved once they are alone together. Our interest in the scene begins in act 4, scene 3, line 18.

EMIL. I would you had never seen him!
DES. So would not I. My love doth so approve him
That even his stubbornness, his checks, his frowns—
Prithee, unpin me—have grace and favor in them.
EMIL. I have laid those sheets you bade me on the bed.
DES. All's one. Good faith, how foolish are our minds!
If I do die before thee, prithee shroud me
In one of those same sheets.
EMIL.   Come, come, you talk.
DES. My mother had a maid called Barbara.
She was in love, and he she loved proved mad
And did forsake her. She had a song of "willow"—
An old thing 'twas, but it expressed her fortune,
And she died singing it. That song tonight
Will not go from my mind. I have much to do
But to go hang my head all at one side
And sing it like poor Barbara. Prithee, dispatch.
EMIL. Shall I go fetch your nightgown?
DES.   No, unpin me here.
This Lodovico is a proper man.
EMIL. A very handsome man.
DES. He speaks well.
EMIL. I know a lady in Venice would have walked barefoot
to Palestine for a touch of his nether lip.
DES.   [*Singing*]
"The poor soul sat sighing by a sycamore tree,
    Sing all a green willow.
Her hand on her bosom, her head on her knee,
    Sing willow, willow, willow.
The fresh streams ran by her, and murmured her moans,
    Sing willow, willow, willow.
Her salt tears fell from her, and softened the stones—"
        Lay by these—   [*Singing*]
            "Sing willow, willow, willow."
        Prithee, hie thee, he'll come anon.—   [*Singing*]

"Sing all a green willow must be my garland.
Let nobody blame him, his scorn I approve—"
Nay, that's not next. Who is't that knocks?

EMIL. It's the wind.

DES.   [*Singing*]
"I called my love false love, but what said he then?
Sing willow, willow, willow.
If I court moe women, you'll couch with moe men."
So get thee gone, good night. Mine eyes do itch.
Doth that bode weeping?

"The Willow Song" has attracted many commentators. All have
agreed that it is an example of Shakespeare's dramatic power at its
peak. It would be impractical to survey here all the criticism and
analyses of the episode, but we should note some of the more recent
studies and review their major conclusions. Before turning to these
comments, however, let us look at the old ballad from which Shakespeare apparently drew the song. While he did not, of course, use all
of the ballad text, he did excerpt enough stanzas to bring "A
Lover's complaint" to the minds of his audience and, by suggestion,
to add to his scene the emotional impact of the lover's plight in the
ballad. There is substantial evidence that the ballad text is older
than the play. This evidence, which will appear when we turn to the
musical settings of the song, supports a date at least as early as 1585.

As H. C. Hart and others have noted, one of the song's texts is
preserved, with a lute accompaniment, in an MS dated c. 1600.[17]
While this text includes some stanzas not used in the play, for a
fuller text we turn to the black-letter ballad, part of Samuel Pepys's
collection, published in Thomas Percy's *Reliques*. . . .[18] In reading
the Pepys text, we should remember that Shakespeare in several
stanzas altered the sex of the lover to make his excerpts applicable
to Desdemona; other stanzas fit without alteration. I omit the Willow
refrain.

1 A poore soule sat sighing under a sicamore tree;
   With his hand on his bosom, his head on his knee:

2 He sigh'd in his singing, and after each grone,
   I am dead to all pleasure, my true love is gone;

17. Shakespeare, *The Tragedy of Othello*, ed. H. Hart, *n*42.
18. Volume 1, pp. 199–203. Cf. Chappell, ed., *The Roxburghe Ballads* 1:171.

3 My love she is turned; untrue she doth prove:
   She renders me nothing but hate for my love.

4 O pitty me (cried he) ye lovers, each one;
   Her heart's hard as marble; she rues not my mone.

5 The cold streams ran by him, his eyes wept apace;
   The salt tears fell from him, which drowned his face:

6 The mute birds sate by him, made tame by his mones,
   The salt tears fell from him, which softened the stones.

7 Let nobody blame me, her scornes I do prove;
   She was borne to be faire; I to die for her love.

8 O that beauty should harbour a heart that's so hard!
   My true love rejecting without all regard.

9 Let love no more boast him in palace or bower;
   For women are trothles, and flote in an houre,

10 But what helps complaining? In vaine I complaine:
   I must patiently suffer her scorne and disdaine,

11 Come, all you forsaken, and sit down by me,
   He that 'plaines of his false love, mine's falser than she.

12 The willow wreath weare I, since my love did fleet;
   O Garland for lovers forsaken most meete.

Part the Second

13 Lowe lay'd by my sorrow, begot by disdain;
   Against her too cruel, still still I complaine.

14 O love too injurious, to wound my poore heart!
   To suffer the triumph, and joy in my smart:

15 O willow, willow, willow! the willow garland,
   A sign of her falsenesse before me doth stand:

16 As here it doth bid to despair and to dye,
   So hang it, friends, ore me in grave where I lye:

17 In grave where I rest mee, hang this to the view
   Of all that doe knowe her, to blaze her untrue.

18 With these words engraven, as epitaph meet,
   "Heer lyes one, drank poyson for potion most sweet."

19 Though she thus unkindly hath scorned my love,
   And carelessly smiles at the sorrowes I prove;

20 I cannot against her unkindly exclaim,
   Cause once well I loved her, and honoured her name:

21 The name of her sounded so sweete in mine eare,
   It rays'd my heart lightly, the name of my deare;

22 As then 'twas my comfort, it now is my griefe;
   It now brings me anguish, then brought me reliefe.

23 Farewell, faire falsehearted: plaints end with my breath!
   Thou dost loath me, I love thee, though cause of my death.

The ballad, with its monotonous repetitions of thought and near-duplication of some lines, shows evidence of oral transmission in the true folk tradition. Also, the stanzas are irregular in quality. Very likely the ballad was an "old thing" when the play was composed.

With Shakespeare's text and the extended ballad before us, we may now review briefly some comments about the dramatic functions of the song. Richmond Noble observed that Desdemona's song aids in making her misery almost unbearable to the spectator.[19] Harley Granville-Barker stated:

> Upon her weariness fancies and memories play freely. Reminder of the wedding sheets (imaging—so she had meant them to—the end as the beginning of their wedded joy) begets the fancy to be shrouded in them some day. From that evolves the memory of her dead mother, and of the maid Barbara and *her* "wretched fortune," and the song which "expressed her fortune"; and this recalls Venice, and for Venice stands the handsome, grave Lodovico.
>
> The sad rhythm of the song, as she sings it, soothes her mind, if it leaves her senses still morbidly acute. . . ."[20]

Ernest Brennecke has noted that Shakespeare invented the maid

19. *Shakespeare's Use of Song*, pp. 125–26.
20. *Prefaces to Shakespeare* 2:69.

Barbara, that he inserted dramatic interjections within the performance of the song.[21] Then, to quote Brennecke:

> Entirely out of its context and rhyme, Shakespeare required
> Desdemona to sing: "Let nobody blame him; his scorn I
> approve" lifting the idea from stanza 7 of the song, and
> recalling, with the audience, how the Moor had so brutally
> struck her in public that very afternoon.
>   Desdemona's subconscious mind has here played her a
> trick.... In her sense of imminent doom she twists the
> words ... so as to apply them to her own tragic situation.
> ... Then, overcome with foreboding, she imagines that she
> hears someone at the door.
>   Finally, Shakespeare causes Desdemona, who only
> vaguely recalls the words "false love" from stanza 11, and
> "She was born to be false" from stanza 7, to improvise an
> entirely original couplet ... "I call'd my love false love,
> but what said he then? / If I court mo[r]e women, you'll
> couch with more men." In spoken utterance Desdemona
> would never spontaneously use so indecorous a word as
> "couch."...
>   But what she cannot say, she sings. The last couplet of
> her song tells us that she is inwardly and explicitly aware
> of the cause of Othello's passion.... Desdemona invents
> and sings the conclusion of her song as if in a dream or a
> deep reverie, thereby revealing more of her subconscious
> awareness than any spoken words could indicate.... The
> scene is analogous to the mad Ophelia's self-revelation in
> her singing of ballad snatches.[22]

Frederick Sternfeld has written of the couplet beginning "I call'd
my love false love: but what said he then?":

> The climax of the song has the most significant variation.
> That the first line is in effect the second line of the model
> is unimportant in comparison with the acid reproach of
> promiscuity that rankles in Desdemona and comes to the
> fore, destroying the lyric integrity of the original. At this

21. "'Nay, That's Not Next!' The Significance of Desdemona's 'Willow
Song,'" p. 36.
22. Ibid., pp. 36–37.

point her version is less song than unwitting self-expression. How ironical and touching that the dying Emilia, in Act V, should return to the burden, "willow, willow, willow." The swan song, turned leitmotif, is the only quotation of its kind in Shakespeare where a fragment of a song is repeated in the same play. Emilia's coda thus becomes an act of transfiguration. Desdemona's variation, on the other hand, depends for its effectiveness on the playgoer's knowledge of the model. By starting with a well-known text to a well-known tune, her deviations become significant. To suggest Desdemona is made to entertain the audience with a familiar song by way of an appropriate interlude would be to misconceive Shakespeare's dramatic plan. It would be equally mistaken, however, to assume that the dramatic and symbolic meaning of the Willow Song could come across without the actual singing.[23]

Throughout these critical and interpretive remarks, four points remain constant: that the song serves as, or aids, a psychological revelation of Desdemona's character and emotions; that it reveals three dominant ideas and emotions—her steadfast love of Othello and her inability to account for his belief that she is not chaste; her foreboding of imminent death; and her expectation of the return of Othello, which inspires mixed emotions of fear and love. There could be no better formula devised for the creation of almost agonizing suspense. Of the four points, the first two present obvious analogues to some of the old ballad stanzas.

At the risk of seeming presumptuous, I suggest that Shakespeare had more in mind than the authorities quoted have stated, in particular, that the *context* of Shakespeare's song was to some extent shaped by the text of the old ballad, and that the swan song leitmotif has a symbolic value not previously noticed.

In the Pepys ballad, stanza 7, the line "Let nobody blame me, her scornes I do prove" is echoed in the statement by Desdemona (Shakespeare reversed the sexes) made in answer to Emilia's criticism of Othello, "I would you had never seen him!" To this Desdemona responds, "So would not I. My love doth so approve him. . . ." Then, in Shakespeare's version of the song, the line of the original is re-

---

23. "Shakespeare's Use of Popular Song," p. 159. See also his *Music in Shakespearean Tragedy*, pp. 23–38. Cutts ("Notes on *Othello*," p. 251) commented on Desdemona's reference to Lodovico.

echoed thus: "Let nobody blame him, his scorn I approve——."

A striking influence of the ballad upon Desdemona's spoken lines may be traced to stanzas 15, 16, and 17 of the ballad, where the lover requests that a willow garland be hung above his grave. Desdemona has no willow garland, but her mind turns to an equally symbolic object, the wedding sheets that were witness to her chastity before marriage and symbolic of her fidelity to Othello thereafter. Desdemona hopes that the white sheet with which she wishes to be shrouded, like the willow garland, will remain a mute spokesman for the steadfastness and purity of her love.

The white color of the sheet is linked symbolically to what is, I believe, the major "meaning" of the song that expresses her fortune. Shakespeare explicitly told us what it "means" when he had the dying Emilia say,

> What did thy song bode, lady?
> Hark, canst thou hear me? I will play the swan,
> And die in music.   [*Singing*]
>   "Willow, willow, willow."
> Moor, she was chaste. . . .

Emilia now recognizes that "The Willow Song" was Desdemona's swan song. With her next breath, she vouches for Desdemona's chastity. Did the image of the white swan suggest the purity of Desdemona to her? The swan was a familiar symbol of purity. Lawrence Ross[24] showed a woodcut from a broadside, *The Map of Mortalitie* (1604), of a swan accompanied by the couplet "A Conscience pure, / singes to the last howre." The myth of the swan's death song was, of course, common Elizabethan lore. John Bossewelle, in his book on heraldry, explained:

> The Swanne is of all birdes most whitest, of a shyrle voyce, and singeth moste swetely towardes ye time of hys death, as it were to bewaile hys departure and buriall. Ovid . . .
> > The Swanne doth tune, with mourning breath,
> > Most pleasaunt metres, before his death.
> He is a gentle and quyet birde, His mortall enemye is th'Egle.[25]

Bossewelle's book was published in 1572, some thirty years before

24. "Shakespeare's 'Dull Clown' and Symbolic Music," plate 9, facing p. 121.
25. *Workes of armorie* . . . bk. 3, fol. 7ᵛ.

Shakespeare matched his gentle, quiet, white swan with a black eagle of war.

But in Joseph Barnes's *The Praise of Musick* (1586), John Case added another dimension to the legend by a reference to Plato's *Phaedo*: "the Swanne . . . is therefore saide to bee under the patronage of Apollo . . . she seemeth to have som divination from him,

The poore Soule sat sing - ing by a Sic - a - mour tree Sing all a green wil - lough Sing wil - lough wil - lough Her hand on her bo - some her head on her knee Sing all a green wil - lough must be my Gar - land.

Figure 32.

whereby she foreseing what good is in death, by a naturall instinct, finishes her life with singing and with joy."[26] If we combine the statements of the woodcut, of Bossewelle, and in Barnes, we observe that the swan, the whitest of birds, divining her approaching death, sings most sweetly both in mourning and in joy. The analogy is strong: Desdemona, chaste, innocent, passive, has a foreboding of her death and sings a swan song expressing both sorrow at her fortune and love for the Moor who has become her mortal enemy. "The Willow Song" is Desdemona's "Liebestod."

In turning to the musical settings of the ballad text, we are embarrassed by riches, for where the difficulty usually is to find *any*

26. Pages 49–50.

setting for the play songs, in this case we have *three* pieces of music any one of which might have been heard in the original production of *Othello*. In chronological sequence they are: the tune entitled "All of grene willowe" in the Folger Shakespeare Library MS 448.16, page 18, which was recently published for the first time by Peter Seng;[27] the tune with the title "All a greane Willowe" in the Thomas Dallis Lute Book, Trinity College Library, Dublin, MS 410 (D.3.30), page 26, which has been known for some time and is published in Wooldridge's *Old English Popular Music*;[28] and the familiar tune (with text) from Brit. Mus. Add. MS 15,117, published in Chappell's *Popular Music of the Olden Time*[29] and by many others elsewhere.

All three of the Willow tunes differ one from another. It is almost impossible to set either the ballad text or Shakespeare's version of it to the Folger music. Seng managed to do so, but only by inserting more "willows" than I think the landscape should contain. For this reason, I hesitate to accept the Folger tune as a setting for the received text. The British Museum tune is quite familiar, having been used on the stage for many years. The Dallis air, however, is comparatively unknown and fits both texts snugly; moreover, it is older than the setting in the British Museum and therefore more likely to have been known to Shakespeare's audiences when the play was given its early productions. As Sternfeld has stated, the success of the dramatist's alterations of the ballad text would depend largely on its familiarity to the spectators. His statement about the text would be equally true of the tune. I have, therefore, set the first stanza of Shakespeare's text to a literal transcription of the Dallis lute tablature (see figure 32).

Whereas Shakespeare used a rather sophisticated lutenist's ayre in *Troilus*, he turned again to the popular ballads for his songs in *Othello*. What his choices may signify in terms of the audiences to which Shakespeare was directing these two plays, as well as the effects his choice of music had upon the subsequent popularity, or lack of it, of the plays in question, are certainly points worth pondering.

---

27. "The Earliest Known Music for Desdemona's 'Willow Song.'" For an extensive description of the various musical settings and their notation, see Sternfeld, *Music in Shakespearean Tragedy*, appendices 1–4, pp. 38–52. Most recently, John Ward has found a fragmentary setting of music and text, closely related to the Folger MS version, in a Western Reserve MS. See Ward, "Fragments at Western Reserve University," pp. 845–53.

28. Volume 1, p. 110.

29. Volume 1, p. 106.

ELEVEN

King Lear

HAKESPEARE'S WAY WITH HIS SOURCES VARIES FROM a close following, as he treated Plutarch, to a short nod in their direction as in *The Tempest*. Many of his rubrics for the music in *Antony and Cleopatra* are suggested directly by Plutarch; in *The Tempest*, so far as anyone knows, Shakespeare's use of the music was entirely independent of his sources. He was also original in planning the musical elements in *King Lear*. The two major sources of the plot and the Gloucester subplot are, respectively, Holinshed's *Chronicles* and Sidney's *Arcadia*. These sources provide no suggestions for the music in the play. By examining the musical additions, we gain a glimpse of the playwright's creative power as it was exercised uninfluenced by prior ideas or models. What this glimpse reveals is a partial view of the play's structural pattern—a few narrow beams of light tracing some of the great flying buttresses which support this magnificently Gothic tragedy. And occasionally, sometimes unexpectedly, a few finely wrought details, when isolated in our thin shaft of light, assume a fresh aspect of imagination all compact. Let us then go make our visit to the three *loci*—the term "worlds" with its earthbound connotations seems inappropriate—of this great poem.

For reasons best known to himself Shakespeare associated music in performance only with Lear or the main plot; and for the most part, music sounds only in the presence of the old king. The pattern of the main plot seems to have dictated the performance of all the music in the play. As I read it, the Lear plot presents three dramatic *loci*, none of them necessarily spatial or temporal. The first locale is represented by the court of King Lear at the moment he publicly divests himself of his royal prerogatives—and responsibilities—and divides his realm. Before these unnatural acts, as Elizabethan political theorists would consider them, Nature was in a balanced, well-tempered state. As a consequence of his acts, however, the great bonds of Nature crack, Lear disowns his daughter Cordelia and banishes his loyal and trustworthy adviser, Kent; and these are merely the first rents in the tremendous fabric of order and dignity represented by Lear's kingdom, family, person, and mind, which come to total wrack in the storm on the heath. The royal court with Lear as king has its music, the music of ceremony and ritual, music in its public function, which in this case is to elevate human actions and to mark the orderly processes of state.

This locale, when King Lear reduces himself to next to nothingness, gives place to a vast scene of disorder as Lear's mind becomes unhinged and the skies are untuned as Nature itself falls into chaos. Madmen, fools, bestial men and women who rend their proper selves, haunt the storm-tossed scene. This disintegrating universe also has its music, and its music accompanies Lear as he enters the darkness, as he staggers gropingly through his insanity, and as he emerges, following a sea-change to something rich and strange, into the safe harbor of Cordelia's love. In contrast to the public music in the first locale, the song scraps which are scattered throughout the unredeemed Nature that is the second locale reflect the anguished mind of Lear. The songs of the Fool, Edgar as Tom o' Bedlam, and (by report) the king himself (act 4, scene 4) as he wanders, crowned with weeds and chanting old lays, around the countryside near Dover, provide one means by which we are made to hear as well as see, and therefore to feel more intensely, the nightmare and her ninefold. As in *Hamlet*, the vocal music aids us in probing the depths of a distracted mind. But it is to the therapeutic music of an instrumental consort that Lear escapes from his untuned mind to the harmony of Cordelia's love which redeems Nature itself.

The third locale I cannot describe, as I have not perceived it myself. But, as Lear describes this locale, it, too, has its music. Keats said that "Heard music is sweet, but that unheard is sweeter." We cannot hear the music Lear describes, but we know it burst forth from the throat of wronged Philomela, brought consolation to an emperor of Cathay, and gave momentary surcease to the sadness of death-doomed young Keats.[1] But let Lear speak:

> Come, let's away to prison.
> We two alone will sing like birds i' the cage.
> When thou dost ask me blessing, I'll kneel down
> And ask of thee forgiveness. So we'll live,
> And pray, and sing. . . .

1. For a discussion of the Renaissance concept of "unheard music," see Ross, "Shakespeare's 'Dull Clown' and Symbolic Music."

The final act of the great drama returns us—the wheel of fire having turned full circle—to the first locale, and we hear the formal trumpet calls that herald a triumph of temporal justice and the return of order and right to a world now transcended by Lear and Cordelia. The consort music which aurally presents the king's return to sanity, and the trumpet fanfares announcing the trial by combat in act 5, are thus balanced like opposite spokes of a great wheel against the sennet and flourishes heard in act 1.

Now let us consider the specific instances.

The stage direction for the sennet that brings Lear and his court onstage (1. 1. 34) is:

> [*Sennet. Enter one bearing a coronet,* KING LEAR,
> CORNWALL, ALBANY, GONERIL, REGAN, CORDELIA, *and*
> ATTENDANTS.]

The sennet provides the ceremonious music appropriate to bring the courtly procession in with pomp and dignity. It may be a bit of fore-shadowing, a warning that Lear's majesty is unstable, that the royal flourish is missing. Indeed, no flourish is heard until line 190, when trumpets peal to announce the entrance of the king of France, the duke of Burgundy, Gloucester, and assorted attendants. The trumpets sound another flourish when the actors excepting Cordelia, France, Goneril, and Regan leave the stage (line 269). We might expect a sennet to be used again here, but it is not.

Once Lear divides his kingdom, things go from bad to worse. As they do so, the Fool, like a nagging conscience to Lear, appears on the scene. True to form, the Fool expresses himself using bits of ancient folklore—wise saws, riddles, and fragments of ballads and old songs. He is the only intimate of Lear who can tell the old king the truth with impunity; even so, the Fool frequently uses indirection. The song scraps he offers are part of his general gnomic-choric function. They suggest a moral or comment on an action by reminding Lear and the audience of analogous situations in the folk-histories —the ballads.

It is difficult to determine which of the Fool's jingles and rhymes are sung and which are spoken. There is no stage direction in either the Q or F texts to indicate that the Fool sings at all. The first song we can be sure he sings occurs in act 1, scene 4, when he twits

Lear about his foolishness in giving his kingdom to his two daughters. The antic sings two stanzas (beginning at line 181):

> "Fools had ne'er less wit in a year,
>   For wise men are grown foppish,
> And know not how their wits to wear,
>   Their manners are so apish."

LEAR. When were you wont to be so full of songs, sirrah?

FOOL. I have used it, Nuncle, ever since thou madest thy
    daughters thy mother. For when thou gavest them the
    rod and puttest down thine own breeches,

[Singing]

> "Then they for sudden joy did weep,
>   And I for sorrow sung,
> That such a king should play bopeep,
>   And go the fools among."

We can be almost certain that these two stanzas are sung, because, not only does Lear refer to the Fool as being "full of songs," but at least two lines of the second stanza were drawn by Shakespeare from the pack of Autolycus. These two lines provide a clue that will lead us to two tunes either of which could well have been the music to which the Fool sang his impudent scraps.

The lines in question are "Then they for sudden joy did weep, / And I for sorrow sung." They are variants of lines from a godly ballad on the death of John Careless, martyred for his religious beliefs in the reign of Bloody Mary. The ballad was first published in Bishop Miles Coverdale's *Certain most godly, fruitful, and comfortable letters* (1564).[2] The first two stanzas of Coverdale's ballad follow:

> Some men for sodayne ioye do wepe,
>   And some in sorow syng:
> When that they lie in daunger depe,
>   To put away mournyng.
>
> Betweene them both will I beginne,
>   Being in ioy and payne:

2. Pages 634–38. Cf. H. Rollins, "'King Lear' and the Ballad of 'John Careless.'" For general discussion of the songs in *Lear*, see Sternfeld, *Music in Shakespearean Tragedy*, pp. 174–92.

In sighing to lament my sinne,
But yet reioyce agayne.[3]

A broadside "ballad of John Careles &c" was licensed for printing on Aug. 1, 1586.[4] Then another ballad appeared, "The Confession of a Paenitent Sinner," which was directed to be sung "To the Tune of *O man in desperation*; or, *Some men for suddaine joyes doe weepe*."[5] Here the first of the two lines is listed as the name of a tune, presumably the tune to which the "ballad of John Careles &c" was sung. Hyder Rollins expressed the belief that the tunes "Diana" and "O man in desperation" were probably identical and certainly interchangeable; moreover, that a ballad, "The History of Diana and Acteon," dated 1624, was to be sung to the tune "Rogero" and that "Rogero" could thus be equivalent to or interchangeable with "Diana" and "O man in desperation."[6] The tune "Rogero," which will be considered later, is in Chappell's *Popular Music of the Olden Time*.[7] Then, if "Rogero" is also the tune to which "Some men for suddaine joyes doe wepe" was sung, we have found in "Rogero" a possible setting for the "ballad of John Careles &c" and also, possibly, for the two stanzas sung by Lear's Fool.

But there is another possibility we should consider. It seems that by the time *King Lear* was on the boards, the two lines Shakespeare borrowed from the good bishop also had been borrowed by others and, in fact, had been absorbed by other ballads and songs. George Steevens observed that in Thomas Heywood's *Rape of Lucrece* (1608) Valerius sings the following stanza:

When Tarquin first in court began,
And was approved king:
Some men for sudden joy 'gan weep,
But I for sorrow sing.[8]

While we recognize immediately the last two lines, the first two should also jog our memories, for they parody the first two lines of the ballad "Sir Lancelot du Lake." Falstaff sings the lines (*2 Henry*

3. Chappell, ed., *The Roxburghe Ballads* 3:168.
4. Rollins, " 'King Lear' and the Ballad of 'John Careless,' " p. 87.
5. Ibid., p. 88.
6. Ibid.
7. Volume 1, p. 93; Shakespeare, *The Tragedy of King Lear*, ed. W. Craig, p. 190, note to line 189.
8. Chappell, ed., *The Roxburghe Ballads* 6:714–16.

IV, act 2, scene 4) as they are found in the ballad: "When Arthur first in court began, / And was approved king. . . ." "Sir Lancelot du Lake" is directed to be sung to the tune "Flying Fame," which is interchangeable with the old tune celebrated by Sir Philip Sidney, "Chevy Chace." It follows that, since the last two lines of Heywood's parody and the first two lines of the Fool's stanza are slight variants, both may share the same tune—in this case, "Flying Fame." (Incidentally, the ballad "King Leare and his Three Daughters" is directed to be sung to "Flying Fame." A tune with this title is printed by Chappell, but it is dated no earlier than 1707.)[9] If the two lines beginning "Then they for sudden joy did weep" can be sung to this tune, then the Fool's stanzas can also be set to it. Thus, as a possible setting for the two stanzas in *King Lear*, we now have the tune "Flying Fame" and the tune "Rogero."

Peter Seng has found still another musical setting for our two lines, but again, the lines are parts of a song different from any mentioned previously. In this case they are found in what Seng believed is a round or catch for two or more voices composed by John Hilton.[10] The music is an MS entry on one page of the British Museum copy of *Pammelia, Musicks Miscellanie*, published in 1609.[11] Seng dated the entry at about 1646.[12] The text of the round is as follows:

> Late as I waked out of sleepe
> I harde a prety thinge
> some men for suddaine ioy do weepe
> and some for sorrow singe fa la la. . . .

It would appear that Shakespeare wrote the two-stanza song for Lear's Fool and parodied in the second stanza a popular, catchy phrase in order to make the point that the Fool for sorrow sings when he beholds the foolishness of King Lear.[13] The preceding line, "Then they for sudden joy did weep" may be the Fool's reference to Goneril and Regan.

Of the three possible tunes discussed—"Late as I waked out of

---

9. *Popular Music of the Olden Time* 1:199.
10. "An Early Tune for the Fool's Song in 'King Lear.'"
11. Ibid.
12. "The Dramatic Function of the Songs in Shakespeare's Plays," pp. 512–13.
13. Sternfeld ("Music and Ballads") listed and discussed several "echoes" of the tag in other plays and ballads of the time.

sleepe," "Flying Fame," and "Rogero"—the last is, I think, the best choice. The Fool's song can be sung to "Flying Fame" and to "Rogero" with equal ease or to many another ballad tune, because the "tumbling meter"—four and three—is a common ballad characteristic. I choose "Rogero" because the evidence supports my belief that it is the oldest of the three tunes and therefore probably the most familiar to Shakespeare and his audience when the play was first produced.

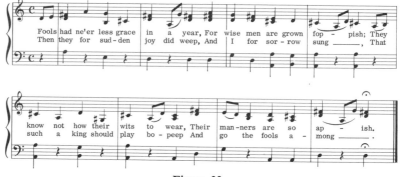

Figure 33.

"Rogero" was frequently used as a ballad tune when Shakespeare wrote *King Lear*, a fact which in itself indicates its popularity and which suggests that the tune was an old one. The title, however, supplies the best argument. Originally, the name was "Ruggiero" or the "Aria di Ruggiero," so-called because it was a "ground" or bass melody, to which a passage in *ottava rima* from Ariosto's *Orlando Furioso* was set by Italian musicians.[14] Brought to England some time in the first quarter of the sixteenth century, the melody was absorbed by the English folk music and its title was anglicized. By 1585 the tune served both as music for popular songs (an interesting example of folk borrowing) and as a tune that lutenist-composers made a subject for variations or "divisions." For example, the tune "Rogero," shown in figure 33, is the ground used by Thomas Dallis in his lute book, on which he or another composer wrote a division found elsewhere in the MS.[15] The transcription of the lute tablature is literal.

The next song is also sung by the Fool. As Lear, the Fool, and

14. See Byler, *Italian Currents*, pp. 14–15, 97.
15. Trinity College (Dublin) Libr. MS 410 (D.3.30), p. 20.

Kent wander in the storm on the heath (act 3, scene 2), Kent finds a hovel and urges the maddened monarch to take shelter in it. In reply, Lear turns to his jester (line 68):

LEAR.   My wits begin to turn.
               Come on, my boy. How dost, my boy? Art cold?
               I am cold myself. Where is this straw, my fellow?
               The art of our necessities is strange,
               That can make vile things precious. Come, your hovel.
               Poor fool and knave, I have one part in my heart
               That's sorry yet for thee.
FOOL.   [*Singing*]
               "He that has and a little tiny wit—
               With hey, ho, the wind and the rain—
               Must make content with his fortunes fit,
               For the rain it raineth every day."
LEAR. True, my good boy.

Shakespeare placed this song at what is, I believe, the turning point in the regeneration of the proud and willful king. In one of the great dramatic ironies of a play replete with ironies, Lear for the first time shows compassion precisely at the moment that his wits begin to turn. The first instance of madness, of alienation from the world in which he had held unquestioned sway—the world of Cornwall, Albany, Edmund, Goneril, and Regan—makes Lear aware that he is not alone in pain, that unaccommodated man is a great society, wherein the king and the Fool are equal in their capacities for suffering. The Fool's song scrap gently underscores the point: both he and his master are equally fools (as the Fool had claimed all along), but now this equality extends into the realm of physical and mental torment (the wind and the rain) which those who have a little tiny wit (Everyman) must endure as long as life lasts ("For the rain it raineth every day"). Thus, life for the poor forked animal that is biological man is simply an existence to be endured. To which the old king answers simply, "True, my good boy."

The Fool's song is an altered version of a stanza Shakespeare gave Feste, another fool, to sing as an epilogue to *Twelfth Night*. The traditional tune to which the song is set appears in the first volume of this series.[16] The song, like the other vocal music in the play, is sung without accompaniment.

The Fool enters the hovel and is almost frightened out of his

16. Page 182.

remaining wits by Edgar disguised as a Tom o' Bedlam. Edgar then emerges from the hut mumbling random bits of old gnomic verses, shouting wild commands to the fiends which supposedly torment him, and singing bits of old songs. It would seem that the stage bedlamites also conventionally sang ballad medleys or disjointed fragments of old songs.[17] There is a distinct class of ballad, the Bedlam songs, that was popular in the Elizabethan and Jacobean years; several ballad tunes entitled "Tom o' Bedlam" may be found in various lute books. But these bedlam songs differ from those which Shakespeare gave to Edgar. The bedlam songs are *about* distracted persons; Edgar's bits of songs are sung by a character acting the part of a madman.[18] In this sense, Edgar's vocal snatches do not fall into the category of the bedlam songs but, rather, into the traditional practice of the stage fool. In his use of songs, Shakespeare seems to have made little or no distinction between madmen and fools or jesters. Ophelia, in *Hamlet*, is a case in point; although she is clearly mad when she sings her plaintive lays, she sings them in the same manner as Feste, Touchstone, and Lear's Fool. Therefore, when Edgar first meets Lear and the Fool (3. 4. 46), he completes his Mad Tom disguise by interlacing song snatches among other fragmentary mouthings:

> EDG. Away! The foul fiend follows me!
> "Through the sharp hawthorn blows the cold wind."
> Hum! Go to thy cold bed and warm thee.

Some editors, including G. L. Kittredge, also an authority on ballads, have believed that Edgar's second sentence may be a line or refrain from an old song. Edgar repeats it, slightly altered (in line 102). The line can be easily set to a strain of the ballad tune "Drive the Cold Winter Away" (see figure 34). The music is taken from Chappell, who found the earliest version of it in John Playford's *The English Dancing Master* (1651).[19] Chappell quoted an earlier, godly parody of the ballad text, which he felt may have been composed in the sixteenth century.[20]

17. For an extended discussion of the traditional links between the stage fools and the ballad medley, see chap. 5.
18. For an example of a bedlam song containing lines reminiscent of some sung by Edgar, see Wells, "Tom O' Bedlam's Song and *King Lear*," pp. 312–13.
19. Chappell, ed., *Popular Music of the Olden Time* 1:193–94.
20. Ibid., p. 194.

A few lines later in the same scene (line 119), Gloucester enters carrying a torch. Mad Tom takes him for "the foul fiend Flibbertigibbet" and chants an old charm supposedly used by St. Withold against the nightmare, or incubus.[21] This incantation differs from Shakespeare's usual practice; in writing charms or spells, he frequently employed a regular trochaic tetrameter verse such as that in act 3, scene 6, line 69. The St. Withold verse does not follow this pattern. On the other hand, it does follow a normal song pattern which can be set without difficulty to either of two distinct Tom o' Bedlam tunes.

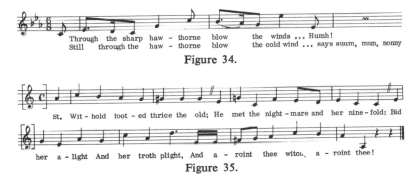

Through the sharp haw - thorne blow the winds ... Humh!
Still through the haw - thorne blow the cold wind ... says suum, mun, nonny

Figure 34.

St. Wit-hold foot - ed thrice the old; He met the night - mare and her nine - fold: Bid

her a - light And her troth plight, And a - roint thee witch, a - roint thee!

Figure 35.

These tunes, written as lute pieces, appear without texts in Brit. Mus. Add. MS 38,539, fols. 14^r and 29^r. Both seem to be descriptive instrumental pieces. The first tune, that of fol. 14^r, appears also in John Playford's *Musick's Delight on the Cithren* ... (1666), no. 33, with the title "Tom a Bedlam." It is there transcribed to a different key and much abbreviated from that in the MS. The fact that there are two versions of this tune argues for its popularity. It probably was the tune to which several ballads were set in Shakespeare's day.[22]

If Edgar, or Mad Tom, sang the St. Withold charm, it is likely that he would have chosen a tune associated with the Tom o' Bedlam tunes, especially if the piece of music were familiar to his audience. I have therefore set the incantation to the first eight measures of the lute piece (fol. 14^r) entitled "Tom of Bedlam" (see figure 35).

As the wild convocation of Fool, mad Lear, and Tom o' Bedlam enters the hovel (line 187), Mad Tom interjects an interesting parallel

21. Shakespeare, *King Lear*, ed. H. Furness, p. 195.
22. For example, "The Cunning Northern Begger" (Chappell, ed., *The Roxburghe Ballads* 1:137), "A Jovial Tinker," c. 1628 (Rollins, ed., *The Pepys Ballads* 1:332), and "The famous Ratcatcher," 1615 (R. Dyboski, ed., *Songs, Carols, and Other Miscellaneous Poems* ... p. 61).

of the mean hut on the heath to a "dark tower." Tom sings or speaks a snatch from what, Kittredge has written, may or may not be a piece of an old ballad now lost:[23]

> EDG. "Child Rowland to the dark tower came.
> His word was still 'Fie, foh, and fum,
> I smell the blood of a British man.' "
>
> [*Exeunt.*]

The first line could well have been sung; the bit of song would serve as an exit song as Kent, Lear, Tom, and the Fool leave the stage. At the same time, this line and the familiar couplet from "Jack the Giant-killer" might be a bridge from act 3, scene 4, into act 3, scene 5, particularly since Mad Tom's doggerel lines seem to anticipate the opening of scene 5. The setting of this scene is Gloucester's castle, which has become morally and symbolically a "dark tower." When Cornwall opens the dialogue with the line "I will have my revenge ere I depart his [Gloucester's] house," we may understand that his house will become a tower even darker and the blood of a British man will flow, when Gloucester's eyes are so cruelly extinguished.

Assuming that the line "Child Rowland to the dark tower came" is from a ballad and also assuming that Edgar sang it, what tune might he have used? I have not found any ballad having Roland as its subject, excepting the highly dubious song published by Chappell "as a curiosity, but without vouching for its authenticity."[24] In *The Shirburn Ballads*, though, is a ballad called "Rowland's god-sonne" to be sung to the tune "Loth to depart."[25] If we make the risky assumption that the tune "Loth to depart" was also the musical setting for a ballad about Roland, as well as about the song "Rowland's god-sonne" (in keeping with the frequent practice of balladeers to set ballads having a common subject to one or two tunes previously associated with the subject), then we may make the wild surmise that Edgar could have sung his line to "Loth to depart." As a matter of fact, the line fits snugly the first two measures of the tune as given by Chappell (see figure 36).[26]

23. Shakespeare, *The Tragedy of King Lear*, pp. 186–87. H. Craig (Shakespeare, *The Complete Works*, p. 1002, note to line 187) stated that the lines in question are "fragments of the ballad *Child Rowland and Burd Ellen*." The evidence seems weak. Cf. H. Sargent and G. Kittredge, eds., *English and Scottish Popular Ballads*, p. 636.
24. *Popular Music of the Olden Time* 1:7.
25. Clark, ed., *The Shirburn Ballads, 1585–1616*, p. 354.
26. *Popular Music of the Olden Time* 1:173.

If the authenticity of the preceding musical setting leaves much to be desired, we need not be suspicious of the music for the next ballad stanza introduced by Shakespeare. In the magnificent scene (act 3, scene 6) wherein Lear conducts the grotesque trial of the imaginary Goneril and Regan, we find pathos and broad comedy so blended as to produce a tragic force that transcends rational analysis. The Tom o' Bedlam becomes a "most learned justicer," the Fool is addressed by Lear as "sapient sir," and, indeed, the Fool is sapient enough to recognize the joint-stool which Lear takes for Goneril. As a part of this mad comedy, Edgar and the Fool sing one stanza of an ancient ballad, "Come over the bourn, Bessy." Ingram saw this bit of music as a weak vestige of rationality barely surviving the ruins of natural

Child Row - land   to   the   dark   tow - er   came;

Figure 36.

order. He said, "Amid the ruin of moral stability and the rending of nature in *King Lear*, the slight music that is heard maintaining the part of faith and reason, is endowed with tremendous meaning ... all recognised standards seem to crumble ... so music itself which symbolises that stability seems almost stripped of its powers. ... The weak and pitiful singing of this pair marks the highest triumph of unreason against the powers of music."[27] The music is not, I think, a symbol of stability worn thin but, in the decorum of the ballad medley, the traditional musical signature of the madman and the natural. The music is a symbol of a mad, torn world and is sung with great glee by the Fool and Tom o' Bedlam.

As Lear arraigns his imaginary she-foxes, Edgar plays along with the demented old king and asks of the nonexistent Goneril or Regan, "Wantest thou eyes at trial, madam?" and then speaks or sings the first line of the ballad "Come o'er the bourn, Bessy, to me." The Fool, delighted, sings his version of the remainder of the stanza: "Her boat hath a leak, / And she must not speak / Why she dares not come over to thee." Edgar, seeing a chance to garnish his mad act, makes a comparison that only a fool or clown would think of if the Fool's voice is, as we might expect, considerably short of melodious. "The foul fiend haunts poor Tom in the voice of a nightingale." As we remember, this is the same kind of musical jest that Shake-

27. *"Hamlet, Othello,* and *King Lear*: Music and Tragedy," p. 171.

speare used in *A Midsummer Night's Dream*, act 3, scene 1, when he gave the enchanted Titania, awakened from sleep by Bottom's singing, the line "What angel wakes me from my flowery bed?"

The stanza altered by the Fool is certainly from an old love song popular in England before the birth of Shakespeare. It was already old enough to become part of a ballad medley sung by a stage clown, Moros, as we recall, in W. Wager's interlude *The Longer Thou Livest the More Fool Thou Art* (c. 1559). Moros sings:

> Com ouer the Boorne besse
> My little pretie Besse,
> Com ouer the Boorne besse to me.

J. Payne Collier listed two ballads, "a Dyaloge sett furthe by twene the quenes maistie and Englonde Come ouer the born Bessy" (1558–59) and "A Saynge betwene the quene and Englonde Called comme ouer the browne Bessye to me" (1564).[28] The latter ballad, by William Birche, begins with this stanza:

> Come ouer the born Bessy,
> Come ouer the born Bessy,
>   Sweete Bessey come ouer to me;
> And I shall thee take,
> And my dere Lady make
>   Before all other that euer I see.[29]

A musical setting for "Come o'er the bourn, Bessy," contemporary with Shakespeare, has been known for some time.[30] This setting, written for the lute, is in University Library, Cambridge, Lute MS D.d.xiii.11. In another lute MS (Univ. Cam. MS D.d.2.11) 1595?–1605? is a variant of the tune (no. 247) by Francis Cuttings, who used the old tune as a theme for a series of divisions or variations. The composition is entitled "Toy—Francis Cuttings," with a subscription "——ouer the broome Bessy." The melody is essentially the same as the one published by Wooldridge, but since Cuttings' "Toy" has not, to my knowledge, been published, I have extracted

28. *Broadside Black-Letter Ballads . . .* pp. 56, 205.
29. As quoted by Kittredge (Shakespeare, *The Tragedy of King Lear*, p. 190).
30. H. Wooldridge, ed., *Old English Popular Music* 1:121. Cf. Sternfeld, *Music in Shakespearean Tragedy*, pp. 184–88.

Figure 37.

from it the two-part melody and to this almost literal extraction have set the lines of Edgar and the Fool (figure 37).

About the next song offered by Poor Tom (3. 6. 42–46), Kittredge remarked: "Edgar assumes the air and manner of a dignified judge, but instantly breaks into song and follows his song with a mad exclamation, as if he saw a demon in the shape of a gray cat. . . ."[31] The song, which has not been otherwise identified, is this:

> Sleepest or wakest thou, jolly shepherd?
> 　Thy sheep be in the corn,
> And for one blast of thy minikin mouth,
> 　Thy sheep shall take no harm.

This apparent song stanza may be an early version of a nursery rhyme which, as I recall, begins "Little boy blue come blow your horn. / The sheep's in the meadow, the cow's in the corn." George Steevens, in his edition of *King Lear*, noted that the first line of Edgar's song resembles closely the title of a song performed in *The*

31. Shakespeare, *The Tragedy of King Lear*, p. 191.

Interlude of the Four Elements (c. 1510) previously discussed.[32] In the interlude, Ignorance sings a ballad medley. One song scrap is the line "Sleepyst thou, wakyst thou, Geffery Coke." J. O. Halliwell noted a similar line in the ballad "King Arthur and the King of Cornwall." The line occurs in the following stanza:

> And when he came to the King's chamber,
> he cold of his curtesie, says,
> "sleepe you, wake you, noble King Arthur?
> & euer Jesus waken yee!"[33]

It seems that here we have another example similar to the Fool's song beginning "then they / For sudden joy did weep," that is, a song employing a catchy line common to several other ballads. If so, we are now given a clue to the tune, or at least *a* tune, which could have been used as a setting for Edgar's song.

The early balladeers habitually set ballad texts with similar subject matter to one or two tunes previously associated with the subject. For example, ballads about fools were often set to the tune variously called "Tarleton," "Tarleton's carroll," or "Tarleton's Medley."[34] Ballads with kings or queens as their subjects were set to the tune "Flying Fame" mentioned earlier.[35] Confessions of criminals and accounts of executions were set to the tunes "Fortune my foe" or "Aim Not Too High." If we may assume that the ballad "King Arthur and the King of Cornwall" was sung to the same tune as "The Noble Acts of Arthur," and we know that the latter ballad was to be sung to the tune "Flying Fame"; then the former ballad may also be sung to the tune "Flying Fame." Then, if the two songs mentioned above and Edgar's song share similar lines, there is a good chance that they may also share a common tune. We may then try "Flying Fame" as a setting for "Sleepest or wakest thou, jolly shepherd?" The result, shown in figure 38, is that the tune and Shakespeare's text fit quite snugly together. Of course, almost any text written in the common "tumbling meter" could be fitted with any one of many ballad tunes.

32. Shakespeare, *King Lear*, ed. Furness, act 3, scene 6, *n*40.
33. As quoted ibid.
34. See Clark, ed., *The Shirburn Ballads, 1585–1616*, p. 351; *Ballads from Manuscripts* 2:92; T. C., *Laugh and Lie Downe* ... sig. D^i; Rollins, ed., *A Pepysian Garland* ... p. 451.
35. Chappell, ed., *The Roxburghe Ballads* 3:211, 6:714–15; also Deloney, *The Works of Thomas Deloney*, p. 297; Rollins, ed., *The Pepys Ballads* 1:12; *A Catalogue of an Unique Collection* ... p. 116.

I only suggest, in this case, that "Flying Fame" is the most likely tune, among many, to which Edgar sang the shepherd song, if indeed he sang the lines.

Our examination of the music in act 3 of *King Lear* has involved an excursion into balladry somewhat more extensive than has been the case in other plays, with the possible exception of *Hamlet*. The reason is that, as ballads are the common denominator of Elizabethan music, just so the ballad scraps sung by Shakespeare's madmen and

Sleepest or wakest thou, jol - ly, shep -herd Thy sheep be in the corn; And for one blast of thy min - i - kin mouth, Thy sheep shall take no harm.

Figure 38.

fools are the lowest common denominator of the English popular music in his time. In act 3, scenes 4 and 5—practically a single scene, since scene 5 is quite brief—we have grouped a madman, a character disguised as a madman, and a fool. We should then expect to hear performed many more ballad patches than usual, and such is the case.

We may also note that, as Lear slips more and more deeply into insanity, Shakespeare assigns the bulk of the song scraps to Tom o' Bedlam. The Fool's song bits have some rationality, and we can relate them to the jester's efforts to make Lear realize his folly. Once Lear makes the dramatic discovery that suffering is also a common denominator of human nature, Shakespeare assigned the subsequent pieces of song, with one exception, to Poor Tom. Also, from the same point in the play, the fragments sung by Edgar and the Fool are, within their context, completely irrational, as though the songs mirrored Lear's deeper descent into madness.

By far, most of the vocal music is performed in act 3. Not only is this act the drama's structural center; it also contains the "discovery" which I think is also the turning point of the tragedy's main plot. We have observed Shakespeare on numerous occasions underscoring turning points and climaxes with music. *King Lear* furnishes another example of this practice, for not only does act 3 contain a turning point—the beginning of Lear's regeneration—but it also contains the climax of the conflict between Lear, still a monarch in his own mind, and a world turned hostile, cruel, and disordered, in which he is nothing but a poor forked animal. The scenes of the anguished king defying unredeemed Nature in the storm on the heath, and his trial of that same Nature in the imaginary shapes of Goneril and Regan, are both mad—but sublimely mad. With this deranged world the Fool and the bedlamite are familiar; their patches and scraps of songs are one means by which the poet creates the "scenery"—the tempestuous and disordered jarring of elements—central to the drama.

With the return of Lear to sanity (but certainly not a return to his former self) in act 4, scene 7, we see the broken pieces of music in act 3 replaced by a harmonious consort, whose sweet concord of sounds wafts Lear's scattered wits into the safe harbor of Dover. Cordelia prays for his recovery, requesting that his wits be brought back into tune as a musician tunes a viol by turning its pegs:

> COR. O you kind gods,
> Cure this great breach in his abusèd nature!
> The untuned and jarring senses, oh, wind up
> Of this child-changèd father!

Lear is brought in, arrayed in fresh garments, and the Doctor calls for the music of the consort to awaken the sleeping old man: "Please you, draw near. Louder the music there!" To the sound of the music, Cordelia kisses her father, and he gradually emerges from both sleep and madness.

The use of music here can be seen as a symbol representing the return of Lear's discordant mind to harmony and wholeness, just as the broken songs of the Fool and Edgar reflect the derangement of Lear's mind earlier in the play.[36] In Elizabethan psychology, however, the use of music for mental therapy was a practical and accepted treatment. And, since the music probably continued through part of the conversation between Lear and Cordelia, Shakespeare could increase the emotional impact of the beautifully simple lines in which the two are reunited. It was Cordelia who was to redeem all the sorrows that Lear had suffered; her redemption of Lear, and through him all Nature, is accomplished to the sound of sweet music.

The context within which the music is performed suggests that the music was played by a "whole" consort of recorders—a combination

---

36. Provost ("On Justice and the Music in *Richard II* and *King Lear*") contrasted this scene with *Richard II*, act 5, scene 5.

of instruments appropriate to solemn scenes in Elizabethan stage practice.[37] From Antony Holborne's *Pavans, Galliards, Almains, and Other Short Aeirs* (1599), I have selected a consort piece called "Paradizo," no. 17, which I think satisfies the requirements of the scene (figure 39). With added inner voices, Holborne's score may be arranged for three recorders—alto, tenor, and bass—with a sackbut or trombone to sound the lower bass notes. No stage direction calls for the musicians to appear onstage; their music probably was played "within."

Figure 39.

In act 5, scene 3, the clarion call of trumpets blown in ceremonious vein returns us to a world of dignity, order, and formality. The battle (act 5, scene 2) is indicated aurally by the noise of an *Alarum and retreat within,* and a flourish (5. 3. 39) announces the victorious entry of Albany, Goneril, Regan, and Soldiers. Albany throws down his gauntlet before Edmund and commands that a

37. See Long, *Shakespeare's Use of Music ... Seven Comedies,* pp. 22, 37.

trumpet summon the unknown champion who will prove by combat
the villainy of Edmund.

> ALB.   . . . [*Enter a* HERALD.] Come hither, herald.—
> Let the trumpet sound.—
> And read out this.
> CAPT. Sound, trumpet!   [*A trumpet sounds.*]
> HER.   [*Reads.*] "If any man of quality or degree within the
> lists of the army will maintain upon Edmund, supposed
> Earl of Gloucester, that he is a manifold traitor, let him
> appear by the third sound of the trumpet. He is bold in
> his defense."
> EDM.   Sound!   [*First trumpet.*]
> HER.   Again!   [*Second trumpet.*]
> Again!   [*Third trumpet.*]
>   [*Trumpet answers within.*]
>   [*Enter* EDGAR *at the third sound, armed, with a trumpet
>   before him.*]

A trumpet sounds a fifth time to punctuate the combat between the
rightful heir to, and the false claimant of, Gloucester's name and
estate. As Edmund falls, mortally wounded, the brassy music abruptly
is silenced. "That's but a trifle here." The death of Cordelia and
Lear and the ordering of the succession to the crown follow. With
Albany's words, "The oldest hath borne most. We that are young
/ Shall never see so much, nor live so long," the actors from their
"great stage of fools" [*Exeunt, with a dead march*].

The trial by combat, a practice long sanctioned by chivalric tradition and usage, is here portrayed in its formal dress. Law and order
must prevail, and order is the basis of ceremony. We observe the
herald accompanied by his trumpeter; we note also the formal
soundings of three trumpets followed by an answer from Edgar's
trumpeter; the combat takes place to the shrill clamor of a trumpet.
In other words, we are witnesses to a legalistic ritual, and the music
augments the ceremony with brassy color. Justice triumphs, right
prevails, order is restored. But Cordelia, her ministry accomplished,
and Lear, released from his rack, are no longer concerned with the
world. To the solemnity of a funeral march, Shakespeare's Great
Nature, so tragically redeemed, is removed from the stage.

The retreat and flourish were doubtless the standard trumpet calls.
The notes sounded just before and during the trial by combat are not

identified; I would guess that the Herald's trumpeter sounded a parley three times. Edgar's answering call was probably a tucket. The trumpets blown during the combat could well have used a "charge." The dead march would have been played on military drums, probably muffled. The notations for all of these pieces of music are given in Appendices I, II, and IV.

The striking quality of the music in *King Lear* is the symmetry with which it is placed throughout the structure of the drama. The music falls into four general sections—the ceremonious instrumental music in act 1, the songs of the Fool and Edgar in acts 3 and 4, the therapeutic consort music at the close of act 4, and the ritualistic music of act 5. These four sections are balanced one against another. The trumpets which add to the pomp of Lear's court in act 1 have their counterparts in the formal music which surrounds his death in act 5 —Alpha to Omega. The scraps of old songs that accompany the madness of Lear are balanced against the harmonious consort music that underscores his return to sanity. The dramatic functions of the music are also balanced. The trumpets in act 1 and the trumpets and drums in act 5 are a means for a dramatic presentation of the outward shows, the pomp, that walls in a king; they are an integral part of the setting. The songs and consort piece take us into the tormented, irrational inner world of Lear—a great stroke of characterization. Thus, the music frames Lear at the height of his pride; it aids in directing our dark journey through Lear's insanity; it marks for us the end of that journey as he emerges from mental darkness; and it returns us to a universe precariously ordered and redeemed once more. As Edmund's dying words have it, "The wheel has come full circle; I am here."

TWELVE

Macbeth

T IS COMMON KNOWLEDGE THAT SHAKESPEARE SEEMS to have written *Macbeth* with the interests of King James in mind. He wrote a tragedy that is (1) brief; (2) based on Scotch "history," witchcraft, the powers of the imagination, and other known interests of the king; and (3) lacking, as far as Shakespeare's authorship is concerned, even a minimum of music or dance, in neither of which James had much interest. But the third characteristic does not quite describe the play according to the earliest text, that of the First Folio. Five or six years after its original production (presumably before the king), the play was revived and elaborated, most authorities agree, with some spectacular songs and dances, including music and song also found in Thomas Middleton's tragicomedy *The Witch*. It is this altered text, as is now believed, that appears in the First Folio. We shall examine the additional music later, but first let us observe Shakespeare's use of music in the play as staged without the added (probably non-Shakespearean) music and its context.

The general impression given by the play's music (other than that in the later alterations) is one of economy. There are no songs or song fragments and no dances—a most unusual omission by Shakespeare. Even the instrumental music is limited to the basic drums, trumpets, and hautboys that, perhaps by necessity, made up the musical resources of the early tragedies. A band of hautboists, or waits, could be found in almost every English town; the acting company that offered only the music of hautboys, drums, and trumpets could hardly be accused of musical extravagance. Therefore, the relative poverty of music in the play is remarkable when we consider that the tragedy was written by Shakespeare with a royal performance in mind. On such an occasion, presumably, the players would feel it their duty to make the extravagant display which protocol suggested and court resources—musical and otherwise—permitted. Shakespeare, as an artist, certainly had no objection to spectacle and music, but in this case he seemed to have aimed at brevity and economy in all respects. Even so, the music in *Macbeth*, at least that attributable

(182)

without question to Shakespeare, is largely spectacular—music that adds color and "scenery" without impeding in the least the thrust of the action.

The first music heard in the play is the flourish sounded before the entrance of King Duncan (act 1, scene 4) and again as he exits at the end of the scene. At the risk of being unbearably repetitious, I call attention to this trumpet fanfare not because its dramatic functions—to separate, during continuous performance, scenes laid in different settings, and to evoke the "presence" of a true king— are exceptional, but because in *Macbeth* the royal flourish sounds only for Duncan and Malcolm. Macbeth never hears it while he wears the crown. Other than the two flourishes that sound for Duncan, the royal fanfare is heard three times at the end of the final scene of the play—when Malcolm enters in triumph, when he is hailed King of Scotland by his troops, and when he sets forth to Scone for his coronation. At no point in the play is Macbeth accorded a flourish. Shakespeare had earlier used, though not always consistently, the flourish as a mark distinguishing a true monarch from a usurper. Here the device is clear and unmistakable. Perhaps Shakespeare was prudent. After all, the play was written to be seen and judged by James, who was not apt to be pleased by any hint that a crown gained by murder and usurpation might be legitimate. Moreover, Macbeth also murders Banquo, supposedly a lineal forebear of King James. In such circumstances, the reckless use of a stage direction could have unpleasant consequences.

The next performance of music (act 1, scene 6) is by a band of hautboys playing for Duncan's entrance into Macbeth's castle at Inverness. The folio stage direction opening the scene is

Scena Sexta

Hoboyes, and Torches. Enter King, Malcolme, Donalbaine, Banquo, Lenox, Macduff, Rosse, Angus and Attendants.

This description suggests several purposes to be served by the hautboys: their music bridges the change of scene, suggests a brief passage of time between the arrival of Macbeth and that of the king, functions as a sennet to move the large group of actors onto the stage. But there is something else. Elizabethan audiences would have assumed that the hautboys were a part of the castle *menie* provided by Macbeth in honor of his royal kinsman Duncan. It is not likely that the band of waits was part of the king's train. In the first place, Duncan was engaged in a military campaign, and hautboys had no part in military music; in the second place, hautboys were usually associated with civic affairs and frequently doubled as the town watch. Their music, then, may be considered a part of the general air of harmony and sweetness which the king, ironically, remarks

Figure 40.

upon as he enters the castle gate that ere the next sunrise will become a porter's Hellgate: "This castle hath a pleasant seat, the air / Nimbly and sweetly recommends itself / Unto our gentle senses."

The musicians, apparently, are present on the stage; F's direction couples them with the torches that were, of course, to be seen by the audience. For their music, I suggest an arrangement of the opening half of "The First of the Queenes Maskes," found in Robert Dowland's *Varietie of Lute-lessons* . . . (1610), no. 24, shown in figure 40. This composition is one of three "maskes," or brief instrumental marches, composed for Ben Jonson's *The Masque of Queens* (1609). This masque is an appropriate source of music for *Macbeth*, for, as we shall see later, some of the music originally required by the First Folio text of the play was borrowed from *The Masque of Queens*.

The hautboys play again at the opening of the next scene (act 1, scene 7). In this case, however, they are used for different purposes, an examination of which reveals a neat bit of stagecraft.

The stage direction before this scene is apt to give us a false impression. It directs, according to F:

Scena Septima.

Ho-boyes. Torches. Enter a Sewer, and diuers Seruants with Dishes and Seruice ouer the Stage. Then enter Macbeth.

If we keep in mind that the action of the play was continuous, the change in scenes may have been accomplished in a manner different from the practice to which we are accustomed. Here is the way it was most likely done. At the end of scene 6, all of the actors *except* the hautboists and torchbearers leave the stage. As they file out, the hautboys strike up a march—the music suggested for the opening of scene 6 is satisfactory. Once the stage is empty, save the musicians and torches, the hautboys end their processional music and immediately begin to play a more festive, less solemn consort piece something like the "Scotche gayliarde" scored for lute in Thomas Dallis' "Lessons for the Lute" (1583), no. 26, Trinity College Library, Dublin, MS 410 (D.3.30). A reduced transcription appears in figure 41. A few moments later, the servants pass over the stage as though on their way to a banquet in an adjoining hall. With no effort, we now understand that there has been a lapse of time, that a welcoming banquet for Duncan is in progress, and that the convivial music creates an atmosphere of comfort, fellowship, and security such as Duncan would expect from a kinsman upon whom he had lately heaped great honors. Then the music ceases, and the musicians either slip away or become part of the scenery as Macbeth paces from the banqueting hall onto the stage. To the sound of the merriment "within" and as the harmony of the dinner music still rings in the ears of the spectators, Macbeth begins the soliloquy, "If it were done when 'tis done, then 'twere well / It were done quickly. . . ."

No more music is heard until the dark deeds at Inverness are accomplished. Then, toward the beginning of act 3, scene 1, at line 10, the stage direction for the entrance of Macbeth reads, in F:

Senit sounded. Enter Macbeth as King, Lady Lenox, Rosse, Lords, and Attendants.

Again we have a large body of actors coming onstage, and the sennet
(played either by the band of hautboys or by trumpets) provides the
requisite processional. But we note the omission of the royal flourish.
Shakespeare seems to have carefully omitted any sign that Macbeth
is a legitimate ruler. Even the rubric is circumspect: it does not state
"Enter King" or "Enter King Macbeth," but *Enter Macbeth as King*.
The flourish is also missing when Macbeth exits at the end of the
scene.

Figure 41.

After the murder of Banquo, Macbeth pays his visit to the three
Weird Sisters. They do not answer the question Macbeth asks, but
they show him three "Apparitions," the last of which prophesies that
"Macbeth shall never vanquished be until / Great Birnam Wood to
high Dunsinane Hill / Shall come against him." Macbeth then asks
another question:

MACB.   . . . Shall Banquo's issue ever
         Reign in this kingdom?

ALL.	Seek to know no more.
MACB.	I will be satisfied. Deny me this,
	And an eternal curse fall on you! Let me know.
	Why sinks that caldron? And what noise is this?

[*Hautboys.*]

1. WITCH.	Show!
2. WITCH.	Show!
3. WITCH.	Show!
ALL.	Show his eyes, and grieve his heart.
	Come like shadows, so depart!

[*A show of eight* KINGS, *the last with a glass in his hand,*
BANQUO'S GHOST *following.*]

These stage directions pose a problem. It is clear that the "noise" Macbeth hears is the music played by the hautboys called for in F's marginal stage direction. But what is the reason for the music? The music obviously accompanies the sinking of the witches' cauldron, but, again, why does the cauldron sink? There is no explanation given for its disappearance. Also, the five lines—three consisting of one word each—provide precious little time for the hautboys to be heard, for the music apparently ends at the appearance of the first of the eight kings. If it continued beyond this point it would obscure Macbeth's lines in which he comments on each king as he appears. The witches' "show" is not a dumb show to be accompanied by music; in fact, here the skirling of shawms would blur the statement giving the lineal descent of each king from Banquo—the lines that Shakespeare probably hoped would catch the ear of King James— as Macbeth traces the links between Banquo and his descendants.

I propose one explanation that may solve these problems. Obviously, the sinking of the cauldron requires a trap door in the stage floor. The lowering of the cauldron serves no dramatic purpose, as far as I discern, *unless* the lift is needed to bring something up from beneath the stage. What it elevates are the eight kings and Banquo, a procedure that doubtless would have been rather noisy and time-consuming. To fill the interval of time while the lift was descending with the cauldron and then ascending with the "show," and to mask the sound of the machinery (the Weird Sisters had commanded the apparitions to appear "like shadows"), the hautboys played as directed. As soon as the elevator reached stage level, the music ended and the eight kings and Banquo turned, one by one, to face Macbeth.

At the conclusion of the show, as Macbeth turns to the witches and asks, "What, is this so?" the First Witch answers, "Aye, sir, all this is so." At this point (line 125) the three hags joined the actors on the trap lift and, with them, were lowered below the stage, again to the music of the hautboys. There is no stage direction that the hautboys play at the end of the "show," probably because the direction was replaced by the *Musicke* and the *Witches Dance* later interpolated, as most authorities believe, from Middleton's *The Witch*.

The music played by the hautboists for the witches' show would have been, I suggest, something like "The Divells dance," no. 84 in Brit. Mus. Add. MS 10,444, a collection of masque and theatrical music. The notation is given in figure 42.

The remaining music in our reconstructed play consists of several drum marches in act 5 (scenes 2, 4, 5, and 6), all aimed at adding aural excitement to the battle. Then in act 5, scene 8, line 34, immediately after the death of Macbeth, a retreat and a flourish (see Appendices I and IV) signal the end of the battle and the entrance of Malcolm, rightful successor to Duncan, and his followers. The royal flourish, symbolizing all for which Macbeth has hazarded so much, sounds only after his death. As Macduff shouts, "Hail, King of Scotland" and is joined in acclamation by the assembled soldiers, another flourish is directed (line 59). And after Malcolm's concluding lines, "So thanks to all at once and to each one, / Whom we invite to see us crowned at Scone," the final stage direction is [*Flourish. Exeunt*].

Now that we have examined the music in *Macbeth* as Shakespeare may have originally created the play, that is, without the supposed interpolation of the witches' songs and dance, let us turn to the text as found in the First Folio. This text contains the two songs and the witches' dance directed to be performed in act 3, scene 5, line 33; act 4, scene 1, line 43; and act 4, scene 1, line 132; respectively. These musical garnishes were probably taken from Middleton's play. He placed the songs in his unsuccessful tragicomedy *The Witch* sometime around 1609. No one is certain of the date Middleton composed his play nor of the time at which the songs and their contexts were interpolated into *Macbeth*, but the year 1611 seems about right.[1] Recently, Richard Flatter, perhaps relying too heavily on the F

1. See Chambers, *William Shakespeare* 1:472; Shakespeare, *Macbeth*, ed. K. Muir, pp. xxxv–xxxvi; Shakespeare, *Macbeth*, ed. J. Wilson, pp. xxvii–xxviii; H. Paul, *The Royal Play of Macbeth: When, Why, and How It Was Written by Shakespeare*, pp. 72, 275–76; Sternfeld, *Music in Shakespearean Tragedy*, p. 88.

Figure 42.

text, asserted his belief that no interpolation had occurred, and that F is completely the work of Shakespeare.[2] John Cutts, in reply, supported the non-Shakespearean authorship of the songs and their immediate contexts.[3]

2. " 'The Other Three Witches,' and Their Songs." Cf. Flatter, "Who Wrote the Hecate-Scene?" and "Professor Flatter's Reply."
3. "Who Wrote the Hecate-Scene?"; and " 'Speak—Demand—We'll Answer': Hecat(e) and 'The *Other* Three Witches.' "

Students of the play have almost universally damned the inserted matter as a blot on the play's beauty. They take much pleasure in imagining Shakespeare's stage hags singing with croaking voices, and dancing with beldame legs, to lift up Macbeth's spirits, the last thing these Powers of Evil would want to do for him. But we should not let modern critical standards obscure the fact that by 1610 Jacobean dramatic tastes savored music, dancing, and spectacle in drama. Shakespeare, himself, was writing in the new mode in 1611, as witness his final romantic comedies. While we may look upon the musical additions to *Macbeth* as excrescences upon an otherwise well-unified and arrow-straight plot, the audiences from around 1611 to Sir William D'Avenant's production of the play after the Restoration must have enjoyed the music. Samuel Pepys (Apr. 19, 1667) called D'Avenant's version (which retained the songs and dances) "one of the best plays for a stage, and variety of dancing and musick, that I ever saw."[4] The music that Pepys heard was the same that Robert Johnson (probably) had composed and that had been used in the Jacobean productions of *The Witch* and *Macbeth*; it was re-arranged and rescored by Matthew Locke for D'Avenant's Restoration production of *Macbeth*.[5]

Some of the interest shown by the early audiences in the play's music may have grown out of sixteenth- and seventeenth-century witch lore. Ben Jonson, who studied the subject while writing *The Masque of Queens*, described the witches' music and dancing in the masque as follows:

> At w^ch, wth a strange and sodayne musique, they fell into a magicall Daunce full of preposterous change, and gesticulation, but most applying to theyr property: who, at theyr meetings, do all thinges contrary to the custome of men, dancing back to back, hip to hip, theyr hands joyn'd, and

4. Halliday, *A Shakespeare Companion*, p. 384.
5. Locke has been credited with the composition of the music for D'Avenant's production of *Macbeth* in 1667. Recently, though, J. Nosworthy ("The Hecate Scenes in *Macbeth*") recognized Locke's music as being, to a great extent, a reworking of the music written originally for, he believed, *The Witch* —probably by Robert Johnson (Shakespeare, *Macbeth*, ed. Muir, p. 196). J. Cutts ("The Original Music to Middleton's 'The Witch,'" p. 204) believed that Locke, a King's Musician, had access to the pre-Restoration scores used by the musicians of the King's Men company of actors. The subject is treated further by R. Moore ("The Music to *Macbeth*"), who concluded (pp. 26–27), "What is certain is that Locke modeled his dance tunes upon the old Johnson score, which was in the theater's possession and which he had obviously studied."

making theyr circles backward, to the left hand, with
strange phantastique motions of theyr heads and bodyes. All
wch were excellently imitated by the maker of the daunce,
Mr Hierome Hernc, whose right it is, here to be nam'd. . . .
These Witches, with a kind of hollow and infernall musique
. . . all wth spindells, timbrells, rattles, or other veneficall
instruments, made a confused noyse, wth strange gestures.[6]

Lewes Lavater, in his *Of Ghostes and Spirites Walking by Night.
1572*, reported:[7]

in many places in the North partes, there are certaine mon-
sters or spirites, whiche taking on them some shape or
figure, use (cheefly in the night season) to daunce, after
the sounde of all manner of instrumentes of musicke:
whome the inhabitants call companies, or daunces of Elves,
or Fairies. . . . In *Mauritania* beyonde the Mount *Atlas*,
many times in the nighte season are seene great lightes, and
that tinkling of Cymbals, and noyses of Pypes arc also
heard, and, when it is daylight no man appeareth.

Also, Thomas Cooper, in his *The Mystery of Witchcraft* . . . (1617),
stated that the devil, in order to hold a witch in his power, heaps
"on *kindenesse upon kindenesse* unto her; fitting her with musicke
and al carnal delights. . . ."[8]

Both Jonson and Middleton, therefore, had ample authority for
supplying their witches with music and dance. The crux of the matter is that dancing and singing witches, while proper in a spectacular
masque or in Middleton's tragicomedy, simply did not, it seems, fit
into Shakespeare's conception of *Macbeth*. The attempt to graft the
music and dancing in *The Witch* to Shakespeare's tragedy could only
be considered unfortunate by serious students of Shakespeare's art.
All of which brings us to another point. Earlier I made the observation that Shakespeare, with two doubtful exceptions, found no place
for the artistic types of songs, such as lutenists' ayres, in his tragedies, but that he confined his music, for tragic purposes, to the
popular songs and ballads of his day. If the songs in *Macbeth* had
been in Shakespeare's original manuscript, their appearance there

6. Jonson, *The Masque of Queens*, p. 30. See also *Ben Jonson* 7:301.
7. Page 93.
8. Page 126.

would have been a distinct departure from his customary practice. But, as we can be reasonably certain, the interpolations containing the songs are not Shakespeare's; hence, *Macbeth* is not one of the exceptions to the rule stated above.

There is probably a direct link between the musical insertions in *Macbeth* and Jonson's *The Masque of Queens*. It has been suggested that *The Witch* was written shortly after Jonson's masque was performed, and that the play made use of the same performers, dancers, and costumes.[9] If so, and the argument is reasonable, the music for one of the witches' dances in *The Masque of Queens* was also probably borrowed by Middleton for his play, and from there was interpolated into *Macbeth*. Let us, then, examine the music which, I think, was shared by *The Witch* and *Macbeth* and, in the case of the dance, by *The Masque of Queens*.

The witches' song "Come away, come away, Hecate" (3. 5. 33 in *Macbeth*) is given with a lengthier text in *The Witch* (3. 3. 39) as follows:

> *Song:* *Come away: Come away:*
> *Heccat: Heccat, Come away* $\Big\}$ *in y^e aire.*
>
> *Hec.* *I come, I come, I come, I come,*
> *with all the speed I may,*
> *with all the speed I may.*
> *wher's Stadlin?*
> *Heere* $\}$ *in y^e aire.*
> *wher's Puckle*
> *heere*
> *And Hoppo too, and Hellwaine too* $\Big\rangle$
> *we lack but you; we lack but you,* $\Big\}$ *in y^e aire*
> *Come away, make up the count* $\Big\rangle$
> *Hecc.* *I will but noynt, and then I mount.*
> *Ther's one comes downe to fetch his dues* $\Big\rangle$
> *A Spirit like* $\Big\}$ *a kisse, a Coll, a Sip of Blood* $\Big\}$ *aboue*
> *a Cat descends* $\int$ *. and why thou staist so long* $\Big\rangle$
> *I muse, I muse.*
> *Since the Air's so sweet, and good.*
> *Hec.* *oh art thou come*
> *what newes: what newes?*
> *All goes still to our delight,*

---

9. Shakespeare, *Macbeth*, ed. Wilson, pp. xxvii–xxviii; W. Lawrence, *Shakespeare's Workshop*, pp. 28–33; Muir (Shakespeare, *Macbeth*, p. xxxvi) disagreed and placed the time of the insertions at about 1615–1616.

Either come, or els
Refuse: Refuse:
Hec. Now I am furnished for the Flight.
Fire: hark, hark, the Catt sings a braue *Treble* in her owne language.
Hec. going up }. *Now I goe, now I flie,*
Malkin my sweete Spirit, and I.
oh what a daintie pleasure 'tis
to ride in the Aire
when the Moone shines faire
and sing, and daunce, and toy, and kiss;
Ouer Woods, high Rocks, and Mountaines,
Ouer Seas, our Mistris Fountaines,
Ouer Steepe Towres, and Turretts,
we fly by night, 'mongst troopes of Spiritts,
No Ring of Bells, to our Eares sounds
No howles of Woolues, no yelps of Hounds
No, not the noyse of waters-breache
or Cannons throat, our height can reache.
No Ring of Bells &c. } *aboue.*[10]

The original music for the song was found at the beginning of the nineteenth century and then was apparently forgotten. Both Edward Francis Rimbault and John Stafford Smith have worked with the MS containing the music. Smith published the music and text of the song in his *Musica Antiqua* (1812).[11] Recently, John Cutts republished the original score as found in the MS [12] The notation shown in figure 43 is my transcription from the same source, New

10. Middleton, *The Witch*, ed. W. Greg, pp. 57–59.
11. Pages 48–49.
12. See this chapter, *n5*.

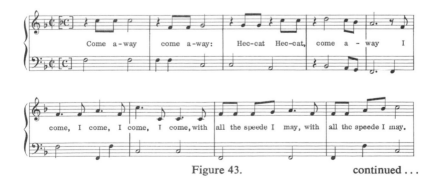

Figure 43.   continued . . .

Figure 43.

continued . . .

dain - tie plea - sure 'tis to ride in the Aire when the Moone shines faire, and

sing, and daunce, and toy and kiss; O - ver Woods, high rocks, and Moun-taines,

o - ver seas, [over cris - tall] Fown-taines, O - ver Steep [les]

Towres, and Tur-retts, we fly by night, 'mongst troopes of Spir-itts,

No ring of Bells, to our Eares sounds, No howles of Woolves, no

yelps of Hounds, No not the noise of wa - ters breache or

Can - nons throat, our height can reach. No ring of Bells, etc.

Figure 43.

York Public Library Drexel MS 4175, "Songs unto the viol and lute," no. 54. As can be seen, the musical setting is composed specifically for the dramatic-dialogue form of the song. The text in my transcription is a collation of that in the play and that in the Drexel MS.

The staging of the witches' songs (act 3, scene 5) in the F text of *Macbeth* was probably much different from the way act 4, scene 1, was originally presented. If Middleton took the witches' songs and dance from his play and put them in *Macbeth*, as some students think he did, he apparently made little change. In *The Witch*, as a part of the dialogue immediately preceding the song "Come away, come away, Hecate," Firestone, one of the witches, says, "hark Mother, they [spirits] are above the steeple already, / flying over your head with a noyse of Musitians." The musicians playing for the song in *The Witch* were doubtless situated in a music room above the stage. Hecate "flies" to join the spirits in the air by means of a lift which raised her to some point above stage level. The same device seems to have been used in the interpolated scenes in *Macbeth*. J. Dover Wilson, in his edition of the play, noted: "It has not been observed that the manner of Hecate's exit as well as the song has been followed. In both plays a car with an attendant spirit bears her aloft, i.e. is lowered and then drawn up by a windlass through a trap in the 'heavens' above the stage. 'Sits in a foggy cloud' (l. 35) shows that, in *Macbeth* at least, the car is concealed in billowing folds of light material such as were commonly used to add mystery to these stage flights. Lastly the music was needed to conceal the noise of the pulleys."[13]

I suggest also that the interpolation calls for an orchestra or consort different in instrumentation from the band of hautboys specified by Shakespeare. The folio stage direction is *Musicke, and a Song*. The term *Musicke* was usually applied to a broken consort of several kinds of instruments. Consorts composed of instruments of the same family were generally designated by their family name, as, for example, *Hoboyes* in *Macbeth*. With the exception of the supposedly interpolated passages, the term *Musicke* does not appear in F's stage directions for *Macbeth*.

The second witches' song, "Black Spirits, &c," occurs in act 4, scene 1, line 43. Only the title is given in F, as is also the case of the preceding song, but the complete text of the song is in *The Witch* (5. 2. 60):[14]

13. Pages 144–45.
14. Middleton, *The Witch*, pp. 87–88.

A Charme Song: about a Vessell.
Black Spiritts, and white: Red Spiritts, and Gray,
Mingle, Mingle, Mingle, you that mingle may.
Titty, Tiffin: keepe it stiff in
Fire-drake, Puckey, Make it Luckey
Liand, Robin, you must bob in
Round, a-round, around, about, about
All ill come running-in, all Good keepe-out.
1. *witch heeres the Blood of a Bat*
Hec.   Put in that: oh put in that
2.   *heer's Libbards Bane*
Hec.   Put-in again
1.   *the Juice of Toad: the Oile of Adder*
2.   *those will make the yonker madder.*
Hec.   Put in: ther's all. and rid the Stench
Fire.   nay heeres three ounces of the red-haird wench.
          all Round: around: around etc.

The music for this song has not been recorded. Moreover, I am unable to find an appropriate substitute. The art form—dramatic dialogue—requires a setting written for the specific text. Probably the music was much like that written for the first witches' song. Like it, also, the second song was accompanied by a broken consort located, probably, above the stage. The folio stage direction is *Musicke and a Song.* At the conclusion of the same song in *The Witch,* Hecate says, "Come my sweet sisters: let the Aire strike our Tune / whilst we show Reverence to yond peeping Moone.—*here they Daunce ye witches Dance & Ex*." There is little doubt that this dance, whose music comes from "the Aire," is the same dance and music, directed to be performed in *Macbeth.*

In Shakespeare's play the witches' dance ends the "show" offered Macbeth by the Weird Sisters (4. 1. 132). The rubric in F is *Musicke. The Witches Dance, and vanish.* If, as I agree, this dance and its music were originally a part of Jonson's *The Masque of Queens,* its movements were wild and grotesque, as Jonson described them. The music for two witches' dances, almost certainly from that masque, is preserved in Brit. Mus. Add. MS 10,444, the collection of masque and theater music made, perhaps, by the musicians of the King's Men.[15]

15. For a more detailed description of this MS, see J. Cutts, "Jacobean Masque and Stage Music."

John Cutts believed the "First Witches Dance" in the manuscript was written by Robert Johnson for the masque and that the "Second Witches Dance" was written by the same composer for performance, along with the first dance, in *Macbeth*.[16] Johnson did write music for the King's Men and for two of Jonson's masques, but the MS scores for the witches' dances are anonymous; also, whereas Ben Jonson credited Alfonso Ferrabosco with the music for *The Masque of Queens*, he did not mention Johnson. The two scores in question have been published by Andrew Sabol in his *Songs and Dances for the Stuart Masque.* . . .[17]

Only one dance is performed by the witches in *Macbeth*, and there is evidence that it was the "First Witches Dance." Jonson's masque was presented at Whitehall, Feb. 2, 1609, at which time no doubt, both witches' dances were performed.[18] Then, sometime between 1609 and 1611, Middleton wrote *The Witch* and included a witches' dance. In 1611 *Macbeth* was revived, probably for a court performance, and the songs and dance from Middleton's play were presumably added. The evidence is that Middleton borrowed the "First Witches Dance" for his play and then it was inserted into *Macbeth*.

The "Second Witches Dance" seems not to have impressed the popular taste of the early audiences, perhaps because its eccentricities in composition (duple time in the treble, triple time in the bass) were rather esoteric by Jacobean standards.[19] The only score for it is in the manuscript cited above—the entry made, possibly, at the time Jonson's masque was produced. The "First Witches Dance" was a popular hit. In 1609, Robert Dowland, son of the famous lutenist-composer John Dowland, was making a collection of lute pieces by his father and other lutenists. One section of his collection consisted entirely of almains. Apparently capitalizing on the popularity of Jonson's *The Masque of Queens*, Robert Dowland added to this section three "maskes" (marches or almains) and the first witches' dance, although it was not strictly speaking an almain—all four, compositions from *The Masque of Queens*. His collection, *Varietie of Lute-lessons* . . . was published in 1610. In it the "First Witches

16. Cutts, "The Original Music to Middleton's 'The Witch,' " pp. 192–93.
17. Pages 121, 123.
18. Paul, *The Royal Play of Macbeth*, p. 408.
19. Perhaps too esoteric to be easily credible. Sabol, like myself, had trouble in transcribing the music from the MS. The mensuration is confusing, perhaps because of an error by the original copyist.

Dance" is no. 27. The music for the first witches' dance was also recorded elsewhere. It appears, written in lute tablature, in an undated manuscript, Brit. Mus. Add. MS 38,539, the eighth entry.

Figure 44.

The versions of the first witches' dance found in all three sources —MSS 10,444 and 38,539, and Dowland's *Lute-lessons*—differ slightly from one another, but they are essentially the same work. Middleton, we may suppose, borrowed the more popular dance, the first dance, for his play, and popularity would explain its use in *Macbeth.*

The music for the "First Witches Dance" is given in figure 44. My transcription is of the version arranged for lute in Robert Dowland's collection cited above. I chose this version because it is the closest in time to the 1611 production of *Macbeth* and because it also provides some of the inner voices missing from MS 10,444. The music does not suggest the wild movements of the witches' dance as Jonson described it; perhaps the dance steps were more extravagant than the music.

The only discernible function of the witches' dance in *Macbeth*, apart from spectacle, is to remove the witches in a striking manner that also creates an illusion of the supernatural. As pure spectacle, the scene probably pleased the early audiences as it pleased Samuel Pepys. It is difficult for us, accustomed as we are to a middle-class, comparatively drab, existence, to realize the drama, color, and excitement fostered by an earlier age. In a very literal sense, the actors on the Elizabethan and Jacobean stages were merely walking shadows of the greater, more vivid and spectacular events that spiced the daily life of Shakespeare's, Middleton's, and Jonson's England.

Macbeth, then, provides us with an opportunity to observe a Shakespeare play with, and without, the suggested interpolations, and to note the dramatic taste to which the F text appealed. It is interesting, also, to watch the casual way in which the dramatists of the time seem to have borrowed, or stolen, from one another in the absence of effective copyrights, particularly as this absence affected the musicians and composers. And, while we may deplore the presumed tampering with *Macbeth*, we should realize, as Shakespeare probably realized, that an occasional play written to please a rather dogmatic and austere monarch might require some musical sweetening to please the general public once the original occasion for the play was past. In any event, we may have *Macbeth* with or without singing and dancing witches.

THIRTEEN

Antony and Cleopatra

OME SEVEN YEARS INTERVENED BETWEEN SHAKE-
speare's writing of *Julius Caesar* and his composi-
tion of *Antony and Cleopatra*. The latter play was
composed in 1607 and entered in the Stationers'
Register in 1608. It was not published until 1623
when it appeared in the First Folio.[1] Yet, despite the lapse of seven
years, the playwright picked up the threads—the destinies of his
characters, Antony, Octavius, Lepidus, and Pompey the Younger—
and, like Lachesis, continued weaving his story of the fall of the
Roman Republic, and with it the decline of the austere virtues which
collectively were termed *romanitas*.

The major source of both plays, Plutarch's *Lives of the Noble
Grecians and Romans . . .*, was a unifying factor, for Plutarch supplied the outlines for the actions and characterizations in both plays.
But Shakespeare increased the unity of *Antony and Cleopatra*,
particularly as he developed the characters of Antony and Octavius
Caesar. In Mark Antony he created a complex and magnificent character. Antony seldom acts in a small or mean way; as a soldier he is
Mars personified, and in peace he revels with bacchic abandon. This
dual quality of Antony's character—his proclivity for the harsh
blows of war, and an equal inclination toward the sensual caresses
of luxurious Venus—Shakespeare found both interesting and dramatically useful. In a larger sense Antony serves to personify the
conflict between a masculine, martial Rome and an effeminate,
sensuous Egypt in the person of Cleopatra. Thus, the general conflict
between Rome and an alien Egypt is made dramatic by Antony's
inner conflict between stern duty (his Roman mood) and sensual
desire (Cleopatra). The character of Antony is hence the major unifying agent of the action, theme, historical background, and spectacle of
the play. It is for these reasons, I suppose, that Shakespeare opened
the drama with Philo's description of Antony's "dotage" in which
"Those his goodly eyes, / That o'er the files and musters of the
war / Have glowed like plated Mars, now bend, now turn / The

1. Chambers, *William Shakespeare* 1:476.

office and devotion of their view / Upon a tawny front. His captain's heart, / Which in the scuffles of great fights hath burst / The buckles on his breast, reneges all temper, / And is become the bellows and the fan / To cool a gypsy's lust."

I have emphasized Antony's character because, as it provides the point of unity for the play in general, so it explains the use of the music in particular. The kinds of music and its performance in this play, especially in the two instances where music is emphasized—the revels on Pompey's galley (act 2, scene 7) and the departure of Antony's genius, Hercules (act 4, scene 3)—are both intimately linked to the inner conflict that destroys Antony. For Antony has not one, but two, geniuses—Hercules, who presides over his Roman thoughts, and Bacchus, who fans his Egyptian desires. As we shall see, Shakespeare employs music to emphasize the presence of these geniuses and to make their presence sensible for his audience. To achieve this result, he again drew upon Plutarch, and in doing so he provided us with a fascinating example of the way a dramatist can use his source.

To comprehend fully the two instances just mentioned, we should consider them within their musical contexts. The first music in the play is the ceremonious trumpet flourish at the entry of Antony and Cleopatra (act 1, scene 1). Here the royal lovers are shown at the height of sovereign sway. They are magnificently imperial, vaunting their great love in comparison to which "Kingdoms are clay." But Philo observes, "Look where they come. / Take but good note, and you shall see in him / The triple pillar of the world transformed / Into a strumpet's fool. Behold and see." As though to illustrate his words, the transformation takes place before our eyes in a pageant whose symbolic significance could hardly be overlooked by an audience familiar with the great Stuart masques. The trumpets proclaim the imperial theme, but when the royal procession advances onto the stage, we see Antony almost surrounded by *Cleopatra, her Ladies, the Traine, with Eunuchs fanning her*, as the First Folio stage direction describes the scene. The breath that sharply sounded the regal and martial trumpets is transformed into the eddying breezes made by sexless slaves to cool Cleopatra. Antony's virility, his manliness, is being squandered in oriental luxury. Once Shakespeare has made his point, we should not be surprised that, upon all but one of the later entrances of Antony and Cleopatra, the trumpet flourishes are conspicuously absent.

Shakespeare frequently used the trumpet flourishes or sennets to mark the opening or closing of councils of state. In act 2, scene 2, occurs such a council involving Antony, Octavius, and Lepidus. The triple rulers make no ceremonious entrance but, to indicate their disunity, enter at different times and from different directions. After some quarreling, they decide to patch up their differences as long as Pompey is a common threat. With this precarious amity, of which Antony's marriage to Octavia is the seal, the council ends in unity. The three depart as one, and a flourish of trumpets salutes the restoration of undivided authority.

The trumpet music, however, is only the first musical manifestation of unity. The second occurs in the form of the music played in the two scenes (act 2, scenes 6 and 7) in which the triumvirs and Pompey meet to do battle but instead agree to a truce and turn the battle into a drinking bout aboard Pompey's galley. This banquet is significant, for it symbolizes an accord obtained, if only briefly maintained, not just between the triumvirs but between all of the jarring factions of the Roman world.

It is at this moment, when a harmony in the Roman affairs is finally achieved, that Shakespeare, I believe, chose to make a statement about the relationships between Antony and his fellow Romans, between Antony and Cleopatra, and between the Roman spirit and the Egyptian spirit. In doing so, he made use of music and spectacle as his most effective means. The statement, in brief, is this. Antony, having succumbed to the enchantment of Cleopatra, carries her charms (and by extension those of Egypt) like an infection.[2] The poison of the "serpent of old Nile" spreads among the Roman leaders (again by extension, Rome) until it is checked by the one Roman immune to her venom—Octavius Caesar. It is this statement, I think, that explains the events and the spectacular elements in act 2, scene 7.

In act 2, scene 6, a ceremonious flourish heralds the meeting between Pompey and the triumvirs before they fall to battle. Instead of trusting to the fortunes of war as befits true Romans, they make

---

2. In describing Cleopatra as an enchantress, I intend no denigration of her dramatic character. She is complex, subtle, and in the last act dramatically magnificent. But it is in her attractive charms that her power lies. I therefore think that she uses a natural witchcraft that, with long and successful practice, she has refined to an erotic art. In this belief I follow many others, notably, G. Kittredge, who should know a witch when he sees one. Cf. Shakespeare, *The Tragedy of Antony and Cleopatra*, ed. Kittredge, pp. x–xi.

an uneasy truce and turn to feasting and drinking. Scene 7 opens with the direction [*Music plays. Enter two or three* SERVANTS, *with a banquet*]. The music, of course, is part of the banquet setting, but it also bridges the change of scene from the battlefield to the galley. In observing this musical bridge, we should remember that Shakespeare wrote the play for continuous performance; there are no act or scene divisions in the First Folio text. We should also note that, in this play, the performed music has a sinister connotation quite opposed to the festivity and social harmony which it usually suggests. In *Antony and Cleopatra* the consort music appropriate to entertainment and banquets is associated with Cleopatra and Egypt. Music is never performed in her presence, but she seems to be surrounded by music; indeed, music is closely linked to her witchcraft. Her first line in act 2, scene 5, is "Give me some music—music, moody food / Of us that trade in love." Later, when she wishes to go fishing (lines 10–15), she says, "Give me mine angle, we'll to the river. There, / My music playing far off, I will betray / Tawny-finned fishes . . . and as I draw them up, / I'll think them every one an Antony, / And say 'Ah, ha! You're caught.'" And we recall that earlier (2. 2. 199–202), Enobarbus, speaking almost directly from the pages of North's *Plutarch*, describes Cleopatra in her barge whose "oars were silver, / Which to the tune of flutes kept stroke and made / The water which they beat to follow faster, / As amorous of their strokes." In brief, Cleopatra's music is that of sensual betrayal, and the banquet music performed on Pompey's galley evokes, like a breath of perfume, her presence.

A sennet (see Appendix IV) sounds processional music to which the Roman leaders troop onstage. With them they bring the source of their infection, Egypt. The Egyptian spirit then dominates the scene. Antony introduces the subject by describing to Octavius the measurement of the Nile's rise and fall. Lepidus and Antony discuss the crocodiles of the Nile. While they converse, Menas makes his proposal to Pompey, offering him the Roman world. Pompey, in deference to his honor, refuses to permit the murder of the triumvirs. The failure of Pompey to seize his opportunity reveals his paralysis— his failure to move in a huge sphere.

Lepidus is the next to succumb, paralyzed not by honor but by drink, and another pillar of the Roman world is removed from action. It is then that Pompey remarks, "This is not yet an Alexandrian feast." Octavius states his objection to drinking heavily, then

Enobarbus proposes to Antony, "Ha, my brave Emperor! / Shall we dance now the Egyptian Bacchanals, / And celebrate our drink?" His suggestion introduces the spectacle which follows.

This bacchanal, for reasons I have already stated, deserves better treatment than it has received from past editors and commentators. Few have even commented on the dramatic significance of the carouse; they have been divided in their attempts to reconstruct its performance, and, in tracing its source, they have either noted that it was "suggested" by Plutarch or, by implication, have left the impression that the scene was completely original with Shakespeare.[3] The dramatic purpose and performance of the music in act 3, scene 3, which depicts Antony's desertion by his genius Hercules, also requires some clarification because commentators leave the impression that Shakespeare was greatly indebted to Plutarch as the source of the scene and its music. The reverse seems closer to the truth. Shakespeare was indebted to Plutarch for the music on Pompey's galley, but he was original in treating the supernatural music in act 3, scene 3. Moreover, Shakespeare's composition of the two scenes was closely linked; he drew heavily upon Plutarch for his treatment of act 2, scene 7—so heavily, in fact, that when he turned to act 3, scene 3, he found it necessary to supply a completely original treatment of Plutarch's account. In other words, the playwright's composition of act 2, scene 7, determined his composition of act 3, scene 3.

In order to illustrate, I shall have to quote rather extensively. We begin with the revelry (2. 7. 111–40):

> ANT. Come, let's all take hands
> Till that the conquering wine hath steeped our sense
> In soft and delicate Lethe.
> ENO.   All take hands.
> Make battery to our ears with the loud music,
> The while I place you. Then the boy shall sing,
> The holding every man shall bear as loud
> As his strong sides can volley.
>   [*Music plays.* ENOBARBUS *places them hand in hand.*]
>   THE SONG
>   Come, thou monarch of the vine,

---

3. On this point I cannot claim to have exhausted all of the Shakespeare bibliography, but I have consulted modern editions and critical studies too numerous to mention here.

       Plumpy Bacchus with pink eyne!
       In thy fats our cares be drowned,
       With thy grapes our hairs be crowned.
       Cup us, till the world go round,
       Cup us, till the world go round!
CAES. What would you more? Pompey, good night. Good
                             [brother,
       Let me request you off. Our graver business
       Frowns at this levity. Gentle lords, let's part,
       You see we have burnt our cheeks. Strong Enobarb
       Is weaker than the wine, and mine own tongue
       Splits what it speaks. The wild disguise hath almost
       Anticked us all. What needs more words? Good night.
       Good Antony, your hand.

The triumvirs and Pompey stumble off the stage leaving Enobarbus and Menas.

ENO. Menas, I'll not on shore.
MEN.   No, to my cabin.
       These drums! These trumpets, flutes! What!
       Let Neptune hear we bid a loud farewell
       To these great fellows. Sound and be hanged, sound out!
                      [*Sound a flourish, with drums.*]
ENO. Hoo! says a'. There's my cap.
MEN. Hoo! Noble Captain, come.   [*Exeunt.*]

The folio text continues without interruption:

     Enter Ventidius as it were in triumph, the dead body of
     Pacorus borne before him.

The scene of drunken revelry thus ends with the ironic flourish that also introduces act 3 and Ventidius returning victorious from his battle with the Parthians.

    Before leaving the bacchanal scene, we note that it is Antony and Enobarbus, fresh from Egypt, who initiate the bacchanal upon Pompey's request for an Alexandrian feast; Enobarbus refers to it as "the Egyptian Bacchanals." Octavius objects; he has no stomach for it. But the carouse begins in spite of him. To the sound of loud music, Enobarbus places the generals hand in hand for the dance, for dance it is if we accept Enobarbus' question, "Shall we dance now the

Egyptian Bacchanals, / And celebrate our drink?" A singing boy then sings the first four lines of the song—to a softer musical accompaniment, one would hope—and all of the company join in the repeated "holding" or refrain. Some grotesque dance, though not indicated by a stage direction, probably followed the song; Octavius, in breaking off the revelry, refers to a "wild disguise" which "almost / Anticked us all." These descriptive references suggest the grotesque or comic dances performed in that part of the court masques called the antimasque. If so, "these great fellows" have truly made a spectacle of themselves before they take their maudlin departure—all but Octavius, who reminds all concerned that "Our graver business / Frowns at this levity." Octavius never forgets business.

The statement made earlier, that the drinking party was intended by Shakespeare to dramatize the broad conflict of Roman virtue and oriental sensualism, is supported by certain changes and additions Shakespeare made in his source. In general, he followed North's *Plutarch* with great fidelity. His departures from Plutarch's account are unusual and, being eccentric, are both interesting and significant. The galley scene, generally believed to be an addition by Shakespeare, is actually a re-arrangement of incidents reported by Plutarch. Shakespeare added little at this point which had not been already suggested or described by Plutarch. Moreover, once his adaptations are recognized as such, both the dramatic significance and performance of act 2, scene 7, become clearer.

Plutarch gave no details of the entertainment on Pompey's galley; he merely stated that, following the agreement on the truce between Pompey and the triumvirs, "one of them did feast an other, and drew cuts who should beginne. It was Pompeius chaunce to invite them first."[4] When Shakespeare determined to exploit the dramatic possibilities of this feast, he recalled other descriptive passages from Plutarch's "Life of Marcus Antonius." For example, Plutarch, describing Antony's martial qualities, mentioned that he had a manly look like Hercules' picture stamped on metal, and that Antony thought he was descended from Anton, a son of Hercules.[5] The dramatist no doubt observed, as is implicit in Plutarch's story, that this martial quality dominates Antony only so long as he remains in the Western (Roman) world. In contrast, Plutarch wrote, when Antony carried his conquests into the Near East, he

4. *Plutarch's Lives of the Noble Grecians and Romans* . . . 6:32.
5. Ibid., p. 4.

easely fell againe to his old licentious life. . . . For every one gave them selves to riot and excesse, when they saw he delighted in it: and all Asia was like to the citie Sophocles speaketh of in one of his tragedies:

> Was full of sweete perfumes, and pleasant songs,
> With woefull weping mingled thereamongs.

For in the cities of Ephesus, women attyred as they goe in feastes and sacrifice of Bacchus, came out to meete him with such solemnities and ceremonies, as are then used: with men and children disguised like Fawnes and Satyres. Moreover, the citie was full of Ivey, and darts wreathed about with Ivey, psalteriones, flutes, and howboyes, and in their songes they called him Bacchus, father of mirth, curteous, and gentle: and so was he unto some, but to the most parte of men, cruell, and extreame.[6]

Likewise, Plutarch stressed the bacchic quality of Antony when he meets Cleopatra for the first time in Alexandria:

> and there went a rumor in the peoples mouthes, that the goddesse Venus was come to play with the god Bacchus, for the generall good of all Asia.[7]

Finally, we know that Shakespeare read Plutarch's description of the night preceding Antony's final battle with Octavius, because the dramatist devoted a full scene (act 3, scene 3) to presenting and explaining the significance of the desertion of Antony by his guardian genius. While it is obvious that Shakespeare found in Plutarch the suggestion for the supernatural action and music (*Musicke of the Hoboyes is vnder the Stage*) which he wrote into the scene, the action, characters, and the music described by Plutarch are much different. Plutarch wrote:

> Furthermore, the selfe same night within little of midnight, when all the citie was quiet, full of feare and sorrowe, thinking what would be the issue and ende of this warre: it is said that sodainly they heard a marvelous sweete harmonie of sundrie sortes of instrumentes of musicke, with the crie of a multitude of people, as they had bene daunc-

6. Ibid., pp. 22–23.
7. Ibid., p. 26.

ing, and had song as they use in Bacchus feastes, with movinges and turninges after the manner of the Satyres: and it seemed that this daunce went through the city unto the gate that opened to the enemies, and that all the troupe that made this noise they heard, went out of the city at that gate. Now, such as in reason sought the depth of the interpretacion of this wonder thought that it was the god unto whom Antonius bare singular devotion to counterfeate and resemble him, that did forsake them.[8]

Now we clearly see why Shakespeare departed from Plutarch in dramatic presentation of act 3, scene 3. He replaced the bacchanal described by Plutarch with the music of hautboys because he had used a bacchanal elsewhere in the play. Specifically, he combined Plutarch's description of the bacchic festivities at Ephesus with that of the supernatural bacchanal just quoted, and from the combination created the feast on Pompey's galley. As we recall, Antony's revelry during Pompey's feast includes instrumental music, a song to Bacchus performed by a singing boy, a wild dance, and concludes with loud music by instrumentalists. The bacchanals in Ephesus and Alexandria both include instrumental music, bacchic songs, and satyr dances— the dance in Ephesus performed by "men and children disguised like Fawnes and Satyres," in their songs calling Antony "Bacchus." It therefore seems quite likely that Shakespeare elaborated Pompey's feast into a bacchanal and that he drew from elsewhere in his source the details for his elaboration. He enlarged the feast merely mentioned by Plutarch, but he added nothing original as far as the music and dance are concerned. In this sense, then, Shakespeare derived the music, dance, and spectacle in act 2, scene 7, entirely from Plutarch.

In view of Shakespeare's fidelity to his source throughout the play, we may assume that the bacchic spectacle on Pompey's galley is as close an imitation of the bacchanals described by Plutarch as Shakespeare thought dramatically effective. The instruments included hautboys, fifes, drums, and, for extra loudness, trumpets. The music for the offstage banquet was probably played by the hautboys. An appropriate consort piece for this occasion is the galliard to "Captain

8. This passage from North's translation is frequently quoted by editors, for example, Kittredge (Shakespeare, *The Tragedy of Antony and Cleopatra*, p. 190) and M. Ridley (Shakespeare, *Antony and Cleopatra*, p. 280). Sternfeld (*Music in Shakespearean Tragedy*, p. 224) believed this description is the source of the song in act 2, scene 7. He does not mention satyr dances.

Pipers' Pavan" in Thomas Morley's *The First Booke of Consort Lessons* . . . (1599–1611).[9] The cantus or treble voice of this galliard appears in figure 45. The sennet which brings the Roman generals onto the stage could have been played by hautboys or by trumpets (see Appendix IV). The instrumentalists play again while Enobarbus places the members of the symposium hand in hand, after, perhaps, crowning their heads with wreaths of ivy or grape leaves. The music performed here was probably used a moment later for the song.

Figure 45.

The performance of the song presents a minor problem. It is sung by a singing boy introduced for the purpose, as the text makes clear. But the instruments mentioned in the text are not suitable to accompany a boy's voice; moreover, the bellowing of the men as they join in the refrain would certainly smother the boy's pure and clear tones. Cecille DeBanke and Richmond Noble attempted to solve the problem with the suggestion that the song to Bacchus is a hymn—a classical version of "Veni Creator"—and hence performed in a solemn and ceremonious manner.[10] Others, Emile Legouis and

9. My notation is taken from the original editions of 1599 and 1611. A full reconstruction of the original score (whose lute part has been lost) may be found in Sidney Beck's edition, *The First Booke of Consort Lessons, 1599 & 1611.*

10. Respectively, *Shakespearean Stage Production*, pp. 267–68; and *Shakespeare's Use of Song* . . . pp. 127–28.

J. Dover Wilson, for example, have believed that the song was a lusty drinking song presented in a boisterous and drunken manner.[11] A more satisfactory explanation appears if we turn again to Plutarch.

In the bacchanal at Ephesus, children and men disguised as fauns and satyrs dance and sing bacchic songs. We may therefore suspect that the singing boy, perhaps costumed as a faun, is a part of Shakespeare's dramatization. Also, taking another cue from Plutarch, he may have directed the boy to accompany his solo portion of the song with a lute or cittern in imitation of the "psalteriones" or psalteries used in the Ephesian bacchanal. The boy may not have sung his solo lustily, but there can be little doubt that the men volleyed out the refrain.

The original musical setting of the song is not known. Obviously, the text presents a drinking song; it is brief, and it has an emphatic rhythm, especially the refrain or "holding." It is hence well suited to the lusty performance Enobarbus requests. Shakespeare's use of a singing boy, however, would normally suggest that the musical setting was an art form complex enough to require a trained chapel chorister for its proper performance. In this particular case, though, I think that the boy is presented not because of any artistic demands made by the musical setting, but because Shakespeare wished to realize, within his dramatic limits, the children whom Plutarch described as singing bacchic songs to Antony in the festival at Ephesus. The original music for Shakespeare's song could well have been a simple ballad tune or other popular ayre common to the taverns of Jacobean London. Certainly the song text is adaptable to a simple tune.

I have, therefore, set the song text to an anonymous popular tune called "Willsons Wylde" (fig. 46). The music shown is a literal transcription from a lute book, University Library Cambridge MS Dd.2.11, fol. 68ᵛ. The manuscript is undated, but, since it includes numerous compositions by John Johnson, Antony Holborne, and John Dowland, and omits such names as Robert Johnson and Robert Dowland, I would guess that the date of the collection falls between 1600–1615. William Chappell has published a version of the tune under the title "Wolsey's Wild" in his *Popular Music of the Olden Time*.[12] Other versions appear in *The Fitzwilliam Virginal*

---

11. Respectively, "The Bacchic Element in Shakespeare's Plays," pp. 15–16; and Shakespeare, *Antony and Cleopatra*, p. 178. For the latest comment, see Seng, "Shakespearean Hymn-Parody?"

12. Volume 1, pp. 86–87.

Book (c. 1600) and Playford's *Musick's Delight on the Cithren* (1666).

At the conclusion of the song, the party grows wilder as the Romans fall into a dance described by Octavius as a "disguising" apt to make antics of them all. This was almost certainly a satyr's dance such as that performed in *The Winter's Tale* and in Ben Jonson's masque *Oberon* (1611)—a rough dance, with leaps and

Figure 46.

bounds, for men only. As we have seen, Plutarch mentioned such dances being performed in both the bacchanals he described. Also, a satyr's dance would have been appropriate for the bacchic reel on Pompey's galley. The dance, by Pompey and the two triumvirs, probably followed immediately after the boy's song. The music was played by a "loud consort" combining hautboys, fifes, drums, and, possibly, trumpets. The notation for a "Satyre's Masque" contemporary with *Antony and Cleopatra* appears in figure 47 below.[13]

13. See also Long, *Shakespeare's Use of Music: The Final Comedies*, pp. 140–41.

Figure 47. continued . . .

Figure 47.

Act 4, scene 3, presents the supernatural departure of Antony's Roman genius, Hercules. The scene was suggested by Plutarch's description of the supernatural bacchanal whose spectral dancers and singers deserted the city of Alexandria the night before the last battle between Antony and Octavius. Plutarch seems to have intended this incident to depict the desertion of Antony by his other genius, Bacchus. But Shakespeare, having used similar music to accompany the bacchanal on the galley, apparently decided to substitute an addition of his own. He gave the scene a military setting (absent in Plutarch's account) by introducing a company of soldiers who station themselves "*in every corner of the stage*." They soon are startled by the music of hautboys played under the stage.

> 4. SOLD. Peace! What noise?
> I. SOLD.   List, list!
> 2. SOLD. Hark!
> I. SOLD.   Music i' the air.
> 3. SOLD.   Under the earth.
> 4. SOLD. It signs well, does it not?
> 3. SOLD.   No.
> I. SOLD.   Peace, I say!
> What should this mean?
> 2. SOLD. 'Tis the god Hercules, whom Antony loved,
> Now leaves him.

This quotation makes it clear that, beyond accepting Plutarch's mention of supernatural music heard by the Alexandrians at this point in his story, Shakespeare completely altered the original description. In the dramatic scene, there is no mention, or presentation, of singers and dancers. Plutarch's anonymous citizens who hear the eerie bacchantes are, in the play, replaced by a group of sentries who provide a martial context and who serve as commentators to explain the significance of the music.

It seems evident, therefore, that the dramatist reconstructed the events and characters of this scene for a threefold purpose: to associate the events specifically with the final destruction of Antony's *virtus*, or Roman spirit, in the form of Hercules; to foreshadow the consequent loss of military command, symbolized by the sentries as they desert their posts and troop off after the departing genius; and to create the atmosphere of military *romanitas*, the quality in Antony which Cleopatra had so frequently mocked. Shakespeare insisted upon a solemnity in the presentation of this scene; the sentries speak in blank verse appropriate to the tragic spiritual bankruptcy of Antony that is the focus of the scene.

In such circumstances, the music played by the hautboys was probably grave, even funereal. A military dead march would not have been out of place. For this reason I have reproduced in figure 48 a funeral march, "The buriing of the dead," from a descriptive suite for virginals called "The Battell" by William Byrd. The illustration is from E. H. Fellowes' edition of *The Collected Works of William Byrd*.[14] An incomplete manuscript of the suite is in Christ Church, Oxf. MS 431, no. 11. There it is titled "Mr. Birds battle." The music shown in figure 48 falls well within the voice range of the Elizabethan and Jacobean consort of hautboys.

In view of the foreshadowing given by Shakespeare of the result of Antony's final battle with Octavius, there is much irony in the trumpet music heard at act 4, scene 4, line 23. The stage direction in F is *Showt. Trumpets Flourish. Enter Captaines, and Souldiers.* The scene shows Antony and his officers and soldiers assembled for the forthcoming conflict. The trumpets could have sounded the entry (Le entree) recorded by Mersenne, followed by the royal flourish saluting Antony and Cleopatra (see Appendices I and IV). Antony's comment on the trumpet music adds a sad poignance to the irony, as the aging general, his glory behind him, exclaims (lines 25–27), " 'Tis well blown, lads. / This morning, like the spirit of a youth / That means to be of note, begins betimes."

Antony goes forth gallantly to his camp, and the trumpet music bridges the shift to the next scene (act 4, scene 5), laid in his camp.

14. Volume 18, p. 123.

As the echoes of the trumpets die mockingly away, Antony is greeted by the old soldier whose advice he had, to his sorrow, earlier ignored. This veteran, obviously recalling the honest Enobarbus, tells Antony of the desertion of Enobarbus, prefigured by the departure of An-

Figure 48.

tony's genius Hercules. When the scene ends, as Antony exclaims, "Oh, my fortunes have / Corrupted honest men!" the trumpets sound a flourish—not for Antony, but to bridge another change of scene to act 4, scene 6, laid in Octavius Caesar's camp.

Another musical bridge occurs between act 4, scenes 6 and 7. The folio stage direction is *Alarum, Drummes and Trumpets. Enter Agrippa.* The military tumult and signals probably included the trumpet call "Le charg conflictus" (see Appendix I). Thus, the alarum, drums, and trumpets provide a bridge between scenes and suggest the offstage battle. The folio [*Retreat*] *Far off* (sounded at line 8) marks the end of the day's engagement and the temporary defeat of Octavius.[15] The bridge from act 4, scene 7, to scene 8 is another alarum followed by F's direction *Enter Anthony againe in a March. Scarrus, with others.* While the direction does not mention music specifically, a lean military march played by drums and fifes

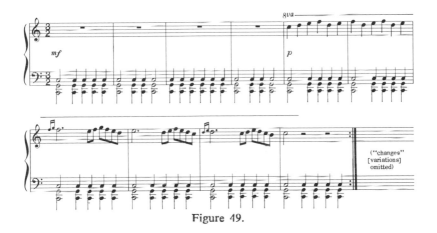

Figure 49.

would fit here. In figure 49 is such a march, "The flute and the droome," taken from Byrd's military suite "The Battell" described above. The illustration is written for virginals, but a military drum may be substituted for the bass, and a fife (playing an octave higher) for the treble voice.

The consistent use of musical bridges between scenes 4, 5, 6, 7, and 8, coupled with the brevity of each scene, makes for a continuous and swift movement. The bridge music also serves to set the tone or mood of the scenes thus introduced since the brevity of the scenes prevents much use of dialogue or actions for this purpose. The musical resources in these scenes are limited to drums and trumpets, but their use by Shakespeare is deft and efficient.

In act 4, scene 9, Enobarbus, the ultimate surrogate of Antony's lost Roman virtues, destroys himself. As his body is borne away by

15. The Norton Facsimile omits the word "Retreat" in this stage direction, leaving only *Far off*. Obviously, something should be *Far off*. See other facsimiles of the First Folio.

Caesar's sentries, a whispered roll of muffled drums is heard sounding a reveille (line 30) to awaken the sleeping armies for the last battle. From this point on, no music is associated with Antony. There are two flourishes (5. 2. 110 and 5. 2. 190) as the victorious Octavius and his train enter and depart from Cleopatra's monument. This time the trumpets give both final salutes to Caesar and, by implication, the knell of Cleopatra. As Iras says (lines 193–94), "Finish, good lady. The bright day is done, / And we are for the dark."

The music in *Antony and Cleopatra*, we may conclude, originates from two distinct sources, Plutarch and Shakespeare, and serves two distinct purposes. Shakespeare used the music suggested by Plutarch to enrich the characterization of Antony, but he supplied the military signals which provide ironic comments and speed the action of the play. The music for the banquet scene on Pompey's galley seems to have originated in Plutarch's description of the bacchanal performed in honor of Antony at Ephesus and, perhaps, óf the supernatural bacchanal at Alexandria. Shakespeare, perhaps noting the elements common to the bacchanals and to scenes in the court masques of his day, combined music, song, dance, costume, and especially allegory, to create a miniature masque, whose allegorical theme is the infection of "honest men" by the poison of that serpent of the Nile, Cleopatra. Likewise, the suggestion for the ghostly music that underscores the desertion of Antony by his genius Hercules came from Plutarch; but again Shakespeare, completely changing the action, characters, and type of music, altered the original incident to serve a symbolic and dramatic purpose of his own.

The various trumpet calls, flourishes, alarums, and other military signals do not appear in the broad sweep of Plutarch's narrative. These are technical devices and serve purely dramatic purposes. They are original additions by Shakespeare who, we must admit, knew what he was doing.

FOURTEEN

Coriolanus

ORIOLANUS IS NOT A POPULAR PLAY, NOR IS THE CHAR-
acter of its protagonist always attractive. The story
presents a patrician Roman general who carries his
pride, austerity, and integrity near to the point of
egomania. Only his mother, Volumnia, can crack
his rigid self-possession, and she, the stern Roman mother, having to
choose between the destruction of Rome or the death of her son,
chooses to save Rome.

This astringent story, caviar to the general, seems suited to the
audiences of the Blackfriars theater, who, we are told, were more
sophisticated than those who attended the public playhouses. Later,
we shall see evidence that some stage directions in *Coriolanus* were
intended for a performance at the Blackfriars theater, which had
been taken over by the King's Men from Nathaniel Giles and his
Children of the Chapel in 1608 or 1609. This play may have been one
of the first Shakespeare's company produced in the new quarters.
Chambers, looking at interior evidence, guessed that the play was
written between *Antony and Cleopatra* and *Pericles*, and he placed
its first production sometime in the early part of 1608.[1]

It had long been customary for the Blackfriars Children of the
Chapel, and other choirboy companies, to augment their plays with
musical performances, both throughout the action of the plays and
during the "act time"—intermissions between acts.[2] The King's
Men, after they began playing in Blackfriars, did not continue the
rather lavish music formerly offered by the choristers, probably because the adult company lacked some of the musical resources
provided by the musically trained children and other musicians
associated with them. But the King's Men did increase the music, in
their Blackfriars productions, beyond that normally offered at the
Globe, at least in one respect. In *Coriolanus*, we shall see some
evidence of the change.

1. *William Shakespeare* 1:479–80.
2. See T. Graves, "The 'Act Time' in Elizabethan Theatres"; and J. Moore,
"The Songs of the Public Theaters. . . ."

Shakespeare dramatized in this dour play the life of Coriolanus as translated in North's *Plutarch's Lives of the Noble Grecians and Romans*. . . . It is not a play that offers much scope for social or entertaining music. Most of the music called for is military or ceremonious, in keeping with the character of Coriolanus. Three points of interest emerge, however: (1) stage directions at the opening of act 1, scene 10, at act 2, scene 1, line 220, at act 2, scene 2, line 158, and at the opening of act 3, scene 1, specify music by a consort of cornets—instruments seldom called for in the earlier plays of Shakespeare, though frequently used in the productions given by the choirboy company recently displaced from the Blackfriars theater; (2) Shakespeare found in Plutarch's account no suggestion for the music he calls for in *Coriolanus*—the music and its use is an addition by Shakespeare uninfluenced by his source; (3) the musical support is unusually strong: the theater musicians used instruments including trumpets, drums, hautboys—the same combination used in *Antony and Cleopatra*—and a consort of cornets. Barring the possibility that the hautboists doubled in playing the cornets, the full theater orchestra included from twelve to fifteen instrumentalists.

The music in the play begins with the military signals incidental to the battle between Marcius (Coriolanus) and the Volsces (act 1, scene 4). At line 12 is a parley sounded by the Roman trumpeters; in answer, senators appear on the walls of Corioli. A distant drum signals the approach of the Volsces' main army returning to lift the siege of their city. The home guard then issues from the city gates to engage the Roman besiegers. The battle takes place offstage and is merely suggested by the alarums called for by the stage directions. The scene then shifts, after the Romans led by Marcius have taken the city, to a reunion of the armies of the Roman general Cominius and Marcius, his lieutenant. The victorious forces are introduced by the rubric opening act 1, scene 9:

> [*Flourish. Alarum. A retreat is sounded. Enter from one
> side,* COMINIUS *with the* ROMANS; *from the other side,*
> MARCIUS, *with his arm in a scarf.*]

The flourish, alarum, and retreat do not refer to the action in act 1, scene 9, but to the preceding scene. The flourish salutes Marcius' triumph in beating back Aufidius and his Volscian guard; the retreat ends the general battle. These signals not only conclude scene 8, but they are a musical bridge to scene 9, the Roman camp. The action of the latter scene begins as Cominius and Marcius enter. There is little doubt that *Coriolanus* was written for continuous performance within the acts; the First Folio text is divided into acts, but it contains no scene divisions.

To reward Marcius' valor, Cominius offers him a tenth of the booty taken from Corioli. To this generous offer, Marcius returns an oafish answer, unaware that he is actually playing to the common soldiery that he despises.

> MAR. I thank you, General,
> But cannot make my heart consent to take
> A bribe to pay my sword. I do refuse it,
> And stand upon my common part with those
> That have beheld the doing.
> [*A long flourish. They all cry* "Marcius! Marcius!" *cast up their caps and lances.* COMINIUS *and* LARTIUS *stand bare.*]

With the same surly pride, Marcius turns on the soldiers and the excited trumpeters.

> MAR. May these same instruments, which you profane,
> Never sound more! When drums and trumpets shall
> I'the field prove flatterers, let Courts and cities be
> Made all of false-faced soothing!

Marcius, however, does accept the honorary name "Coriolanus" to memorialize his victory over Corioli. Upon its bestowal by Cominius, the rubric is [*Flourish. Trumpets sound, and drums.*], and all the armies hail Marcius Caius Coriolanus. The flourish, of course, salutes Coriolanus—the trumpets and drums supplying the clamor which could not be very well produced by the token few soldiers actually on the stage.

Scene 9 ends with the direction "*Exeunt*" as the Romans disperse to their tents. This direction is followed immediately, in the F text, by the rubric

> *A flourish. Cornets. Enter Tullus Auffidius bloudie, with two or three Souldiors.*

Those editors of the play who insert scene divisions invariably mark the above directions as introducing the following scene 10, a practice which misleads the reader. Actually, the flourish concludes the war council just ended by the Romans. There is no reason for Aufidius, who enters defeated and mourning the loss of Corioli, to be greeted with a fanfare of trumpets. Nor do the trumpeters link the two scenes in this case. That function is performed by the cornetists, who, in my opinion, play a sennet to which the Romans march off the stage.

The naming of the cornets in the stage direction requires a brief digression. It might be argued that the cornets, not trumpets, sound the flourish and that this is the extent of their music. The cornetists could easily have replaced the trumpeters, but I do not believe that they did so in this case. In the other directions calling for flourishes in scene 9, there is no call for cornets; it seems to be understood that the flourishes are to be sounded, as usual, by the trumpets. But, if trumpets were on the spot, why should they not also play the sennet, which, as I suggested, moved the Romans offstage? Trumpeters sometimes played sennets.

The answer to the rhetorical question, I believe, is that, when the King's Men began producing plays in the Blackfriars theater, they inherited the band of adult cornetists that had performed there for the plays acted by the Children of the Chapel—a subject I have discussed elsewhere.[3] Moreover, it is reasonable to assume that the King's Men would wish to employ the cornetists, who, to judge by the frequency with which their music is called for by the stage directions of the Children's plays, had achieved some fame.[4] The use of the cornets in the first few plays offered by the King's Men at Blackfriars would be especially desirable since the spectators they wished to attract were accustomed to a rich musical fare to which the Blackfriars cornetists had earlier contributed. The presence of the cornets in *Coriolanus* does not indicate any departure from the usual conventions of dramatic music practiced by Shakespeare and the King's Men, but it does reveal, I think, an attempt by the company to increase the quantity and variety of music in the plays they offered in their new theater. In the case of *Coriolanus*, there is no dramatic necessity for music that could not have been met by the trumpets, drums, and hautboys. The cornets were used in *Coriolanus*, I would conclude, largely as a concession to an audience more musically

3. See Long, *Shakespeare's Use of Music . . . Seven Comedies*, pp. 23–24, 33–34.

4. This popularity of the Blackfriars cornetists may be inferred from their frequent use in Marston's plays *Antonio and Mellida* (1602), *Sophonisba* (1606), and *The Malcontent* (1604), all written for the choirboy companies performing in the Blackfriars theater.

sophisticated than the mixed following who attended the Globe playhouse.

The triumphal entry of Coriolanus into Rome provides the occasion for the next music in the play. In the midst of a conversation, Menenius and the Tribunes hear a distant bray of trumpets. He exclaims (2. 1. 172), "Hark! The trumpets." The rubric is [*A shout and flourish*]. This signal indicates the entry of the victorious armies into Rome. The triumphal procession then enters the stage (line 178). The folio direction is

> *A Sennet. Trumpets sound, / Enter Cominius the Generall,*
> *and Titus La[r]tius: betweene them Coriolanus,*
> *crown'd with an Oaken / Garland, with Captaines and*
> *Soul- / diers and a Herauld.*

As the F description shows, Shakespeare presented a spectacular state affair. The direction for removing the triumph from the stage (line 220) adds to the description, thus: *Flourish, Cornets. / Exeunt in State, as before.*

The musical portions of the scene may be easily reconstructed. At the opening, the trumpets sound a full flourish. The cornets then play a stately sennet. Cominius, Coriolanus, and the remaining body of soldiers—relatively large in this case—then march onto the stage. The Herald makes his formal proclamation ending with, "Welcome to Rome, renowned Coriolanus," at which point the trumpeters sound another flourish. The procession halts, and Coriolanus speaks to Menenius, Valeria, and Volumnia. Then, upon Cominius' command (line 220), "On, to the Capitol!" the trumpets sound another fanfare, the cornets repeat their sennet, and the military triumph moves offstage. (For the music notation see Appendices I–IV.)

As the action moves to the Capitol, there is another stately procession (scene 2), in which consul, senators, tribunes, and Coriolanus —all preceded by lictors—enter the Capitol (line 40) to the music of a sennet. As is evident, the stage business here is ceremonious and rather lengthy. The sennet, the usual march to which nonmilitary councils assembled, fills the aural gap while the scene is being set. No trumpets or drums are needed for military color since the action here concerns only civic affairs. Here the sennet was probably sounded by the same cornetists who, replacing the more military trumpets, furnish the flourish that ends the council, as the stage direction (line 158) states in F: *Flourish Cornets. / Then Exeunt. Manet Sicinius and Brutus.* By using cornets here Shakespeare made a subtle distinction between flourishes sounded for an individual general or ruler and flourishes sounded for a representative ruling body.

The cornetists play again at the opening of act 3, scene 1. It is difficult to see why, except that the music is a bridge between acts 2 and 3. The folio rubric is *Cornets. Enter Coriolanus, Menenius, all the Gentry, / Cominius, Titus La[r]tius, and other Senators.* Since this gathering of patricians meets in the street and in a casual manner, no formal ceremony, such as was usually accompanied by sennets or other music, seems necessary. We may only conjecture that Shakespeare called for entr'acte music in order to suggest a lapse in time between the events of acts 2 and 3 and also, incidentally, to exploit the skill of the cornetists before the "gentry" in the Blackfriars audience.

Music is heard no more in the play until Coriolanus, driven from Rome by the plebeians, seeks shelter with his old enemy Aufidius. When he enters the Volscian's house, a banquet is in progress. The rubric is [*Music within. Enter a* SERVING-MAN]. The music identifies the offstage banquet and also bridges the change from scene 4, a street before Aufidius' house, to scene 5, within the house. The banquet here emphasizes, by contrast, the wretchedness of the homeless and rag-clad Coriolanus. Some kind of jolly music would have been appropriate to the festivity. In the original production the music was played, I surmise, by the hautboys. Not only would their performance at a banquet conform to the customary use of hautboys at English banquets, but it would give some work to the hautboists who, until this scene, had been standing around in the wings or engaged in a hot game of draughts.

There is a possibility that the musicians who used the cornets also doubled in playing the hautboys, especially since at no time in the drama are hautboys and cornets directed to be played simultaneously. But I do not think that doubling occurred here. In the first place, a consort of hautboys had long been associated with the King's Men before they began playing at Blackfriars. Also, a band of cornets had been performing at Blackfriars before the King's Men took over that theater. W. J. Lawrence long ago argued this point and concluded that those few stage directions calling for cornets in the early plays of Shakespeare, for example, *The Merchant of Venice,* were inserted for revivals of those plays at Blackfriars after 1608. Moreover, cornetists took much training; the instrumental family required a unique and difficult embouchure not easily picked up. It is therefore easier to believe that the hautboys and the cornets were played by two distinct bands of musicians. The music played for Aufidius' banquet was probably some merry galliard such as "Michels Galliard," no. 16 in Thomas Morley's *The First Booke of Consort Lessons* . . . (1599). The notation in figure 50 is a literal transcription of the treble viol and pandora parts. The full score is reconstructed in Sidney Beck's edition.

Figure 50.

The hautboists are given another opportunity to perform when in act 5, scene 4, a messenger meeting Menenius and Sicinius in the streets of Rome reports the success of Volumnia and Valeria in dissuading Coriolanus and his Volscian army from sacking the city. To portray the relief and consequent great joy of the Roman citizenry, Shakespeare called for a loud consort of instruments to create tumultuous music throughout the final portion of the scene. The music begins as the Second Messenger concludes his report to Sicinius (line 50):

> Ne'er through an arch so hurried the blown tide
> As the recomforted through the gates. Why, hark you!

                    [*Trumpets, hautboys, drums beat, all together.*]
        The trumpets, sackbuts, psalteries, and fifes,
        Tabors and cymbals and the shouting Romans,
        Make the sun dance. Hark you!

Seven lines later, Menenius ends his comments on the news by again
calling attention to the joy of the plebeians. The direction (line 60)
is then [*Music still, with shouts*]. At line 65, Menenius, Sicinius, and
the two messengers exit ending the scene. The music, bridging to
scene 5, is still heard while in this very brief scene (laid elsewhere in
the streets of Rome) two senators and the other lords conduct
Volumnia and Valeria across the stage before a gaggle of towns-
people. One of the senators proclaims:

> I. SEN. Behold our patroness, the life of Rome!
>   Call all your tribes together, praise the gods,
>   And make triumphant fires, strew flowers before them.
>   Unshout the noise that banished Marcius,
>   Repeal him with the welcome of his mother,
>   Cry "Welcome, ladies, welcome!"
> ALL.   Welcome, ladies,
>   Welcome!
>   [*A flourish with drums and trumpets. Exeunt.*]

Thus we see that the mother and wife of Coriolanus, and in their
persons Coriolanus himself, are accorded a triumph befitting saviors
of their country. But in calling for the music and thus underlining
the happiness and relief of the Romans, the playwright was also
preparing for a moment of greater dramatic impact.

The music bridges again to scene 6, where we are shown, in
Corioli, Aufidius and his followers reacting to Coriolanus' decision
to prevent the destruction of Rome. Naturally, they are not pleased,
and they conspire to assassinate the Roman general. Their decision is
reached as, offstage, they hear the public welcome given to Coriolanus as he enters their city. This civic welcome, purposely, I think, is
a parallel to that which greeted the Roman ladies, Volumnia and
Valeria, and it causes Aufidius to proclaim his anger against
Coriolanus (5. 6. 46):

> AUF. At a few drops of women's rheum, which are
>   As cheap as lies, he sold the blood and labor
>   Of our great action. Therefore shall he die,

And I'll renew me in his fall. But hark!
> [*Drums and trumpets sound, with great shouts of the
> people.*]

I. CON. Your native town you entered like a post,
And had no welcomes home, but he returns,
Splitting the air with noise.

The parallel receptions offered the Roman ladies and Coriolanus provide a fine example of dramatic irony. The women's appeal to Coriolanus gives life to Rome, and they are adulated by plebeians and patricians alike. Yet it is Coriolanus who holds the power of life or death over every Roman, and it is he who gives them life. The irony, of course, is that in saving Rome he must forfeit his own life. The triumphal music and shouting Volscians in Corioli marshal him to knavery and death, as Shakespeare emphasized by making the two scenes so similar in other respects, such as the music and shouts.

Aufidius and his fellow conspirators carry out their plot and murder Coriolanus before the lords and commons of Corioli. Then, conscience-stricken, Aufidius delivers the conventional eulogy (line 148) which also describes the dead march that concludes the play.

My rage is gone,
And I am struck with sorrow. Take him up.
Help, three o' the chiefest soldiers, I'll be one.
Beat thou the drum, that it speaks mournfully.
Trail your steel pikes. Though in this city he
Hath widowed and unchilded many a one
Which to this hour bewail the injury,
Yet he shall have a noble memory.
Assist.
> [*Exeunt, bearing the body of* CORIOLANUS. *A dead march
> sounded.*]

The music and its instrumentation in act 5, scenes 4, 5, and 6, is much the same. The festive music played by the trumpets, hautboys, and drums in scenes 4 and 5 requires a jaunty piece that can be played by valveless trumpets and hautboys. These requirements are well met by a composition of William Byrd called "The souldiers' dance," reproduced in figure 51.[5] The open notes of the same tune, if assigned to trumpets with a drum accompaniment, could be used in

5. *The Collected Works* 18:126.

scene 6. The repetition might remind the audience of the festivity in the preceding scene and thus musically enhance Shakespeare's irony.

We should now consider the discrepancies between the instruments required by the stage direction (5. 4. 51)—trumpets, hautboys, and drums—and the instruments described as sounding by the Messenger (lines 52–53)—trumpets, sackbuts, psalteries, fifes, tabors, and cymbals. Here, it seems, we have a case of verbal augmentation. Just as a

Figure 51.

standard and a few soldiers could, on the Renaissance stage, represent an army described in the spoken lines (as in *Coriolanus,* act 1, scene 4), so could a few instruments represent a lavish collection of musicians. The early patrons of the play accepted, as we do, this dramatic convention as a matter of course.

Having surveyed the musical resources apparently available to Shakespeare and the King's Men for their production using the stage directions in the First Folio text, we may now reach several conclusions. As stated in the opening of this chapter, the presence and use of cornets in the play marks a change in the instrumental composition of the company's customary orchestra. If W. J. Lawrence was correct in his argument that cornets were not employed by the King's Men until they moved their stage to Blackfriars, then the earliest date for the production of *Coriolanus* using the First Folio text must have been between 1608 and early 1609, the time the company moved to the Blackfriars theater. This date would support E. K. Chambers' opinion, based largely upon interior evidence, that the first performance of the play occurred "early in 1608," and also W. A. Neilson's choice of "late in 1608 or early in 1609 as the period of composition."[6]

In contrast to his use of music in *Antony and Cleopatra*, Shakespeare made little or no attempt to use music as a means of delincating Coriolanus' character. Perhaps the comparative simplicity of the protagonist's character may have made the musical characterization found in *Antony and Cleopatra* unnecessary. But it is true, also, that the dramatist found no suggestion for such music in his source, North's *Plutarch*. Anyway, he seems to have limited his use of music to solving problems in stagecraft, such as the presentation of crowd scenes, battles, or ceremonies. For these purposes, instrumental music alone was quite satisfactory.

An unusually large force of musicians played, as the First Folio stage directions indicate, for *Coriolanus*; but the additional consort of cornetists seems to have proved an embarrassment to Shakespeare. He apparently thought he should use them, but he did not quite know how to employ them to the best advantage. He had them alternate with the trumpeters in sounding some of the flourishes, called on them to play several sennets, and in one instance used them for entr'acte music between acts 2 and 3, a practice foreign to productions in the Globe. The music, in every instance where cornets are called for, could have been supplied by the easily available trumpets and drums or by the hautboys. The cornet music was largely a superfluous, but fashionable, ornamentation—at least, as Shakespeare used it in *Coriolanus*.

6. *The Complete Plays and Poems of William Shakespeare*, p. 1287; Chambers, *William Shakespeare: A Study of Facts and Problems* 1:478–80.

FIFTEEN

Timon of Athens

THE SKETCHY, OR PERHAPS INCOMPLETE, NATURE OF *Timon of Athens* may explain why it is infrequently performed and why comparatively little critical attention has been given to it. Yet the outlines of its structure are reasonably clear, and, fortunately for our purposes, the performed music in the play is as rich as in most of Shakespeare's more finished dramas. The first half of *Timon of Athens* portrays the protagonist as a noble and generous man beloved by his retainers, respected by his peers, and flattered by the Athenian artisans. He uses his wealth to aid all who seek help from him. The second half provides a dramatic contrast in which Timon, having lost his wealth, turns to his erstwhile friends for aid, expecting a return of his generosity toward them. When he finds neither gratitude nor aid, he slips into complete misanthropy, separates himself from all mankind, and dies alone in the wilderness.

The music in the play is an aid to spectacle, but it primarily points to a closer relationship (than the text alone reveals) between Timon, Alcibiades, and the latter's feminine companions Phrynia and Timandra. The First Folio text also provides a structurally complete Jacobean masque in addition to the usual ceremonious and military music. The masque, in turn, supplies a link between Timon and the two women—a link otherwise not established in the play.

The trumpets, as usual, provide the first music in the play. They sound before the entrance of Timon to greet his guests, noble Athenians whom he has invited to a banquet. The trumpets probably did not waste breath in blowing a formal flourish here since Timon has no claim to royalty or leadership. A short signal to attract attention would have sufficed. The stage direction (1. 1. 94) is simply [*Trumpets sound*]. Later (1. 1. 247) the rubric is [*Trumpet sounds. Enter a* MESSENGER]. In this case, as the messenger announces, the trumpet heralds the approach of the general Alcibiades and a company of cavalry come to join the banqueters. The single trumpet here suggests that the call it sounds is a tucket, a personal signal which identifies Alcibiades.

In act 1, scene 2, after several lines of dialogue, the banquet begins with this F text direction:

Exeunt.

*Hoboyes Playing lowd Musicke. A great Banquet seru'd
in: and then, Enter Lord Timon, the States, the Athenian
Lords, Ventigius which Timon redeem'd from prison. Then
comes dropping after all Apemantus discontentedly like
himselfe.*

The music of the hautboys is used to help a change of scenes. As F indicates, Timon and his guests, excepting two lords, earlier left the stage ostensibly to go into an adjoining banquet hall. The two remaining lords comment on Timon's nobility and bounty for some thirty lines, then they also exeunt. The stage is now bare. When the hautboys are heard, we are to understand that the bare stage, formerly presented as an anteroom in Timon's house, is now to be considered the banquet hall, and, to the sound of the music, servants begin bringing onstage the table, chairs, and other properties necessary for the banquet. This shift in scenes is, of course, aided by the hautboys' music—the kind of music customarily associated with formal banquets in the minds of Shakespeare and his contemporaries. The "lowd Musicke" also suggests that the music was employed not only for its intrinsic value and for its power of suggestion, but also to fill the hiatus in the action of the play. Once the scene is set, Timon and his guests enter, and the action continues.

This festive occasion calls for genial, cheerful music; all is harmonious in Timon's home and heart. The score shown in figure 52 is a previously unpublished galliard called "The Two Merry Lasses" taken from Brit. Mus. Add. MS 10,444, fol. 1^r. Its lilting air should furnish a fitting introduction to the banquet that follows.

As a part of his entertainment, Timon presents his guests with a Mask of Amazons. The late Otto Gombosi has observed that this masque, though brief, is patterned on the formal structure of the Stuart court masques as composed by such writers as Ben Jonson and Thomas Campion.[1] All the major elements of the court masque are present excepting the "antimasque" or fantastic dances performed by professionals. The absence of the antimasque is probably not an omission made by Shakespeare. The little masque he provided is

---

1. "Some Musical Aspects of the English Court Masque."

Figure 52.

composed in the form that he knew; the antimasque, as a formal element of the Stuart masque, was not added under that name until it was introduced by Jonson into *The Masque of Queens* in 1609.[2] The following quotation (1. 2. 119) describes well the structural parts of the Stuart masque as Shakespeare presented it in *Timon of Athens*:

[*Tucket, within.*]

TIM.   What means that trump?

[*Enter a* SERVANT.]
How now!

SERV.   Please you, my lord, there are certain ladies most
              desirous of admittance.

TIM.   Ladies! What are their wills?

SERV.   There comes with them a forerunner, my lord,
              which bears that office to signify their pleasures.

TIM.   I pray, let them be admitted.

2. Sabol, ed., *Songs and Dances for the Stuart Masque* . . . p. 1.

[*Enter* CUPID.]

CUP. Hail to thee, worthy Timon! And to all
That of his bounties taste! The five best Senses
Acknowledge thee their patron, and come freely
To gratulate thy plenteous bosom. Th' Ear,
Taste, Touch, and Smell, pleased from thy
　　　　　　　　　　[table rise.
They only now come but to feast thine eyes.

TIM. They're welcome all. Let 'em have kind
　　　　　　　　　　[admittance.
Music, make their welcome!　　[*Exit* CUPID]

I. LORD. You see, my lord, how ample you're beloved.

[*Music. Re-enter* CUPID, *with a mask of* LADIES *as Amazons,
with lutes in their hands, dancing and playing.*]

APE. Hoyday, what a sweep of vanity comes this way!
They dance! They are mad women.
Like madness is the glory of this life,
As this pomp shows to a little oil and root.
We make ourselves fools to disport ourselves,
And spend our flatteries to drink those men
Upon whose age we void it up again
With poisonous spite and envy.
Who lives that's not depravèd or depraves?
Who dies that bears not one spurn to their graves
Of their friends' gift?
I should fear those that dance before me now
Would one day stamp upon me. 'T has been done.
Men shut their doors against a setting sun.

[*The* LORDS *rise from table, with much adoring of* TIMON;
and to show their loves, each singles out an AMAZON,
*and all dance, men with women, a lofty strain or two
to the hautboys, and cease.*]

TIM. You have done our pleasures much grace, fair
　　　　　　　　　　[ladies,
Set a fair fashion on our entertainment,
Which was not half so beautiful and kind.
You have added worth unto 't and luster,
And entertained me with mine own device.
I am to thank you for 't. . . .
Ladies, there is an idle banquet attends you,
Please you to dispose yourselves.

ALL LADIES. Most thankfully, my lord.
　　　　　　　　　[*Exeunt* CUPID *and* LADIES.]

This rather lengthy quotation presents the complete little masque.

The entrance of the masquers conforms to the custom followed in the early Tudor masques as well as in the later Jacobean versions (see chapter 1). The tucket sounds offstage to announce the ladies' arrival. A servant takes their request for admittance to Timon, who, after expressing the conventional surprise, grants it. Cupid, the "presenter," appears and states the purpose of the masque. The masque proper begins as the Amazons enter performing a ballet-like dance to the music of their lutes and, perhaps, an instrumental consort. The second half of the masque begins with the "Revels," when each lord chooses a partner from among the Amazons, and they dance one of the familiar ballroom steps, such as a pavane or galliard. The revels conclude the masque, and the masquers are given a banquet.

The performance of the music is fairly clear. When Timon commands his music to welcome the ladies, the Amazons enter, dancing to the music of their lutes and to the music played by Timon's musicians. The score they played was possibly "The Amazonians Masque" given in figure 53. This piece of music, found among other masque and theatrical music in Brit. Mus. Add. MS 10,444 (no. 71), was not included by Andrew Sabol in his collection *Songs and Dances for the Stuart Masque* . . . nor is the composer's name known. This negative evidence admits the possibility that the score was composed for Shakespeare's play, but since the play seems incomplete and there is no record of a Jacobean production, the possibility must remain remote.

The dramatic significance of the masque and its music is rather obscure. Obviously, the masque is one means of showing Timon at the peak of his good fortune—wealthy, generous, admired, envied, a patron of the arts. It may also be Shakespeare's re-creation of a classical symposium in which the lute-playing and dancing Amazons suggest the flute girls and *hetairai* who entertained the wealthy men of Periclean Athens. But the masques usually contained a symbolic or allegorical statement about the person in whose honor the masque was given. Timon says that the ladies "entertained me with mine own device." The word "device" may refer to some visual heraldry or inscription as well as to the masque.

Still another significance of the masque should not be overlooked. Timon's banquet is a love-feast: it includes a masque introduced by the God of Love, and the lords dance with the Amazonian ladies to show their love of Timon, who has provided the entertainment out of his bounty and his love for them. But there is something wrong: we see a curious reversal in the conduct of the masque itself. In the masques which Shakespeare knew before 1609, the masquers were almost invariably men, and it was they who performed the main figure-dance and, following it, invited ladies from among the spectators to join them in the revels. In the Mask of the Amazons it is the classical masculine-women warriors who perform the main dance and

Figure 53.

then, with the spectator-lords, dance the revels. Moreover, though they are presented by Cupid, mythological Amazons were not noted for their love of men: to the contrary, as warriors they fought mankind and were, in this sense, also misanthropes.

Leigh Hunt, reviewing one of the infrequent performances of *Timon of Athens*, the Drury Lane production of Edmund Kean, objected to the presence of the Amazons:

> We must protest however against the dance of young Amazons, clashing their swords and shields. Shakespeare,

we allow, has specified Amazons for the occasion; but if
Amazons there must be, they should at least have had lutes
in their hands, which he has specified also, instead of
weapons. We are at a loss to conjecture why Shakespeare
introduced Amazons at all, which seem to be no more to
his taste in general than they were to old Homer's. . . . At
all events, we should like to have as little of these unfeminine feminines as possible; lutes would make them more
human, and might act as a sort of compliment to *Alcibiades*,
who is one of the guests, or to the spirit of sociality in general, as much as to say—a spirit of harmony corrects what
is barbarous.[3]

While Hunt stated his inability to explain Shakespeare's intentions
in using the Amazons, his guess, pointing to some connection with
Alcibiades, may be closer to the explanation than Hunt realized.
When we turn to the last scene shared by Timon and Alcibiades, a
possible explanation for the presence of the Amazons emerges. But,
first, we should observe the mock banquet—the antithesis of the
preceding banquet—which Timon serves to his false friends.

Timon, having exhausted his substance, turns for aid to his
friends. All but his loyal steward prove ungrateful and turn their
backs upon him. The distraught Timon, now bitterly misanthropic,
invites his former associates to a final banquet, consisting of luke-
warm water, and then denounces and renounces mankind to live
alone in the forests like a wild animal. In contrast to the love-feast
shown earlier, this banquet is a hate-fest that marks the turning point
of the tragedy. On this occasion, we should not expect to find the
consort music and dances with their connotations of harmony in
melody and movement; nor do we find them.

As Timon greets his guests (3. 6. 26), who do not expect the fare
of invective and abuse which he will serve them, he turns to two lords:

> TIM.   With all my heart, gentlemen both. And how fare you?
> 1. LORD. Ever at the best, hearing well of your lordship.
> 2. LORD. The swallow follows not summer more willing than
> we your lordship.
> TIM.   [*Aside*] No more willingly leaves winter. Such summer
> birds are men.—Gentlemen, our dinner will not
> recompense this long stay. Feast your ears with the

---

3. L. Hunt, *Leigh Hunt's Dramatic Criticism, 1808–1831*, pp. 138–39.

music awhile, if they will fare so harshly o' the
trumpet's sound. We shall to 't presently. . . .
                              [*The banquet brought in.*]

While no rubric calls for music here, Timon's lines make it clear
that music of some kind accompanied the serving of the banquet.
All the editors I consulted have inserted directions calling for music
at the opening of the scene and, apparently, throughout the dinner.
This practice, I think, is misleading to the reader and contrary to
Shakespeare's intention, since the general term "Music" used by the
editors might cause one to expect the same kind of music directed for
the previous banquet scene. But Timon's lines, if we accept Kenneth
Deighton's interpretation, "if the guests can be content with such harsh
fare as the sound of the trumpet," refer only to the blasts of a single
trumpet.[4] This harsh fare would be more in keeping with the other
rough courses—the covered dishes of water and the tongue-lashing
which Timon gives his guests. In this case, melodic harmony, such as
that produced by a group of instrumentalists playing in consort,
would be singularly inappropriate, whereas the trumpet clamor would
add to the scene a warlike atmosphere suitable to Timon's following
declaration of hatred for all mankind. It is the violent contrast
between the love-feast and the hate-fest that Shakespeare intended;
we should therefore be safe in assuming that he provided a similar
contrast in the kinds of music he wished to accompany each banquet.
    Another, more prosaic, purpose of the trumpet music is again to
fill the pause in the dialogue and action while the banquet is brought
onstage. And, since no actor would like to speak his lines in compe-
tition with the blasts of a nearby trumpet, I assume, contrary to the
usual directions inserted by editors, that the trumpet sounded only
while the dinner was being set before the lords. Royal or state feasts
were often accompanied by trumpet music in Shakespeare's England,
but the trumpets played only before the feast began and during the
intervals when the dishes of one course were being removed and those
of the next course were being brought in. While each course was
being eaten, and as a background for social talk, dinner music was
played by a broken or whole consort of instruments whose music was
softer and sweeter than the strident trumpet.[5]
    I have no idea what original trumpet music Shakespeare had in

4. Shakespeare, *Timon of Athens*, ed. K. Deighton, p. 84nn35–36.
5. See Galpin, *Old English Instruments of Music . . .* p. 200.

mind for the mock banquet. One of the longer military calls such as "La Chamade (The Parley)" might serve the purpose (see Appendix I).

After the banquet of water, we hear no more music until Alcibiades, marching with an army to repeal his unjust banishment from Athens, meets the self-banished Timon crouching over a hoard of gold he has just discovered buried in the woods (4. 3. 44):

> TIM. . . . [*March afar off.*] Ha! A drum? Thou'rt quick,
> But yet I'll bury thee. Thou'lt go, strong thief,
> When gouty keepers of thee cannot stand.
> Nay, stay thou out for earnest.   [*Keeping some gold.*]
>   [*Enter* ALCIBIADES, *with drum and fife, in warlike manner;*
>   PHRYNIA *and* TIMANDRA.]

The dramatic impact of this scene is described by Leigh Hunt:

> The finest scene in the whole performance was the one with *Alcibiades*. We never remember the force of contrast to have been more truly pathetic. *Timon*, digging in the woods with his spade, hears the approach of military music; he starts, waits its approach sullenly, and at last comes the gallant *Alcibiades* with a train of splendid soldiery. Never was scene more effectively managed. First, you heard a sprightly quick march playing in the distance; Kean started, listened, and leaned in a fixed and angry manner on his spade, with frowning eyes, and lips full of the truest feeling, compressed but not too much so; he seemed as if resolved not to be deceived, even by the charm of a thing inanimate; the audience were silent; the march threw forth its gallant note nearer and nearer; the Athenian standards appear, then the soldiers come treading on the scene with that air of confident progress which is produced by the accompaniment of music; and at last, while the squalid misanthrope still maintains his posture and keeps his back to the strangers, in steps the young and splendid *Alcibiades*, in the flush of victorious expectation. It is the encounter of hope with despair.[6]

It is apparent that Hunt believed Alcibiades to be a dramatic foil to Timon, and that one of the major themes of the play is the contrast

6. Hunt, *Leigh Hunt's Dramatic Criticism, 1808–1831*, pp. 137–38.

between the two—between youthful hope and aged despair; and he has convincingly described one dramatic effect of the drum and fife march. When we recall the Mask of the Amazons, which accompanied the only preceding appearance of Alcibiades and his soldiery before Timon, other contrasts and parallels appear woven about the theme discerned by Hunt. For example, we note (1. 2. 146) that Apemantus, in his sour comment on the dance of the Amazons (provided by Timon as a compliment to Alcibiades, as Hunt surmised), predicts:

APE. . . . Who dies that bears not one spurn to their graves
Of their friends' gift?
I should fear those that dance before me now
Would one day stamp upon me. 'T has been done.
Men shut their doors against a setting sun.

The apparently abbreviated nature of *Timon of Athens* makes criticism difficult, but we may observe that the meeting of Timon and Alcibiades in the woods can be construed as fulfilling Apemantus' prophecy. Timon is certainly a "setting sun." The presence of Phrynia and Timandra in Alcibiades' military expedition is never explained by Shakespeare; Timon calls them whores and camp-followers, but, since they are women engaging in the masculine practice of war, we might see them as two of Hunt's "unfeminine feminines" or Amazons, and the verbal abuse they exchange with Timon as a form of stamping upon him. Thus, the dance of the Amazons, in contrast, becomes, in the scene in act 4, a "spurn" to Timon delivered by the companions of Alcibiades, formerly Timon's dearest friend, which pushes him closer to despair and to his lonely grave.

The dramatic juxtaposition of the earlier masque of Amazons with the meeting of Timon with Alcibiades' "Amazons" in the woods could be enhanced if the drum and fife play "The Amazonians Masque" earlier suggested as the music for the Mask of Amazons. The score is, appropriately, in march time, and the melody need only be raised an octave for the fife.

The final music in the play again points up the contrast between Alcibiades and Timon, a process which, indeed, appears throughout the play. A soldier, searching the woods for Timon, finds Timon's tomb and epitaph. As he exits (5. 3. 10), trumpets sound to bridge a change of scene to that showing Alcibiades and his forces before the walls of Athens:

[*Trumpets sound. Enter* ALCIBIADES *with his powers.*]
ALC. Sound to this coward and lascivious town
        Our terrible approach.   [*A parley sounded.*]
                                    [*Enter* SENATORS *upon the walls.*]

The senators give the city to Alcibiades, begging him to temper his
revenge. At this moment of triumph, a messenger brings word of
Timon's death and a copy of his epitaph. The young general reads
the bitter words contained in the epitaph, then speaks, in gentle contrast, his final words (5. 4. 79):

ALC.   Dead
        Is noble Timon, of whose memory
        Hereafter more. Bring me into your city,
        And I will use the olive with my sword,
        Make war breed peace, make peace stint war, make each
        Prescribe to other as each other's leech.
        Let our drums strike.   [*Exeunt.*]

For the trumpet music which sounds as Alcibiades and his troops
appear before the walls of Athens, I suggest the "Solemn cavalcade,"
no. 6 in Appendix I, to be followed by the "Parley," no. 10.[7] The
final drum march could be the "English Drum March" shown in the
same appendix.

The unique feature of Shakespeare's music in *Timon of Athens*
is its integral association with Timon and Alcibiades as protagonist
and dramatic foil. With the single exception of the trumpet signal
announcing the first entrance of Timon, the music in the play is
heard at points when either Timon and Alcibiades are shown together or when they are otherwise associated (as when the banishment of Alcibiades from Athens is announced at the mock banquet
given by Timon to mark his self-banishment from Athens). The
two major characters are thus linked by the music primarily at four
important points in the drama—the Mask of Amazons, when Timon
is at the height of fortune; the trumpet music at the mock banquet,
which is the turning point of the action; the military march that

7. Mersenne (*Harmonie Universelle* . . . trans. R. Chapman, p. 332) remarked, "there must be noted that only about seven or eight kinds of tunes
are used in war. The first is called the *cavalcade*, used when the army . . .
approaches towns, through which it passes going to a siege or places of combat,
to warn the inhabitants and make them participants in the cheerfulness and
expectation of winning the victory."

emphasizes the contrast between the despair of Timon and the youthful optimism of Alcibiades at their last meeting; and the military signals and drum march that accompany the triumph of Alcibiades and, again, are a tragic contrast to the utter spiritual exhaustion revealed in Timon's epitaph.

If *Timon of Athens*, as some students believe, is an incomplete draft, then it provides an opportunity for us to observe some of the process followed by Shakespeare as he composed the play, in particular his treatment of the music—at least, in one example. He apparently wrote the first and last acts with rather full details, leaving the mid-portion of the play as a sketch to be further developed. That the music was conceived as an integral part of the tragedy from its inception we may be reasonably certain. The stage directions concerning the music are particularized; the Mask of Amazons is completely constructed; the directions controlling the music for the mock banquet and the military activities of Alcibiades follow a clear dramatic logic. There is, therefore, little reason to believe that any of the music in *Timon of Athens* was added as an afterthought or intended to be an extradramatic diversion. Rather, its main purpose is to help develop the characterization of Timon and Alcibiades—certainly an important and purely dramatic element of the play.

SIXTEEN

Henry VIII

N JUNE 29, 1613, THE GLOBE PLAYHOUSE BURNED
to the ground. Its thatch roof was ignited by a dis-
charge of "chambers" during a performance of
Henry VIII, and within an hour the great Globe
was an insubstantial wrack.[1] The fire was, no
doubt, the most spectacular event in a play designed by Shakespeare
to be a magnificent historical drama which would re-create the great
moments in the reign of the eighth Henry, with all the verisimilitude
of which the King's Men were capable.[2] "All is True," the play's
subtitle proclaims, and one would agree that, to judge from the carefully detailed stage directions in the play, the authors intended it to
reflect the pomp and pageantry of the Tudor Age. Indeed, most commentators have described this drama as a chronicle epic, a historical
pageant, or a collection of historical episodes but slightly unified by
their common subject. In spite of its episodic structure, however, the
play does achieve a kind of unity, an integrity resting more upon its
pervading tone and purpose than upon the classical unity of action,
an organizing principle more akin to the medieval mystery cycles
than to Aristotelean tragedy.

Henry VIII is a great hymn praising the English monarchy, especially the Tudor dynasty as represented by Henry and his daughter
Elizabeth. Just as the medieval Corpus Christi plays were unified by
the common theme of redemption by the blood of Christ and by their
common religious fervor in the worship and glorification of God, so
Henry VIII achieves a unity much in the same manner. If we remember that Henry VIII became not only the political, but also the spiritual ruler of England, that he was the Vicar of Christ as head of the
Anglican church, then we should not be surprised that Shakespeare
composed his play as a blend of historical, political, and religious

1. For contemporary accounts of the burning of the Globe playhouse, see
Chambers, *William Shakespeare* 2:343–44; and also Chambers, *The Eliza-
bethan Stage* 2:419–23.
2. Concerning the authorship of the play, see Shakespeare, *Henry VIII*, ed.
R. Foakes. Also see Cutts, "Shakespeare's Song and Masque Hand in *Henry
VIII*."

matter in which, under the wise and just rule of Henry, all England becomes a heavenly realm, and voices and instruments sound harmonious paeans of praise such as the heavenly hosts arc wont to sing around the throne of God. This exalted, almost sacrilegious, simile goes far to explain the ritual and pageantry in the play, and, as a part of the ceremonies, the music in the play.

In comparison with the preceding histories and tragedies, the music in *Henry VIII* is, with two exceptions, purely ceremonial in quality and is associated with public events. The two exceptions are the performances of music associated with Queen Katherine— both musical episodes intended to reveal something of her character. But Katherine does not sing as did Desdemona and Ophelia: kings and queens do not sing on Shakespeare's stage—for them to do so would violate dramatic decorum. Her character is not revealed by her performance of music but by her reactions to music performed before her. With the assumption, then, that music is intended to contribute to the pageantry and, to some extent, the characterization in *Henry VIII*, we may now consider the particular uses of music in the play.

The direction describing Henry's entrance at the opening of act 1, scene 2, is:

> [*Cornets. Enter* KING HENRY, *leaning on the* CARDINAL'S *shoulder, the nobles, and* SIR THOMAS LOVELL. *The* CARDINAL *places himself under the* KING'S *feet on his right side.*]

Normally, a flourish would introduce the king, but in this case the cornets may have sounded the flourish followed by a brief sennet to bring the group of actors into the council chamber. Cornets could, and frequently did, imitate other instruments; they may have replaced the trumpets in this case. Yet it is curious that they should do so in this scene, since trumpets were certainly available for the purpose. Apparently, we find here another example of sheer musical extravagance, the use of a band of cornets simply because it was available. Notations for a flourish and sennet appear in Appendix IV.

Act 1, scene 4, one of the most spectacular scenes, presents the revelry in progress at Cardinal Wolsey's York Palace in direct contrast to the somber betrayal and unjust execution of Buckingham by Wolsey. In the course of the scene, the complete outline of a court

Figure 54.

masque appears, and in the midst of the masque Henry meets and is attracted by Anne Boleyn. The scene opens with banquet music played by a consort of hautboys. The direction is:

> [*Hautboys. A small table under a state for the* CARDINAL, *a longer table for the guests. Then enter* ANNE BULLEN *and divers other* LADIES *and* GENTLEMEN *as guests, at one door; at another door, enter* SIR HENRY GUILDFORD.]

The music of the hautboys both sets the festive atmosphere of the occasion and fills the time while the cardinal's state, the tables, and other props are placed on the stage. Once they are placed, Anne, the other guests, and Sir Henry Guildford enter. The music continues until all of the party are in their places; it ceases with Sir Henry's first words of welcome. This banquet music should be, of course, light and merry. In Brit. Mus. Add. MS 10,444, fols. 3^r and 58^r, among the instrumental pieces for masques and plays, is a catchy tune entitled "The Huming Batchelor." The cantus and bassus voices are transcribed in figure 54.

The guests are seated at the table, the hautboys sound again, and to their music the cardinal sweeps onto the stage and takes his seat on the throne. The direction is [*Hautboys. Enter* CARDINAL WOLSEY, *and takes his state*]. Quite obviously the cardinal is attempting to rival the king in pomp. He could not usurp the royal flourish of trumpets, but he could have his hautboists play processional music to attend him to his throne. A short march or "masque" would have been played for this purpose. Such a piece of brief pomposity is the instrumental piece "Stephen Thomas his Almaine" found in the collection previously described, Brit. Mus. Add. MS 10,444, fols. 8^v, 8^r, and 63^v. Only the cantus and bassus parts are there given. A literal transcription of these voices appears in figure 55.

After a few lines of social chatter, the banquet is again interrupted by the sounds of trumpet, drum, and cannon salutes offstage. The direction is [*Drum and trumpet. Chambers discharged*]. It was the discharging of these "chambers," we recall, that started the fire which destroyed the Globe. But, to our purpose, the trumpet, drum, and cannon announce the opening of the masque. Since the author attempted to follow his source, Holinshed's *Chronicles*, as closely as possible, we also should turn to the source. According to Holinshed:

when it pleased the king for his recreation to repaire to the cardinals house (as he did diuerse times in the yeare) there wanted no preparations or furniture: bankets were set foorth with maskes and mummeries, in so gorgeous a sort and costlie maner, that it was an heauen to behold. There wanted no dames or damosels meet or apt to danse with the maskers, or to garnish the place for the time: then was there all kind of musike and harmonie, with fine voices both of men and children.

On a time the king came suddenlie thither in a maske with a dozen maskers all in garments like shepheards . . . hauing sixteene torchbearers, besides their drums and other per-

Figure 55.

sons with visards. . . . And before his entring into the hall, he came by water to the water gate without anie noise, where were laid diuerse chambers and guns charged with shot, and at his landing they were shot off . . . they receiued them . . . with such a noise of drums and flutes, as seldome had been heard the like. . . . Then the king tooke his seat under the cloth of estate. . . . Thus passed they foorth the night with banketting, dansing, and other triumphs, to the great comfort of the king, and pleasant regard of the nobilitie there assembled.[3]

As the masque is staged, following the offstage trumpet and cannon

3. Holinshed, *The Third Volume of Chronicles* . . . (1587), pp. 921–22.

salutes, a servant enters the banquet room and reports that a "noble troop of strangers, / For so they seem . . . as great ambassadors" is approaching. The cardinal directs the Lord Chamberlain to receive them and to conduct them "Into our presence, where this Heaven of beauty / Shall shine at full upon them." The direction is then [. . . *All rise, and tables removed*]. The hautboists then sound again or, as the rubric has it:

> [*Hautboys. Enter the* KING *and others, as masquers, habited like shepherds, ushered by the* LORD CHAMBERLAIN. *They pass directly before the* CARDINAL, *and gracefully salute him.*]

The hautboy music in this case covers the awkward removal of the tables and brings the maskers marching into the supposed banquet room. This music continues while the maskers pass before the cardinal and render some formal salute to him. This "movement" and the welcome given by the Lord Chamberlain might be considered the opening half of the masque, that is, the portion of the masque performed by the maskers without feminine partners. For proper music to open the stage masque, the "first dance" from an actual masque should be appropriate. Again drawing from Brit. Mus. Add. MS 10,444, fols. 19^v, 73^v, and 73^r, I have chosen the piece titled therein "The Ladies Masque. 1" from a suite of three dances having the general title "The Ladies Masque." The dances are anonymous, and the original masque, at least by this name, is unknown. The date of entry in the collection is also unknown, but the collection itself is believed to have been made between 1600 and 1630.[4] A literal transcription of "The Ladies Masque. 1" appears in figure 56.

With F's direction *Choose Ladies, King and An Bullen*, the maskers choose partners from the spectator-ladies, and the revels—the second half of the masque—begin. As King Henry takes the hand of his future wife and queen, he exclaims, "The fairest hand I ever touched! O Beauty, / Till now I never knew thee!" The direction then states [*Music. Dance.*], and Henry and Anne, with the other maskers and their ladies, perform a courtly dance to open the revels. The

4. For descriptions of this MS, see Cutts, "Jacobean Masque and Stage Music"; and Sabol, ed., *Songs and Dances for the Stuart Masque*, p. 168, note to line 39. The earliest account of the MS is given by W. Lawrence, "Notes on a Collection of Masque Music," pp. 49–58.

Figure 56.

direction calls for *Music* rather than for hautboys; this general rubric indicates that the dance music is to be played by a broken consort of strings and woodwinds. Since the maskers are attired as shepherds, in keeping with Holinshed's description, I have provided for the dance music here an anonymous masque dance, "The Sheapheards

Masque" (Brit. Mus. Add. MS 10,444, fols. 36ᵛ and 87ᵛ), transcribed in figure 57.

Figure 57.

After the dance, Henry learns the name of the lady he danced with and kisses her. Wolsey announces the customary banquet to be served the maskers in an adjoining room, then he remarks to the king, "Your Grace, I fear, with dancing is a little heated." To which the king replies, "I fear, too much."[5] As the party troops offstage, Henry proclaims to all:

5. This quotation and the two immediately following occur in lines 99–108.

KING.   I have half a dozen healths
              To drink to these fair ladies, and a measure
              To lead 'em once again; and then let's dream
              Who's best in favor. Let the music knock it.
                                                [*Exeunt with trumpets.*]

Henry's concluding command is that the "*Musicke*" play again, as F has it. His expression is a form of the cue found often at the end of acts in the choirboy plays, "Knock up the Musicke,"[6] that is, start the entr'acte music. But the direction calls not for the music of a broken consort, to which Henry alludes, but for trumpets. This apparent non sequitur can be explained if the dramatic purpose of the scene as a whole is considered.

The dramatic point of the scene is the meeting of Anne and Henry. Their meeting must be shown to be dramatically significant, since the conclusion of the play, the christening of their daughter, Elizabeth, is the dramatic result of this meeting. Shakespeare therefore selected what he considered an appropriate occasion as reported by Holinshed, the masque described above, and used it to provide a properly symbolic setting for the origin of the royal lovematch. Holinshed, of course, said nothing about Anne being present at the masque in question. The symbolism of the scene was perhaps suggested by Holinshed's description of the masque as "an heauen to behold" and wanting "no dames or damosels meet or apt to danse with the maskers . . . then was there all kind of musike and harmonie. . . ."[7] To the Elizabethans, dancing symbolized the act of matrimony, music signified harmony, the ladies signified heavenly beauty.

While we might have some difficulty in seeing the union of Henry and Anne Boleyn in such terms, the Elizabethans probably found such associated concepts more compatible. Besides, every masque was expected to offer some allegorical or didactic message. Thus, at the conclusion of the masque in act 1, scene 4, when Henry says, "let's dream / Who's best in favor. Let the music knock it," we may believe that he refers to Anne as best in favor and also to the music they will make together in addition to the music of the consort. Then, as they exit together, the trumpets blow not a royal flourish but, as I think, a solemn series of peals that serve as an announcement—not

6. For example, at the end of each of the first four acts of William Percy's *The Cuck-queanes and Cuckolds Errants* (1601) is the direction "*Here they knockt up the consort.*"
7. See this chapter, *n*3.

Henry VIII

to Anne, of course, but to the audience. I would therefore suggest that the trumpets sound the "Solemn Chant," no. 6 in Appendix I.

Act 2, scene 4, spectacularly presents the consistory which is to determine the legality of Henry's divorce from Katherine. The extensive stage directions call for at least twenty-two persons (excluding musicians) in the processional that opens the scene, and for a high solemnity in the movements of the actors about the stage. The requisite music is described at the beginning of the directions as [*Trumpets, sennet, and cornets . . .*]. This direction has, I believe, confused some editors, who have assigned the sennet to the trumpets and left the cornets in a vacuum. It is possible that the trumpets play the sennet; but, if so, what is left for the cornets? The two kinds of instruments were seldom played in consort. I rather think that the trumpets brayed out the customary royal flourish and that the cornets then played a sennet to which the procession of actors entered and found their proper positions on the stage. The cornets, frequently used to accompany chapel choirs, would have contributed to the ecclesiastical setting and atmosphere of the scene.[8] At the end of the scene the rubric is [*Exeunt in manner as they entered*]. We may therefore assume that the trumpet flourish and cornet sennet are repeated as a recessional. For the notation of a flourish and sennet, see Appendix IV.

The character of Queen Katherine is drawn with sympathy and pathos. The major characters, excepting Wolsey, all speak of her as blameless—sinned against rather than sinning. And yet, not sinned against, either, since King Henry could not be shown as guilty of ingratitude or injustice. Perhaps we are to think of her as a Queen Dido losing her Æneas by the will of the gods—a martyr to the future welfare of England. Following her impassioned defense in act 2, scene 4, in the face of the full power of church and state as represented by the spectacular ceremony described above, the first scene of act 3 opens in dramatic contrast to reveal Katherine, in her private apartment and attended by a few ladies, listening to the quiet sweetness of a lute song:

[*The* QUEEN *and her* WOMEN, *as at work.*]
Q. KATH. Take thy lute, wench. My soul grows sad with
[troubles.
Sing, and disperse 'em if thou canst. Leave working.

8. Galpin, *Old English Instruments of Music . . .* p. 192.

SONG

Orpheus with his lute made trees,
And the mountain tops that freeze
   Bow themselves when he did sing.
To his music plants and flowers
Ever sprung, as sun and showers
   There had made a lasting spring.

Every thing that heard him play,
Even the billows of the sea,
   Hung their heads, and then lay by.
In sweet music is such art,
Killing care and grief of heart
   Fall asleep, or hearing die.

The sharp contrast of this picture and music with the music in the preceding scene emphasizes the loneliness and helplessness of Katherine. We no longer see her as a queen, but as a deserted housewife mechanically carrying on her work and momentarily checking her grief by attention to the song. We are reminded of Mariana, forlorn by the moated grange; but, as W. H. Auden has observed, Katherine is trying to forget her unhappiness by attending to an *encomium musical* having little bearing on her situation, whereas Mariana is indulging her sadness by sucking melancholy out of a song.[9] John Cutts has noted that the song "prepares the way for the 'masque-vision' in which Katherine finds compensation in heavenly harmony."[10]

Katherine listens to what is obviously a set song—a lutenist's ayre —though the song was not necessarily written for the play. It was doubtless intended to please the audience by its intrinsic musical worth as well as to achieve dramatic ends. It was sung by a boy, probably a well-trained choirboy who accompanied himself with a lute. Katherine, we note, does not sing.

There is no evidence that the song is not by Shakespeare, although some students believe its author to be John Fletcher. They point to a passage analogous to the song text, that appears in *The Captain* (act 3, scene 1) by Francis Beaumont and John Fletcher:

> *Jul.* . . . And when she speaks, oh
>   Angelo, then musick
>   (Such as old Orpheus made, that gave a soul

9. "Music in Shakespeare," pp. 513–14.
10. "Shakespeare's Song and Masque Hand in *Henry VIII*," p. 186.

To aged mountains, and made rugged beasts
Lay by their rages: and tall trees that knew
No sound but tempests, to bow down their branches
And hear, and wonder; and the Sea, whose surges
Shook their white heads in Heaven, to be as mid-night
Still, and attentive) steals into our souls
So suddenly, and strangely, that we are
From that time no more ours, but what she pleases.[11]

The original lute music for the song text has disappeared. Matthew Locke, Charles II's Composer in Ordinary, who arranged much theater music including that for the D'Avenant-Dryden version of *The Tempest* (1667) and for D'Avenant's revival of *Macbeth* (1672), made a three-voice setting of the song that was published in John Playford's *Catch as Catch Can, or The Musical Companion* in 1667. There is a growing body of evidence that Locke, as a member of the King's Musick, may have reworked some theatrical music he inherited from the pre-Restoration King's Men or, at least, that he revised music believed to have been originally composed by Robert Johnson (?) for Shakespeare's *Macbeth*.[12] If Locke had access to the early music played by the King's Musick or by musicians of the King's Men, and if he habitually adapted the early music for Shakespeare's plays for Restoration revivals, then his setting of "Orpheus with his Lute" may be an adaptation of the original setting. The evidence is so tenuous, however, that I have chosen to set the text to the cantus and orpharion (lute) accompaniment of an ayre, "All my wits hath will inwrapped," no. 7 in John Bartlett's *A Booke of Ayres . . .* (1606), which, I think, is closer to the early seventeenth-century lutenist ayre than is Locke's setting (see figure 58).

The music of spectacle and ceremony returns to the stage with Anne's coronation procession at the opening of act 4, scene 1. The description of the music is given in the dialogue and in the elaborate stage directions. Two gentlemen are discussing the removal of Katherine to Kimbalton (line 35):

2. GENT.   Alas, good lady!   [*Trumpets.*]
        The trumpets sound. Stand close, the Queen is coming.
                                                  [*Hautboys.*]

11. *The Works of Francis Beaumont and John Fletcher* 10:263.
12. See chap. 12, *n*9.

THE ORDER OF THE CORONATION

1. *A lively flourish of trumpets.*
2. *Then two* JUDGES.
3. LORD CHANCELLOR, *with purse and mace before him.*
4. CHORISTERS, *singing.* MUSICIANS.

And so on through ten groups or entries in the procession. Then the rubric is:

[*Exit procession; and then a great flourish of trumpets.*]

Orph-eus with his Lute made Trees, and the Moun-taine tops that freeze,

Bow them-selves when he did sing Bow them-selves when he did sing.

Figure 58.

The "order of the coronation" seems to be directions to aid the prompter in organizing the procession. As the scene was acted, a commentary by the two Gentlemen accompanied the appearance of each group in the train. We may then easily reconstruct the performance of the music.

Introducing the procession, a trumpet fanfare sounds offstage, then the hautboys strike up a sennet to which the two judges, the Lord Chancellor, and the bearers of the purse and mace enter. The hautboys cease, and the voices of the choir, probably accompanied by the cornets, are heard singing either a *Te Deum* or a *Gloria*, to which music, perhaps in alternation with the hautboy sennet, the procession moves across the stage and then exits.

The staging of the coronation is patterned closely on Holinshed's description. Of course, Shakespeare dramatized only the return of

Anne from the coronation; the coronation itself is described by the Third Gentleman. According to Holinshed, the choristers were composed of the "kings chapell and the moonks solemnlie *singing* with procession."[13] During the actual coronation, he related, "*the queere soong Te Deum,* &c. . . ."[14] These remarks imply that the choristers included both men and boys. And, since the Third Gentleman reported the singing of the *Te Deum,* we might believe that the choir then followed the *Te Deum* with the *Gloria* as it appeared on the stage. Holinshed then reported that "when she [Anne] was out of the sanctuarie and appeared within the palace, the trumpets plaied maruellouslie freshlie. . . ."[15] This remark no doubt explains the great flourish of trumpets which the stage direction calls for after the procession leaves the stage. The flourish here is to suggest the proclamation, throughout the kingdom, of Anne as queen and also to give an audible example of the new harmony and life given the kingdom through Henry's choice.

Music for the introductory trumpet flourish and the cornet sennet is given in Appendix IV. I suggest that the choristers might sing the *Gloria* from a service by Thomas Tallis (figure 59). This work by Tallis is recorded in Brit. Mus. Add. MS 38,539, the *Gloria* on fol. 53ᵛ. The concluding "great flourish" by the trumpets probably was an extended fanfare, not a sennet or a conventional flourish. The "Entrata Imperial" by Fantini shown in figure 29 could serve the purpose in this scene. The trumpets should be placed offstage, of course.

As R. A. Foakes has observed, the next scene (act 4, scene 2) is intended to be both a contrast and a parallel to the preceding scene.[16] Whereas in the first scene we are shown Anne's coronation with all its worldly pomp and pageantry, in the second scene a miraculous vision appears in which the dying Katherine is given a heavenly crown by angelic "spirits of peace" who, in a solemn dance, restore her soul with the divine justice that in its worldly form had been denied her. The staging of this variation of the deus ex machina is

13. *The Third Volume of Chronicles* . . . (1587), p. 202. King Henry's orders to his household Jan. 1525–1526 mention "the Master of the King's Chapell with six of the same children." An earlier account (Feb. 1510–1511) lists twenty-one Gentlemen of the Chapel. Nine singing men and children attended the burial of Henry VIII on Feb. 21, 1547–1548 (see H. Lafontaine, ed., *The King's Musick* . . . pp. 5–7).

14. *The Third Volume of Chronicles* . . . (1587), p. 202.

15. Ibid., p. 203.

16. Shakespeare, *King Henry VIII*, pp. l–lii.

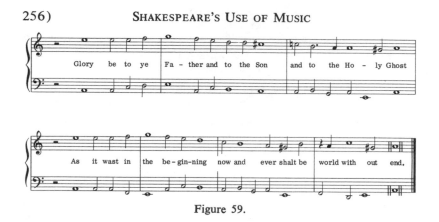

Glory be to ye Fa - ther and to the Son and to the Ho - ly Ghost

As it wast in the be - gin-ning now and ever shalt be world with out end.

Figure 59.

clearly described by the stage direction and its immediate context, beginning with line 77:

KATH.　　　　Good Griffith,
　　　　　Cause the musicians play me that sad note
　　　　　I named my knell, whilst I sit meditating
　　　　　On that celestial harmony I go to.
　　　　　　　　　　　　　　[Sad and solemn music.]
GRIF.　She is asleep. Good wench, let's sit down quiet,
　　　　　For fear we wake her. Softly, gentle Patience.
　　　　　[*The vision. Enter, solemnly tripping one after another, six
　　　　　personages, clad in white robes, wearing on their heads
　　　　　garlands of bays, and golden vizards on their faces;
　　　　　branches of bays or palm in their hands. They first
　　　　　congee unto her, then dance; and, at certain changes, the
　　　　　first two hold a spare garland over her head, at which the
　　　　　other four make reverent curtsies. Then the two that held
　　　　　the garland deliver the same to the other next two, who
　　　　　observe the same order in their changes, and holding the
　　　　　garland over her head; which done, they deliver the same
　　　　　garland to the last two, who likewise observe the same
　　　　　order, at which, as it were by inspiration, she makes in
　　　　　her sleep signs of rejoicing, and holdeth up her hands to
　　　　　heaven. And so in their dancing vanish, carrying the
　　　　　garland with them. The music continues.*]
KATH.　Spirits of peace, where are ye? Are ye all gone
　　　　　And leave me here in wretchedness behind ye?

GRIF. Madam, we are here.
KATH.   It is not you I call for.
      Saw ye none enter since I slept?
GRIF.   None, madam.
KATH. No? Saw you not even now a blessèd troop
      Invite me to a banquet, whose bright faces
      Cast thousand beams upon me, like the sun?
      They promised me eternal happiness
      And brought me garlands, Griffith, which I feel
      I am not worthy yet to wear. I shall, assuredly.
GRIF. I am most joyful, madam, such good dreams
      Possess your fancy.
KATH.   Bid the music leave.
      They are harsh and heavy to me.   *[Music ceases.]*

While the divine coronation of Katherine is obviously intended to be a parallel to Anne's earthly one, a close analysis of the music in this case reveals much more than a simple parallel to the trumpet and cornet and choral music of the preceding scene. Katherine calls for her "knell" to prepare her spirit for "that celestial harmony I go to," but the music also evokes pity in the audience as does the lute song in act 3, scene 1. Moreover, the solemn music then telescopes the time during which Katherine falls asleep—usually an awkward moment on the stage. To the strains of the music then appear the six "personages" who perform their pantomime dance and then depart. Of course, music and the dance are aural and visual symbols of the celestial harmony in store for Katherine, but they are also intended to recall to our minds not only the coronation of Anne but also the masque scene (act 1, scene 4) in which King Henry first meets Anne. We note that the vision takes the form of a dance in which the performers wear vizards; the "blessèd troop" invite Katherine to a banquet; and her reference to the garlands brought to her, which she felt unworthy to wear, remind us of the honors that Anne so modestly accepted from Henry. Surely, the vision and its solemn dance are to suggest that each step in Henry's courtship and marriage to Anne Boleyn, and her coronation, has its counterpart in heavenly beneficence for Katherine, that somehow Katherine's unjust divorce from Henry is, at the same time, a marriage with God, that she becomes the bride of Christ. Then, as Henry has remarked about Anne, "let's dream / Who's best in favour."

Figure 60.

We thus see that the authors have gone to great effort, much of it in the use of music, to assure the audience that Henry's apparent injustice to Katherine is, after all, to her benefit; therefore, Henry is not to be blamed. Drama is not history—fortunately, in this case.

The musical requirements for Katherine's vision would probably have been met by a broken consort performing a piece suitable for the solemn dancers, one grave in tempo and providing the "changes" at which points they hold the garland over Katherine's head. Such music is admirably supplied by Thomas Morley in *The First Booke of Consort Lessons.* . . . There, no. 11 is a program piece called "Allisons Knell," probably composed by Richard Allison, in the form of a pavane and having therefore at least two "changes." A literal transcription of the treble viol and pandora parts is shown in figure 60.

The concluding music performed in the play is again processional and ceremonious. The scene is the christening of the infant Elizabeth (act 5, scene 5), which opens with the procession returning from the christening. The direction is preceded by a cue given by the Lord Chamberlain (line 86), "Hark! The trumpets sound. / They're come already from the christening. . . . SCENE V. *The palace.* [*Enter Trumpets, sounding; then two* ALDERMEN . . .]." Then follows the order of the procession.

If we assume that a complement of nine royal trumpeters was used here, the number of actors and musicians brought onstage was about twenty-eight or thirty, moving with solemn steps and completely traversing the stage. All this movement probably required several minutes to complete. Then, after these actors have found their places and Garter has saluted the princess, the rubric is [*Flourish. Enter* KING *and* GUARD]. Thus the trumpets sound a full sennet for the entrance and positioning of the members of the procession; then they peal the royal flourish for the entrance of King Henry and his guards.

Following the entrance of the king, Cranmer speaks his prophecies, with their glowing encomiums of Henry, Elizabeth, and James, and the play concludes on a joyous note. The stage direction is then simply *Exeunt*, but it is obvious that the same flourish and sennet that open the scene would also be necessary to move the king and the remainder of the actors off the stage. No doubt, it was with ears still ringing from the final trumpet blasts that the spectators heard the Epilogue say, "Some come to take their ease / And sleep an act or two; but those, we fear, / We have frighted with our trumpets. . . ."

In conclusion, it is clear that the music performed in *Henry VIII* may be placed into two general categories in terms of both mood and method of performance. The larger portion of the music is public, ceremonious, social, and associated closely with Henry, Anne Boleyn, and Elizabeth. We see that dance music accompanies Henry's courtship of Anne, and processional music attends Anne at her coronation and Elizabeth at her christening. While these three persons combine in themselves both political and religious attributes, the music linked to them emphasizes their political positions—Henry as father of his country, Anne as his native English consort, and Elizabeth as the fruit of their love destined to become the savior and wise governess of England.

The remaining category of the performed music is private in nature, performed only in the apartments of Katherine and is associated entirely with the pathetic fate of this queen. Katherine, a Spaniard and foreigner, was a dramatic problem to Shakespeare. She could not be ignored, nor was she guilty of any sin or crime that might permit her to be characterized as a villainess and therefore to be put aside justly by Henry. What to do with her without imputing cruelty and injustice to Henry? The solution was for the author to make her a saint and a martyr—society's usual salve for a guilty conscience. The lute song helps to isolate her from the public and political world and to prepare us for the celestial harmonies that attend her heavenly coronation in the vision scene.

Thus, the music heard in this historical pageant play underscores its dualistic quality. The music reminds us that we may view the drama as chronicle and as a mystery play sprung from roots imbedded in English medieval drama and history—a native stock to which Greek, Roman, and Italian classicism was, in this case, little engrafted.

The quantity, as well as the variety, of the music described in the stage directions is impressive. Instrumental music includes a cry of trumpets (probably nine or more), a consort of hautboys, a consort of cornets, a "broken" consort of mixed strings and woodwinds, and (probably a member of the broken consort) a lutenist who played the accompaniment for a song. Vocal music includes a solo singer— perhaps a choirboy—and a choir possibly composed of men and choirboys. Even if some allowance is made for doubling by the musicians playing the hautboys and cornets, the number of musicians still is large by Jacobean standards, about twenty or twenty-five all told.

The variety of the music is also unusually rich. It ranges from the brassy fanfares of the trumpets to the quiet twangling of a lute, from the whine of the hautboy processionals to the sparkle of the broken consort, from the pure voice of a "wench" (choirboy) to the solemn chant of a full choir, from the joyous dance of a masque to the sad measures of a knell. Almost the full musical resources of the day are represented in this one play. In this respect, the music in

Henry VIII reminds us of the rich musical fare present in other plays of Shakespeare's late production—*Cymbeline, A Winter's Tale,* and *The Tempest*—and again marks the great extent to which the dramatic use of music had developed at the end of Shakespeare's productive career.

SEVENTEEN

Conclusion

ENRY VIII IS THE LAST PLAY THAT CAN BE AT-
tributed to Shakespeare with any certainty, and
with it this study is concluded. To summarize the
many functions of the music in the histories and
tragedies would be wastefully repetitious; to attempt
to draw any firm conclusions would be unwise, since much of this
study depends upon circumstantial and conjectural evidence. Therefore, I would rather offer some tentative conclusions about certain
critical matters to which a broad view of the uses of music in
these plays seems pertinent. In the process I shall necessarily review
some of the salient points made throughout this study.

Music in Shakespeare's plays is *an appeal to the immediate experiences of the audience.* Regardless of what specific function the
music may serve in a given instance, its basic purpose is to remind
the audience of experiences and emotional responses to experiences
which the audience knows from everyday life. For example, all
Londoners were familiar with the municipal waits, or band of hautboists. They heard the waits play for civic events such as the in-
stallation of a lord mayor, for festive banquets in the guildhalls, for
solemn processions by the city fathers to Whitehall. Hence, when the
dramatist wished to set his scene in a deliberative council or a banquet, he evoked in his audience a recollection of actual occasions by
having the theater hautboists play a sennet or cheerful dinner music.
The music thus stimulated the imagination of the audience and sup-
plemented other means by which the playwright set his scene.

It is this basic appeal to immediate experience, I think, that explains the frequent anachronisms in the dramatic uses of music by
Shakespeare and his contemporaries—for example, Lucius playing a
lute to soothe the troubled mind of Brutus. It was not important to
these dramatists that Romans march across the stage to the sound of
actual *bucinae*; their audiences had no association of ideas with
Roman musical instruments. It *was* important that the audience,
literate and illiterate, hear the familiar waits or trumpets and, by
association of ideas, transfer to the actors on the stage the dignity

and pomp which the spectators had observed with their own eyes and ears in the streets of London. As a poet chooses particular words for their connotative values, so Shakespeare and his fellows seem to have chosen various kinds of performed music for the same purpose.

Performed music also suggested abstract ideas or concepts. In this sense, it could be used for symbolic purposes. The Elizabethan definition of music included all forms in which harmony could be expressed; that is, music or harmony included the idea of the perfected relationships between all things, from the musical triad to the Trinity. This broad definition included such areas of human activity as politics, psychology, religion, and ethics. Therefore, the sounding of a flourish by the stage trumpeters could evoke from the audience not only an emotional response proper to the appearance of a monarch but could also symbolize the harmony of the state, the perfected political relationships associated with the idea of monarchy. The harmonious music that sounds as Prince Hal, at the bed of his dying father, crowns himself as rightful successor is an example of music used for a rhetorical purpose—to enhance the emotional impact of the prince's soliloquy—and a symbolic use in that it suggests the political and national harmony that was denied Henry IV but which by legal succession is granted his son. Conversely, the fact that Shakespeare never assigned a royal flourish to Macbeth or, after the murder of Duncan, associated any form of music directly with him, is a negative symbol of the illegitimacy of his crown and the lack of harmony within him. In ethical terms, the absence of music associated with Macbeth, as with Othello and Cassius, who both dislike music, symbolizes the dark and discordant qualities within their natures.

To turn to a textual matter, the use by Shakespeare of musical bridges from one scene to another deserves restatement. That he used musical bridges should not surprise us when we recall that the plays were written for continuous performance on stages lacking, as far as anyone knows, front curtains which could be drawn to indicate scene changes on the outer stage. In many cases, as we have seen, musical elision smooths what might otherwise be a difficult transition. And, as he often did, Shakespeare made the maximum dramatic use of these elisions, often by using them to create dramatic irony or intentional ambiguity. Surely it was a stroke of great art when, in *Antony and Cleopatra*, he placed not only the drunken revels of the triumvirs in marked contrast to the appearance of Ventidius triumphant over the Parthians, but also directed the shrill clamor of trumpets that concludes the revels on Pompey's galley to bridge over and become the martial music sounding for Ventidius' victory. Then we may better understand the sarcasm in Ventidius' statement when he remarks that "Caesar and Antony have ever won / More in their officer than person." This one musical episode thus provides a climax to the revelry, elides the scene into the following one, and, by linking in contrast the carouse and the triumph of Ventidius, helps to produce a stroke of irony in which Ventidius' remarks are rhetorically enhanced. If, as seems very probable, Shakespeare was using intentional ambiguity to link his scenes in this case, then scene divisions inserted by editors have in many instances obscured or thwarted his intention, not only in this instance but perhaps in many others.

The problem of classification in Shakespearean criticism is sometimes a vexing one, particularly when we try to determine Shakespeare's definition of the broad terms "comedy," "history," and "tragedy." If we knew, for example, that he intended *Measure for Measure* to be a comedy or *Troilus and Cressida* to be a tragedy, then criticism of these plays could be more logical and objective. Some of the problems of the "problem" plays might be solved. The habitual uses of music by the playwright may provide us an additional factor in arriving at Shakespeare's use of these terms.

What, if any, distinction did Shakespeare make between a "history" play and a tragedy? May we classify *Richard II* as a tragedy and the two parts of *Henry IV* a history simply because one has a tragic ending and the others do not? Surely such a distinction is a vast simplification. Is *Julius Caesar* a tragedy, or is it a history play? If a tragedy, then whose tragedy? If a history play, by what definition of "history"? And yet, in the main, Shakespeare seems to have distinguished between the two categories, at least in one respect—characterization. His use of music provides good evidence that tragedy, in Shakespeare's thought, was an intense vision of inner conflict and mental and physical destruction, as A. C. Bradley has claimed. An aging barbarian, perplexed in the extreme; a mad old king; a scarce-sane young prince; Macbeth's moral vacuum turned into a tale told by an idiot—these are the stuff of tragedy. According to this view, Richard II, who baits himself and symbolically shatters his inner harmony on the flagstones of Westminster Abbey, shows us tragedy, but Richard III, whose wolfish appetite moves him from murder to murder until he is himself killed like a mad dog, shows us less a tragedy than a museum of political horrors illuminated by Richard's cynical brilliance, revealing not so much inner conflict as remorseless and unquestioning ambition. And how does the music turn this facet of Shakespearean tragedy to our view? By means of the bits of ballads that provide a window into the minds and spirits of Shakespeare's tragic characters, or by means of the instrumental music such as that to which the doomed Richard II moralizes, or by the use of the serenade scorned by Othello. But especially the ballad snatches—surely one of the most effective dramatic devices Shakespeare used. Not only do they act as gnomic references pointing to this or that action or situation or moral made familiar to the Elizabethan audience by years of exposure to a popular ballad tradition, but they also create, by means of their music, an emotional empathy between actor and audience, a union which can be evoked in no other way. Finally, their piecemeal quality suggests a world in fragments, a mind torn in different directions, a spirit divided and hence in conflict.

One may object, of course, that Shakespeare used fragments of ballads or popular songs because any dramatist would be hard put to find occasion or time for the performance of a complete ballad within the two-hours traffic of the stage. Quite so; but having chopped off bits of ballads, any playwright worth his salt would surely turn the fragments to more than one use. Someone once said that if you have to place a cannon on the stage, be sure to fire it; and, while you are waiting to fire it, be sure that you use it for any other dramatic purpose which might suggest itself. But, of course, we have no evidence that Shakespeare wished to use a complete ballad and then was forced, by the nature of drama, to cut it short. He used single stanzas or single lines of ballads because he had good dramatic reasons for doing so.

And what is the effect? The effect is to furnish certain tragic characters with a language and a mythos through which their inner beings reveal themselves to the audience in a manner far transcending, in emotional power, a similar device—the soliloquy. For example, Desdemona's willow song expresses not only in words and music (that is, lyrical emotion) the plight of all lovers scorned by their loved ones, but it links the fate of Desdemona to all of the rich connotative devices of the popular ballad tradition, for example, the willow tree image and the various legends associated with willows

and forsaken lovers. In this sense, the popular ballads and their traditional content—the betrayal of love, the reversal of fortune, death
by violence, the coming of May, the anticlerical jests and fabliaux,
the adventures of Robin Hood or brave knights—were old enough
and familiar enough to Shakespeare's audience to provide a popular
mythology more or less native to England, and hence to furnish
points of reference that could be caught by the most illiterate Elizabethan with as much ease as the most literate courtier would catch a
reference to Dido or Priam. Moreover, the ballad mythology was
known by high and low alike. Desdemona and Ophelia are familiar
with this ballad lore, though they seem to recollect it from childhood.
And Edgar and Lear's Fool match ballad lines with no effort.

When we recall that the vocal music in the tragedies is composed
almost entirely of ballad bits or parts of old popular songs, whereas
the vocal music in the comedies is composed largely of art songs or
complete lute songs, the suggestion is strong that Shakespeare
considered tragedy a more popular form of drama than comedy.
Moreover, there is strong evidence that Shakespeare's most powerful
tragedies grew from popular, hence native, roots; whereas his comedies grew from classical or continental roots and hence were somewhat foreign in the same sense that the culture in the courts of
Elizabeth and James was somewhat foreign.

In contrast to the tragedies with their ballads and emphasis on
inner conflict, the histories use music, for the most part, in its public,
social, and ceremonial vein. This music is, of course, largely instrumental—the flourishes of trumpets, the sennets of cornets, the banquet music of hautboys, or the dance music of the broken consort.
The dramatic actions which the music accompanies and enhances—
the actions which, we may assume, the author thought most important
in his production—are usually those most public. The importance of
spectacle and pageantry cannot be over-emphasized. Judging by the
music performed in the histories, then, we may believe that Shakespeare thought of the history or chronicle play in terms mainly of
action rather than character, and the more spectacular the action,
the better.

By an examination of the performed music, we may thus be able
to make some distinctions between some of Shakespeare's plays
which are difficult to classify according to the conventional categories, tragedy, history, and comedy. Thus, according to a single
criterion—the most prominent type of music the author calls for in a

play—*Troilus and Cressida* is *essentially* a comedy, because its music is entirely courtly and "artificial"; *Richard III*, though usually called a tragedy, is *essentially* a history or chronicle play because its music is entirely public and ceremonious in nature. *Measure for Measure* is *essentially* a comedy because it contains an art song; *Hamlet* and *King Lear* are *essentially* tragedies because their vocal music is composed entirely of ballad snatches. In few cases may anything be classified on the basis of a single criterion—certainly not literary works, and the value of any classification has its limits; but a consideration of the type of music employed in a Shakespeare play, along with other criteria, should be of aid in those instances where sharp definition is necessary.

Finally, the study of performed music as a part of Shakespeare's dramatic craftsmanship should teach us to regard the music in the plays not as an addition made simply for the intrinsic pleasure music affords, not just to add to the excitement or emotional force of the action, but as an integral part of the dramatic structure. Genius exploits to the fullest the materials it chooses to work upon. If Shakespeare was a genius, then we should expect his shaping power to be apparent in his use of music as well as in his powers of language or characterization. Music was only one tool in his workshop, but it was effective, efficient, and popular. On a stage bare, for the most part, of scenery and lighting effects, the aural appeals of language and music were of prime importance. The world knows what Shakespeare accomplished with the art of language: it is my hope that this study may reveal, even if inadequately, some of what he accomplished with the art of music.

Appendix

Appendices I–V—Military and Ceremonious Music

Field signals and ceremonious military music of the kinds called for in Shakespeare's plays are rather rare. The field signals for the cavalry trumpet, however, may be found in the second part of Marin Mersenne's *Traité de l'Harmonie Vniverselle* ... (1627) and in the recent edition of a portion of his works entitled *Harmonie Universelle: The Books on Instruments* (*1635*) (1957). The notation of the various calls shown in Appendix I, however, is not taken from either of these two sources but from a manuscript in the British Museum—Brit. Mus. Harl. MS 6461, fols. 58^b and 59—which was copied from Mersenne's original edition, I believe, around the middle of the seventeenth century. I present the MS copy here because it contains descriptive titles for each call—descriptions not found in the published editions—in a garbled mixture of Latin, French, and Greek. In the notation below, I give the original Latin and French of the MS (the Greek was too obscure for trustworthy transcription) and, in brackets, the translations.

Distinct from the field signals are the various kinds of ceremonial and processional music, such as the drum march Edward Naylor reprinted from Sir John Hawkins' *A General History of the Science and Practise of Music*. This march is apparently a very old one revived by Prince Henry in 1610. The Royal Warrant quoted by Hawkins describes the march as being grave and majestic. Naylor reproduced it in *Shakespeare and Music* ..., p. 201. I reproduce it below (Appendix II) for the convenience of the reader.

Another type of ceremonious military music are the three "posture" tunes shown in Appendix III. The music, to be played by drum and fife, was used to accompany a military drill performed as a part of a martial pageant given Oct. 18, 1638, by "Certain Gentlemen of the Artillery Garden London." The description of the pageant, and the music notation, was reported by William Bariffe in *Mars, his Trivmph* (1639). Bariffe used the terms "tune" and "almain" as synonyms, referring to the "Posture Almayne," p. 17, and to "the

Almaine tune for the *motions*," p. 18. Obviously, the almain, usually described as a kind of dance music, is in this case associated with the military as a march. The notation of the "posture" tunes was republished in M. J. D. Cockle, *A Bibliography of English Military Books . . .*, but since Cockle's book is almost as rare as the work by Bariffe, I reproduce the tunes below.

The three ceremonious types of music most frequently called for by the stage directions in Elizabethan plays are the flourish, the sennet, and the tucket. Unfortunately, no notation for any of these can clearly be ascribed to Renaissance England. I have attempted to supply a sennet by transcribing Thomas Morley's "De la Tromba Pauin" for instruments which usually played, I surmise, the sennets —trumpets, sackbut, and drum. Morley called his piece a "trumpet pavan" or "trumpet march," but he scored his version for a broken consort as he did all the other compositions in *The First Booke of Consort Lessons . . .* (1599, 1611). I have taken the liberty of re-scoring the pavan as a trumpet march which meets all of the dramatic and musical requirements of the sennet. The complete score is given below in Appendix IV.A–E.

Another musical work which I believe is a sennet is a march called "The Parlement." The work is apparently a redaction for lute of a trumpet march used on ceremonious or state occasions. The music appears in lute tablature in Folger Shakespeare Library MS 1610.1, which is a collection of lute music made, I would guess, between 1590 and 1625. The "parlement" contains in its ninth and tenth measures the same trumpet figure used by Morley in his "De la Tromba Pauin." The modern notation for "The Parlement" is given below in Appendix V.

The fact that the trumpet figure mentioned above appears in two distinct compositions of, roughly, the same day suggests that the figure was well known by Elizabethans. And, since Morley as-cribed it to trumpets, I believe that the musical figure as it appears in measures 2–8 of the last strain of the "De la Tromba Pauin" may have been a flourish. This figure is shown between brackets in Appendix IV.A. The tucket, also shown in Appendix IV.A., is simply a part of the flourish above, since, in its dramatic use, the tucket should be brief.

APPENDIX I.

1. Le entree (Entry)

2. Bouteselle ad Ephippia (Boots and Saddles?)

3. Ad ephima aliter (Advance)

4. Ascento in equos indicatur a cheval (Mount Horses)

5. Le simple cavalquot. A la estandart (Procession to the Standard)

6. Le simple cavalkot cantus pomposus (Solemn Procession)

7. Le dobl cavalyr aliter (Double Processional)

8. La charg conflictus (The Charge to Battle)

9. La chamade alui conflictus (The Parley after the Battle)

La chamade (The Parley)

continued . . .

APPENDIX I. (cont.)

10. La Retraite Receptui Cavitur (Retreat—Rein in Horses)

11. La quet vigilid (Recall of the Watch)

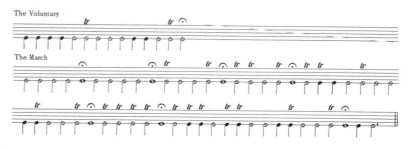

APPENDIX II.

The Voluntary

The March

Postures and Motions

The $\left\{ \begin{array}{l} \text{Muskettiers ftand refted,} \\ \\ \text{Pikes ordered.} \end{array} \right.$

The Pofture tune.   .)

The poftures divided into 3. to make them fit
to keep time with the Drum and Phife.

1
POISE YOUR MUSKETS.

$\left\{ \begin{array}{l} \end{array} \right.$ 1 *Turn the butt ends of your Muskets to the right.*
1 $\left\{ \begin{array}{l} \end{array} \right.$ 2 *Raife up your Muskets with the help of your*
       Refts.
     3 *Sever Muskets and Refts and Poife.*

2
SHOULDER YOUR MUSKETS.

   $\left\{ \begin{array}{l} \end{array} \right.$ 1 *Slip your left hands down from the heads of your*
       Refts.
2 $\left\{ \begin{array}{l} \end{array} \right.$ 2 *Bring Muskets and Refts before you, placing your*
       Refts croffe the ftocks of your Muskets.
     3 *Lay your Muskets properly on your fhoulders.*

Vnfhoulder

18   FACINGS.

begin the *Almaine* tune for the *motions* : and the second time the Tune is played over, they begun their motions as followeth.

The Tune for the Motions.

FACINGS.

1.

The figures of number in the margent declare how many times the whole tune is played over throughout the exercise,

Face all to the right, and march 6 paces.

With the end of the first streyne, all face to the Front againe, and order Armes.

Face all to the left and march 4 paces.

This is to bring you into the midst of the Hall : then face to the Front, and order as before with the close of the second streyne.

Face all to the right about and march sixe paces.

2.

These foure facings intire.

In this motion you are to keepe your Aspects to the Reere, and order Armes with the Close of the first streyne.

Reducement.

Face

of the Musket.

23
Give fire Breſt high.

23 {
1 *Levell your Muskets on yonr Reſts.*
2 *Set the butt-ends to your ſhoulders.*
3 *Draw your Trickers and give fire.*

24
Vncock your Matches.

24 {
1 *Mount the muzels of your Muskets.*
2 *Vncock and return your Matches.*
3 *Shut your Pans.*

Having thus performed their *poſtures*, the *Phife* and *Drum* play the *falling of Tune* ; in the interim whereof the *Muskettiers* perform their *Saluting poſture*, and *wheel* of by *diviſion*, two to the *right*, and two to the *left* , placing themſelves in the *reere* of the *Pikes*.

After this maner the Tune is playd *once over* to every R*ank*.

The Falling of Tune.   )

APPENDIX IV.A.

De la Tromba Pauin (Sennet)

APPENDIX IV.B.

De la Tromba Pauin (Sennet)

APPENDIX IV.C.
De la Tromba Pauin (Sennet)

APPENDIX IV.D.

De la Tromba Pauin (Sennet)

APPENDIX IV.E.

De la Tromba Pauin (Sennet)

APPENDIX V.
The Parlement

Appendix VI—Hunting Music

"The measures of blowing . . ." shown here are taken from George Turberville's *The Noble Arte of Venerie or Hunting . . . (1575)*. Originally intended for the hunting horn, the signals consist of one note blown in various rhythmical patterns. The tempo is indicated by the number of "windes" or breaths required for each group of notes; that is, the notes must be sounded quickly and sharply.

APPENDIX VI.A.

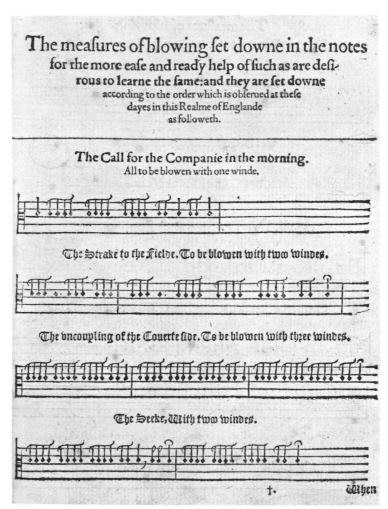

The meafures of blowing fet downe in the notes for the more eafe and ready help of fuch as are defirous to learne the fame: and they are fet downe according to the order which is obferued at thefe dayes in this Realme of Englande as followeth.

The Call for the Companie in the morning.
All to be blowen with one winde.

The Strake to the Fielde. To be blowen with two windes.

The vncoupling of the Couertfide. To be blowen with three windes.

The Seeke, With two windes.

APPENDIX VI.B.

The measures of blovving.

APPENDIX VI.C.

The measures of blovving.

When the Foxe is not couerable, to call away.

The death of a Foxe, eyther in fielde oz couert. With thzee windes.

And the Rechate vpon it.

Foure sundzie calls foz a Keeper, in Parke, Chase, oz Foxrest.

The death of a Deare with Bowe, oz Greyhoundes.

The death of a Bucke with houndes. With two windes.

t.ij.   The

The measures of blovving.

The pryse of an Harte Royall. With three windes.

This to be blowen thrice with three seuerall windes,

and the Rechate vpon it.

I Strake of nyne, to drawe home the companie. With two windes.

To blowe for the Terryers at an earth. With two windes.

APPENDIX VII.

Appendix VII—"The Hobby Horse is Forgot"

This song (cantus only) is reproduced below because it may have been quoted from by Hamlet (see chap. 8). Of course, his quotation may be a cliché used also in the song, but the references to William Kemp provide a link with Shakespeare and also refer to Kemp's tour of the Continent after leaving the Lord Chamberlain's Men. Some implications of the song, and a reproduction of the text and music, are presented by W. Ringler's "The Hobby Horse is Forgot." The song was found by Ringler in Thomas Weelkes' "Ayres or phantasticke spirites made by Master Thomas weelkes, of 3 parts" (1608), New York Public Library MS Drexel 4300.

Bibliography

(Note: Most of the following entries are supplementary to the first two books of this series: *Shakespeare's Use of Music: . . . Seven Comedies* and *Shakespeare's Use of Music: The Final Comedies.*)

Agrippa, H. *Of the Vanitie and vncertuintie of Artes and Sciences.* London: Henry Wykes, 1569.

Arber, E., ed. *A Transcript of the Company of Stationers of London, 1554–1640 A.D.* 3 vols. London: privately printed, 1876.

Auden, W. "Music in Shakespeare." In *The Dyer's Hand and Other Essays.* New York: Random House, 1962.

Bacon, F. *The Works of Francis Bacon, Lord Chancellor of England.* Edited by B. Montagu. 3 vols. Philadelphia: A. Hart, Late Carey & Hart, 1853.

Ballads from Manuscripts. London: Ballad Society, 1868–1873.

Bannatyne, G. *The Bannatyne Manuscript (1568).* 4 vols. N.p.: Hunterian Club, 1896.

Bariffe, W. *Mars, his Trivmph.* London: Ralph Mab, 1639.

Barnes, J. *The Praise of Musick.* Oxenford: Joseph Barnes, 1586.

Bartlett, J. *A Booke of Ayres With a Triplicitie of Musicke.* London: John Browne, 1606. Huntington Library microfilm.

Baskervill, C. *The Elizabethan Jig and Related Song Drama.* Chicago: University of Chicago Press, 1929.

—————. "English Songs on the Night Visit." *PMLA* 36:565–614.

Beaumont, F., and Fletcher, J. *The Works of Francis Beaumont and John Fletcher.* Edited by A. Waller. 10 vols. Cambridge: University Press, 1907.

Berry, F. *The Shakespeare Inset.* London: Routledge & Kegan Paul, 1965.

Bethell, S. *Shakespeare and the Popular Dramatic Tradition.* Durham, N.C.: Duke University Press, 1944.

Bibliotheca Lindesiana: Catalogue of a Collection of English Ballads of the XVIIth and XVIIIth Centuries. Aberdeen: Aberdeen University Press, 1890.

Bossewell, J. *Workes of armorie, devyded into three bookes, entituled, the concordes of armorie, the armorie of honor, and coates and creastes.* London: n.p., 1572.

Brennecke, E. " 'Nay, That's Not Next!' The Significance of Desdemona's 'Willow Song.' " *Shakespeare Quarterly* 4:35–38.

Bronson, B. *The Traditional Tunes of the Child Ballads.* Vol. 1. Princeton, N.J.: Princeton University Press, 1959.

Brown, J. "An Elizabethan Song-Cycle." *The Cornhill Magazine* (May 1920), pp. 572–79.

—————. "Some Elizabethan Lyrics." *The Cornhill Magazine* (Sept. 1921), pp. 285–96.

Bunten, A. "Some Old Scottish Lute Music." *The Scottish Musical Magazine* 3:185–87.

Burney, C. *A General History of Music.* London: n.p., 1776–1789.

Byler, A. *Italian Currents in the Popular Music of England in the Sixteenth Century.* Microfilm of doctoral dissertation no. 1709, University of Chicago Library, 1952.

(287)

Byrd, W. *The Collected Works of William Byrd.* Edited by E. Fellowes. Vol. 18. London: Stainer & Bell, 1950.

C., T. *Laugh and lie downe: or, The worldes Folly.* London: Jeffrey Chorlton, 1605.

Camp, T. "Shakespeare's *Henry IV Part I*, and the Ballad 'Chevy Chase.' " *Notes & Queries* 13:131–32.

Carmel, Sister J. "New Light on Robert Johnson, the King's Musician." *Shakespeare Quarterly* 17:233–35.

Carter, J. *English Dramatic Music to the 17th Century and Its Availability for Modern Productions.* Ph.D. dissertation, Stanford University, 1956. University Microfilms no. 16,016.

Cassirer, E. *The Platonic Renaissance in England.* Translated by J. Pettegrove. Austin: University of Texas Press, 1953.

Chambers, E. *The Elizabethan Stage.* 4 vols. Oxford: Clarendon Press, 1945.
_____. *The Medieval Stage.* 2 vols. Oxford: Clarendon Press, 1903.
_____. *William Shakespeare: A Study of Facts and Problems.* 2 vols. Oxford: Clarendon Press, 1930.

Chappell, W., ed. *Popular Music of the Olden Time.* 2 vols. London: Cramer, Beale and Chappell, [1855–1859].
_____, ed. *The Roxburghe Ballads.* Hertford: Stephen Austin and Sons, 1888.

Child, J., ed. *English and Scottish Ballads.* 8 vols. London: Sampson Low, Son, & Co., 1861.

Clark, A., ed. *The Shirburn Ballads 1585–1616.* Oxford: Clarendon Press, 1907.

Clemen, W. "Shakespeare und die Musik." *Shakespeare Jahrbuch* 102:30–48.

Cockle, M. *A Bibliography of English Military Books up to 1642 and of Contemporary Foreign Works.* London: Simpkin, Marshall, Hamilton, Kent & Co., 1900.

Collier, J. *Broadside Black-letter Ballads, Printed in the Sixteenth and Seventeenth Centuries; Chiefly in the Possession of J. Payne Collier.* N.p.: privately printed by Thomas Richards, 1868.

Cooper, T. *The Mystery of Witchcraft.* London: Nicholas Okes, 1617.

Copley, J. "John Audelay's Carols and Music." *English Studies* 39:207–12.
_____. "Two Notes on Early English Carols." *Notes & Queries* 5:239–40.

Coulanges, F. de. *The Ancient City.* Garden City, N.Y.: Doubleday Anchor Books, 1956.

Coverdale, (Bishop) M. *Certain most godly, fruitful, and comfortable letters.* London: John Day, 1564.

Cowling, G. *Music on the Shakespearian Stage.* Cambridge: University Press, 1913.

Craig, H. *The Enchanted Glass: The Elizabethan Mind in Literature.* Oxford: Blackwell, 1950.

Cutts, J. "A Bodleian Song-book: Don. C. 57." *Music & Letters* 34:192–211.
_____. "Dametas' Song in Sidney's Arcadia." *Renaissance News* 11:183–88.
_____. "Falstaff's 'Heaunlie Iewel.' Incidental Music for *The Merry Wives of Windsor*." *Shakespeare Quarterly* 11:89–92.
_____. "Henry Shirley's 'The Martyred Soldier.' " *Renaissance News* 12:251–53.
_____. "Jacobean Masque and Stage Music." *Music & Letters* 35:185–200.
_____. " 'Mris. Elizabeth Davenant 1624' Christ Church MS. Mus. 87." *Review of English Studies* 10:26–37.
_____. "Music and the Mad Lover." *Studies in the Renaissance.* Publications of the Renaissance Society of America, no. 8. Pp. 236–48.
_____. *La Musique de Scène de la Troupe de Shakespeare. The King's*

Men sous le règne de Jacques Ier. Paris: Éditions du Centre Nationale de la Recherche Scientifique, 1959.
_____. "New Findings with Regard to the 1624 Protection Lists." *Shakespeare Survey* 19:101–7.
_____. "Notes on *Othello*." *Notes & Queries* 6:251–52.
_____. "The Original Music of Middleton's 'The Witch.'" *Shakespeare Quarterly* 7:203–9.
_____. "The Original Music of a Song in *2 Henry IV*." *Shakespeare Quarterly* 7:385–93.
_____. "Peele's 'Hunting of Cupid.'" *Studies in the Renaissance*. Publications of the Renaissance Society of America, no. 5. Pp. 121–29.
_____. "Pericles' 'Most Heauenly Musicke.'" *Notes & Queries* 7:172–74.
_____. "A Reconsideration of the 'Willow Song.'" *Journal of the American Musicological Society* 10:14–24.
_____. "Robert Johnson: King's Musician in His Majesty's Public Entertainment." *Music & Letters* 36:110–25.
_____. "Seventeenth-Century Lyrics." *Musica Disciplina* 10:142–209.
_____. "Shakespeare's Song and Masque Hand in *Henry VIII*." *Shakespeare Jahrbuch* 99:184–95.
_____. "'Speak—Demand—We'll Answer': Hecat(e) and 'The *Other* Three Witches.'" *Shakespeare Jahrbuch* 96:173–76.
_____. "Two Hitherto Unpublished Settings of Sonnets from 'The Passionate Pilgrime.'" *Shakespeare Quarterly* 9:588–94.
_____. "Two Jacobean Theatre Songs." *Music & Letters* 33:333–34.
_____. "An Unpublished Contemporary Setting of a Shakespeare Song." *Shakespeare Survey* 9:86–89.
_____. "Volpone's Song: A Note on the Source and Jonson's Translation." *Notes & Queries* 5:217–19.
_____. "Who Wrote the Hecate-Scene?" *Shakespeare Jahrbuch* 94:200–202.
Davies, Sir J. *Orchestra or a Poem of Dancing*. Edited by E. Tillyard. London: Chatto & Windus, 1947.
DeBanke, C. *Shakespearean Stage Production: Then and Now*. New York: McGraw-Hill Book Co., 1953.
Dekker, T. *The Magnificent Entertainment: Given to King Iames*. London: Tho. Man the yonger, 1604.
_____. *The Non-Dramatic Works of Thomas Dekker*. Edited by A. Grosart. 4 vols. London: Hazell, Watson, and Viney, 1885.
Deloney, T. *The Works of Thomas Deloney*. Edited by F. Mann. Oxford: Clarendon Press, 1912.
Dickinson, A. "Shakespeare in Music." *Durham University Journal* 25:113–22.
Dodsley, R. *A Select Collection of Old English Plays* (*1744*). Edited by W. Hazlitt. 15 vols. London: Reeves and Turner, 1874.
Donington, R. "La Musica y Shakespeare." *Sur* (1964), pp. 82–85.
Doss, E. "The Unity of Play and Song in Shakespeare." Ph.D. dissertation, University of Arkansas, 1958.
Dowland, J. *Lachrimae, or Seaven Teares*. London: John Windet, 1606. Huntington Library microfilm.
Dowland, R. *A Musicall Banquet*. London: Thomas Adams, 1610.
_____. *Varietie of Lute-lessons: ... Whereunto is annexed certaine Obseruations belonging to Lute-playing: By Iohn Baptisto Besardo of Visonti. Also a short Treatise thereunto appertayning: By Iohn Douland Batcheler of Musicke*. London: Thomas Adams, 1610. Huntington Library microfilm.
Duckles, V. "The English Musical Elegy in the Late Renaissance." In *Aspects*

of Medieval and Renaissance Music: A Birthday Offering to Gustave Reese,
edited by J. LaRue. New York: W. W. Norton, 1966.

Dyboski, R., ed. *Songs, Carols, and Other Miscellaneous Poems, from the Balliol MS. 354, Richard Hill's Common-place-Book.* London: Kegan Paul, Trench, Trubner & Co., 1907.

Ebsworth, J., ed. *Bagford Ballads.* 2 vols. Hertford: Ballad Society, 1878.

Edwards, R. *The Dramatic Writings of Richard Edwards, Thomas Norton and Thomas Sackville.* Edited by J. Farmer. London: Early English Drama Society, 1906.

Elson, L. *Shakespeare in Music.* London: David Nutt, 1901.

Evans, P. "Some Reflections on the Origin of the Trope." *Journal of the American Musicological Society* 14:119–30.

Fantini, G. *Modo per imparare a sonare di tromba . . . Francoforte 1638.* Milan: Bollettino Bibliografico Musicale, 1934. Facsimile.

Farmer, J., ed. *Anonymous Plays, Series 3.* London: Early English Drama Society, 1906.

————, ed. *Six Anonymous Plays, Series 2.* London: Early English Drama Society, 1906.

Finney, G. "Ecstasy and Music in Seventeenth-Century England." *Journal of the History of Ideas* 8:153–86.

————. *Music: The Breath of Life.* The Centennial Review of Arts & Sciences, Michigan State University, no. 4. Pp. 179–205.

————. *Musical Backgrounds for English Literature: 1580–1650.* New Brunswick, N.J.: Rutgers University Press, 1962.

————. "A World of Instruments." *Journal of English Literary History* 20 (1953):87–120.

The Fitzwilliam Virginal Book. Edited by J. Fuller-Maitland and W. Squire. Leipzig; reprinted, Ann Arbor, Mich., 1949.

Flatter, R. " 'The Other Three Witches,' and Their Songs." *Shakespeare Jahrbuch* 95:225–37.

————. "Professor Flatter's Reply." *Shakespeare Jahrbuch* 96:192–93.

————. "Who Wrote the Hecate-Scene?" *Shakespeare Jahrbuch* 93:206–10.

Forbes, J. *Cantus, Songs and Fancies.* Aberdeen: John Forbes, 1666.

————. *Cantus, Songs and Fancies.* 3rd ed. Aberdeen: John Forbes, 1682.

Ford, B., ed. *The Age of Chaucer.* Aylesbury: Hazell, Watson, and Viney, 1954.

Foxe, J. *Actes and Monuments . . . An. 1583. Mens. Octobr.* Folger Shakespeare Library copy.

Fraunce, A. *The Arcadian Rhetorike 1588.* Edited by E. Seaton. Oxford: Luttrell Society, 1950.

Friedman, A. "The Late Mediaeval Ballade and the Origin of Broadside Balladry." *Medium Ævum* 27:95–110.

Fuller-Maitland, J. *English Carols of the Fifteenth Century: From a MS. Roll in the Library of Trinity College, Cambridge.* New York: Charles Scribner's Sons, 1891.

Galpin, F. *Old English Instruments of Music: Their History and Character.* London: Methuen & Co., 1911.

Gamble, J. *Ayres and Dialogues.* London: Humphrey Mosley, 1657.

Gibbon, J. *Melody and the Lyric from Chaucer to the Cavaliers.* London: J. M. Dent & Sons, 1930.

Gombosi, O. *The Cultural and Folkloristic Background of the Folia.* Papers of the American Musicological Society (1940), pp. 88–95.

————. "Some Musical Aspects of the English Court Masque." *Journal of the American Musicological Society* 1:3–19.

Granville-Barker, H. *Prefaces to Shakespeare*. 2 vols. Princeton, N.J.: Princeton University Press, 1946–1947.

Graves, T. "The 'Act Time' in Elizabethan Theatres." *Studies in Philology* 12:103–34.

Greene, R., ed. *The Early English Carols*. Oxford: Clarendon Press, 1935.

Greenfield, T. "Nonvocal Music: Added Dimension in Five Shakespeare Plays." In *Pacific Coast Studies in Shakespeare*, edited by W. McNeir and T. Greenfield, pp. 106–21. Eugene: University of Oregon Books, 1966.

Grove's Dictionary of Music and Musicians. Edited by E. Blom. 10 vols. New York: St. Martin's Press, 1955.

Halliday, F. *A Shakespeare Companion 1550–1950*. New York: Funk & Wagnalls Co., 1952.

Halliwell, J., ed. *A Catalogue of an Unique Collection of Ancient English Broadside Ballads*. London: John Russell Smith, 1856.

_____, ed. *A Collection of Seventy-nine Black-Letter Ballads and Broadsides, Printed in the Reign of Queen Elizabeth between the Years 1559 and 1597*. London: Joseph Lilly, 1867.

Harries, F. *The Welsh Elizabethans*. Pontypridd: Glamorgan County Times Printing and Publishing Offices, 1924.

Hartnoll, P., ed. *Shakespeare in Music*. New York: St. Martin's Press, 1964.

Herbert, T. "Shakespeare Announces a Ghost." *Shakespeare Quarterly* 1:247–54.

Holborne, A. *Pavans, Galliards, Almains, and Other Short Aeirs*. London: William Barley, 1599. Huntington Library microfilm.

Holinshed, R. *The Third volume of Chronicles . . . First compiled by Raphael Holinshed, and by him extended to the year 1577. Now newlie recognised, augmented . . . to the year 1586*. [1587]. Folger Shakespeare Library copy.

Hollander, J. *The Untuning of the Sky: Ideas of Music in English Poetry 1500–1700*. Princeton, N.J.: Princeton University Press, 1961.

Hosley, R. "Was There a Music-Room in Shakespeare's Globe?" *Shakespeare Survey* 13:113–23.

Hotson, I. *Shakespeare's Motley*. New York: Oxford University Press, 1952.

Huizinga, J. *The Waning of the Middle Ages: A Study of the Forms of Life, Thought and Art in France and the Netherlands in the XIVth and XVth Centuries*. Garden City, N.Y.: Doubleday & Co., 1954.

Hunt, L. *Leigh Hunt's Dramatic Criticism 1808–1831*. Edited by L. and C. Houtchens. New York: Columbia University Press, 1949.

Husmann, H. "Sequenz and Prosa." *Annales musicologiques* 2:61–91.

Ingram, R. "*Hamlet, Othello*, and *King Lear*: Music and Tragedy." *Shakespeare Jahrbuch* 100:159–72.

_____. "Musical Pauses and the Vision Scenes in Shakespeare's Last Plays." In *Pacific Coast Studies in Shakespeare*, edited by W. McNeir and T. Greenfield, pp. 234–47. Eugene: University of Oregon Books, 1966.

Jackson, K. *Studies in Early Celtic Nature Poetry*. Cambridge: University Press, 1935.

Jacobean Consort Music. Edited by T. Dart and W. Coates. In *Musica Britannica*, vol. 9. London: Stainer and Bell, 1962.

Jones, R. *A Gorgeous Gallery of Gallant Inventions (1578)*. Edited by H. Rollins. Cambridge, Mass.: Harvard University Press, 1926.

Jonson, B. *Ben Jonson*. Edited by C. Herford and P. Simpson. 11 vols. Oxford: Clarendon Press, 1925–1952.

_____. *The Masque of Queenes*. London: The King's Printers, 1930.

Jorgensen, P. *Shakespeare's Military World*. Berkeley: University of California Press, 1956.

Kamphuyzen, D. *Stichtelyke Rymen, Om te lezen of te zingen.* Amsterdam: de Wed. P. Arentsz, 1690.

Kemp, W. *Kemps nine daies wonder.* London: E. A., 1600.

Kiefer, H. "Elizabethan Attitudes toward Music in Shakespeare's Plays." *Dissertation Abstracts* (Columbia University) 22:1177–78.

Knight, G. *The Shakespearian Tempest: With a Chart of Shakespeare's Dramatic Universe.* London: Methuen & Co., 1953.

Lafontaine, H., ed. *The King's Musick: A Transcript of Records Relating to Music and Musicians 1460–1700.* London: Novello and Co., 1909.

LaRue, J., ed. *Aspects of Medieval and Renaissance Music: A Birthday Offering to Gustave Reese.* New York: W. W. Norton, 1966.

Lassus, O. de. *Recveil Dv Mellange D'Orlande de Lassvs . . . Svperivs.* London: Thomas Vatrouller, 1570.

Lavater, L. *Of Ghosts and Spirites Walking by Night. 1572.* Edited by J. Wilson and M. Yardley. Oxford: University Press, 1929.

Lawes, H. *Ayres and Dialogues . . . The First Booke.* London: John Playford, 1653.

Lawrence, W. (J.). "Notes on a Collection of Masque Music." *Music & Letters* 3 (Jan. 1922), pp. 49–58.

Lawrence, W. (W.). *Shakespeare's Problem Comedies.* New York: Macmillan Co., 1931.

————. *Shakespeare's Workshop.* Boston: Houghton Mifflin Co., 1928.

LeComte, E. "Ophelia's 'Bonny Sweet Robin.'" *PMLA* 75:480.

Legouis, É. *The Bacchic Element in Shakespeare's Plays.* Proceedings of the British Academy, 1926.

Levin, H. "The Antic Disposition." *Shakespeare Jahrbuch* 94:175–90.

Long, J. "Music for a Song in Edwards' *Damon and Pithias.*" *Music & Letters* 48:247–50.

————, ed. *Music in English Renaissance Drama.* Lexington: University of Kentucky Press, 1968.

————. *Shakespeare's Use of Music: The Final Comedies.* Gainesville: University of Florida Press, 1961.

————. *Shakespeare's Use of Music: A Study of the Music and Its Performance in the Original Production of Seven Comedies.* Gainesville: University of Florida Press, 1955.

————. "Sneak's 'Noyse' Heard Again?" *Musical Quarterly* 44:76–81.

Lovejoy, A. *The Great Chain of Being; A study of the history of an idea.* Cambridge, Mass.: Harvard University Press, 1936.

Lumsden, D. "The Sources of English Lute Music (1540–1620)." *The Galpin Society Journal* 6:14–22.

McCullen, J. "The Functions of Songs Aroused by Madness in Elizabethan Drama." In *A Tribute to George Coffin Taylor: Studies and Essays, Chiefly Elizabethan, by His Students and Friends.* Chapel Hill: University of North Carolina Press, 1952.

Major, J. "The Moralization of the Dance in Elyot's 'Gouernour.'" *Studies in the Renaissance.* Publications of the Renaissance Society of America, no. 5. Pp. 27–36.

Manifold, J. *The Music in English Drama from Shakespeare to Purcell.* London: Rockliff Publishing Corp., 1956.

Markham, F. *Fiue Decades of Epistles of Warre.* London: Augustine Matthewes, 1622.

Medieval Carols. Edited by J. Stevens. In *Musica Britannica,* vol. 4. London: Stainer and Bell, 1958.

Melvill Book of Roundels, The. Edited by G. Bantock and H. Anderton. London: Roxburghe Club, 1916.

Mersenne, M. *Harmonie Universelle: The Books on Instruments* (*1635*). Translated by R. Chapman. The Hague: Martinus Nijhoff, 1957.

_____. *Traité de l'Harmonie Vniverselle ... Par le sieur de Sermes*. Paris: Gvillavme Bavdry, 1627.

Middleton, T. *The Witch*. Edited by W. Greg. Oxford: Malone Society Reprints, Oxford University Press, 1948 (1950).

Mitchell, A., ed. *A Compendious Book of Godly and Spiritual Songs Commonly Known as 'The Gude and Godlie Ballatis' Reprinted from the Edition of 1567*. London: William Blackwood and Sons, 1897.

Moore, A. *The Secular Lyric in Middle English*. Lexington: University of Kentucky Press, 1951.

Moore, J. "The Songs of the Public Theaters in the Time of Shakespeare." *Journal of English and Germanic Philology* 28:166–202.

Moore, R. "The Music to *Macbeth*." *Musical Quarterly* 47:22–40.

More, Sir T. *A dyaloge of Sir Thomas More knyghte ... (1529)*. Folger Shakespeare Library copy.

Morley, T. *The First Book of Consort Lessons, 1599 & 1611*. Reconstructed and edited by S. Beck. New York: New York Public Library Music Publications, 1959.

_____. *The First Booke of Consort Lessons*. London: William Barley, 1599.

_____. *The First Booke of Consort Lessons ... Collected by Thomas Morley, Gentleman, and now newly corrected and inlarged*. London: John Browne, 1611.

_____. *A Plain and Easy Introduction to Practical Music*. Edited by R. Harman. New York: W. W. Norton & Co., 1952.

Morris, H. "Ophelia's 'Bonny Sweet Robin.'" *PMLA* 63:601–3.

The Mulliner Book. Edited by D. Stevens. In *Musica Britannica*, vol. 1. London: Stainer & Bell, 1954.

Musica: B. M. Additional MS. 14905 (also known by the title "Musica neu Beroriaeth"). Cardiff: University of Wales Press Board, 1936.

Musique et Poesie au XVe siècle. Edited by J. Jacquot. Paris: Éditions du Centre Nationale de la Recherche Scientifique, 1954.

Musique Instrumentale de la Renaissance, La. Edited by J. Jacquot. Paris: Éditions du Centre Nationale de la Recherche Scientifique, 1955.

Nashe, T. *The Works of Thomas Nashe*. Edited by R. McKerrow and F. Wilson. 4 vols. Oxford: Basil Blackwell, 1958.

Naylor, E. *Shakespeare and Music, with Illustrations from the Music of the 16th and 17th Centuries*. New York: E. P. Dutton and Co., 1931.

Nicholson, B. "Willow for the Forsaken." *Notes & Queries* 6:306.

Noble, R. *Shakespeare's Use of Song, with the Text of the Principal Songs*. London: Humphrey Milford, 1923.

Norton, T. *The Dramatic Writings of Richard Edwards, Thomas Norton, and Thomas Sackville*. Edited by J. Farmer. London: Early English Drama Society, 1906.

Nosworthy, J. "The Hecate Scenes in *Macbeth*." *Review of English Studies* 24:138.

Parry, J. *The Welsh Harper. . . .* London: D'Almaine and Co., 1839.

Patrick, J. "The Problem of Ophelia." In *Studies in Shakespeare*, edited by A. Matthews and C. Emery, pp. 139–44. Coral Gables, Fla.: University of Miami Press, 1953.

Paul, H. *The Royal Play of Macbeth: When, Why, and How It Was Written by Shakespeare*. New York: Macmillan Co., 1950.

Percy, T. *Bishop Percy's Folio Manuscript. Ballads and Romances*. Edited by F. Furnivall and J. Hales. 3 vols. London: N. Trübner & Co., 1867.

_____. *The Percy Letters*. Edited by D. Smith and C. Brooks (includes

The Correspondence of Thomas Percy and Evan Evans. Edited by A. Lewis. Vol. 5). Baton Rouge: Louisiana State University Press, 1957.

──────. *Reliques of Ancient English Poetry, Consisting of Old Heroic Ballads, Songs, and Other Pieces of Our Earlier Poets, Together with some Few of Later Date.* Edited by H. Wheatley. 3 vols. London: Bickers and Son, 1876.

Percy Society. *Early English Poetry, Ballads, and Popular Literature of the Middle Ages* (includes Johnson, R. *The Crown Garland of Golden Roses, 1612.* Vol. 6; and Johnson, R. *The Crown Garland of Golden Roses, 1659.* Vol. 15). London: Percy Society, 1845.

Playford, J. *The English Dancing Master.* London: Thomas Harper, 1651. Huntington Library microfilm.

──────. *The English Dancing Master.* London: Mellor, 1933.

──────. *Musick's Delight on the Cithren . . . By John Playford Philo-Musicae.* London: W. G., 1666.

──────. *Musicks Recreation on the Viol, Lyra-way.* London: John Playford, 1669.

Plutarch. *Plutarch's Lives of the Noble Grecians and Romans Englished by Sir Thomas North Anno 1579.* 7 vols. London: David Nutt, 1896.

Prager, L. "The Clown in *Othello.*" *Shakespeare Quarterly* 9:94–96.

Priestman, B. "Music for Shakespeare—Some Practical Problems." *Music & Letters* 45:141–45.

Provost, F. "On Justice and the Music in *Richard II* and *King Lear.*" *Annuale Mediaevale*, Duquesne Studies, no. 2. Pp. 55–71.

Reed, E. *Songs from the British Drama.* New Haven, Conn.: Yale University Press, 1925.

Reliquiae Antiquae. Scraps from Ancient Manuscripts Illustrating Chiefly Early English Literature and the English Language. Edited by T. Wright and J. Halliwell. 2 vols. London: William Pickering, 1841–1843.

Richey, D. "The Dance in *Henry VIII*: a Production Problem." *Bulletin of Furman University*, vol. 35, no. 3, pp. 1–11.

Ringler, W. "The Hobby Horse is Forgot." *Shakespeare Quarterly* 4:484.

Ritson, J. *Ancient Songs, from the Time of King Henry the Third, to the Revolution.* London: J. Johnson, 1790.

──────. *A Select Collection of English Songs.* London: J. Johnson, 1783.

Robinson, C. et al. *A Handful of Pleasant Delights (1584).* Edited by H. Rollins. Cambridge, Mass.: Harvard University Press, 1924.

Rollins, H. "An Analytical Index to the Ballad-Entries (1557–1709) in the Registers of the Company of Stationers of London." *Studies in Philology* 21:1–324.

──────. " 'King Lear' and the Ballad of 'John Careless.' " *Modern Language Review* 15:87–89.

──────, ed. *Old English Ballads 1553–1625.* Cambridge: University Press, 1920.

──────. *The Pack of Autolycus: Or Strange and Terrible News . . . as told in Broadside Ballads of the Years 1624–1693.* Cambridge, Mass.: Harvard University Press, 1927.

──────, ed. *The Pepys Ballads.* 8 vols. Cambridge, Mass.: Harvard University Press, 1929.

──────, ed. *A Pepysian Garland: Black-Letter Broadside Ballads of the Years 1595–1639.* Cambridge: University Press, 1922.

Ross, L. "Shakespeare's 'Dull Clown' and Symbolic Music." *Shakespeare Quarterly* 17:107–28.

Routley, E. *The English Carol.* London: Herbert Jenkins, 1958.

Sabol, A. "A Newly Discovered Contemporary Song Setting for Jonson's *Cynthia's Revels.*" *Notes & Queries* 5:384–85.

_____. "Ravenscroft's 'Melismata' and the Children of Paul's." *Renaissance News* 12:3–9.

_____, ed. *Songs and Dances for the Stuart Masque: An Edition of Sixty-three Items of Music for the English Court Masque from 1604 to 1641.* Providence, R.I.: Brown University Press, 1959.

_____. "Two Songs with Accompaniment for an Elizabethan Choirboy Play." *Studies in the Renaissance.* Publications of the Renaissance Society of America, no. 5. Pp. 145–59.

Sackville, T. *The Dramatic Writings of Richard Edwards, Thomas Norton, and Thomas Sackville.* Edited by J. Farmer. London: Early English Drama Society, 1906.

Sargent, H., and Kittredge, G., eds. *English and Scottish Popular Ballads* (a revision of J. Child's *English and Scottish Ballads*). 2 vols. Boston: Houghton Mifflin Co., 1904.

Seng, P. "The Dramatic Function of the Songs in Shakespeare's Plays." Ph.D. dissertation, Harvard University, 1955.

_____. "The Earliest Known Music for Desdemona's 'Willow Song.'" *Shakespeare Quarterly* 9:295–300.

_____. "An Early Tune for the Fool's Song in 'King Lear.'" *Shakespeare Quarterly* 9:583–85.

_____. "Ophelia's Songs in *Hamlet.*" *Durham University Journal* 25:77–85.

_____. "The Riddle Song in 'Merchant of Venice.'" *Notes & Queries* 5:191–93.

_____. "Shakespearean Hymn-Parody?" *Renaissance News*, vol. 18, no. 1, pp. 4–6.

_____. "Songs, Time, and the Rejection of Falstaff." *Shakespeare Survey* 15:31–40.

_____. *The Vocal Songs in the Plays of Shakespeare: A Critical History.* Cambridge, Mass.: Harvard University Press, 1967.

Sewell, H. "Shakespeare and the Ballad: A Classification of the Ballads Used by Shakespeare and Instances of Their Occurrence." *Midwest Folklore* 12:217–34.

Shakespeare, W. *The Complete Plays and Poems of William Shakespeare.* Edited by W. Neilson and C. Hill. New York: Houghton Mifflin Co., 1942.

_____. *The Complete Works of Shakespeare.* Edited by H. Craig. New York: Scott, Foresman and Co., 1951.

_____. *The First Folio of Shakespeare.* Norton Facsimile, prepared by Charlton Hinman. New York: W. W. Norton & Co., 1968.

_____. *Mr. William Shakespeares Comedies, Histories, & Tragedies. Published according to the True Originall Copies. London Printed by Isaac Iaggard, and Ed. Blount. 1623.* Reduced facsimile. New York: Funk & Wagnalls, 1887.

_____. *The Plays of William Shakespeare.* Edited by Johnson-Steevens. Vol. 4. London, 1793.

_____. *Shakespeare: The Complete Works.* Edited by G. Harrison. New York: Harcourt, Brace & World, 1952.

_____. *Antony and Cleopatra.* Edited by J. Wilson (New Cambridge edition). Cambridge: University Press, 1950.

_____. *Antony and Cleopatra.* Edited by M. Ridley (Arden edition). London: Methuen & Co., 1954.

————. *The Tragedie of Anthonie, and Cleopatra*. Edited by H. Furness (New Variorum edition). Philadelphia: J. B. Lippincott Co., 1907.

————. *The Tragedy of Antony and Cleopatra*. Edited by G. Kittredge. New York: Ginn and Co., 1941.

————. *The Tragedy of Coriolanus*. Edited by J. Wilson (New Cambridge edition). Cambridge: University Press, 1961.

————. *The Tragedy of Coriolanus*. Edited by W. Craig and R. Case (Arden edition). London: Methuen & Co., 1922.

————. *Hamlet*. Edited by G. Kittredge. Boston: Ginn and Co., 1939.

————. *Hamlet*. Edited by H. Furness (New Variorum edition). Philadelphia: J. B. Lippincott & Co., 1877.

————. *Hamlet*. Edited by J. Wilson (New Cambridge edition). Cambridge: University Press, 1936.

————. *The Tragedy of Hamlet*. Edited by E. Dowden (Arden edition). London: Methuen & Co., 1899.

————. *The Tragicall Historie of Hamlet, Prince of Denmarke. By William Shakespeare. Newly imprinted and enlarged to almost as much againe as it was, according to the true and perfect Coppie*. London: N. L., 1604.

————. *The First Part of the History of Henry IV*. Edited by J. Wilson (New Cambridge edition). Cambridge: University Press, 1946.

————. *The First Part of King Henry the Fourth*. Edited by R. Cowl and A. Morgan (Arden edition). London: Methuen & Co., 1919.

————. *Henry the Fourth Part I*. Edited by S. Hemingway (New Variorum edition). Philadelphia: J. B. Lippincott Co., 1936.

————. *The History of Henrie the Fourth; With the battel at Shrewsburie, betweene the King and Lord Henry Percy, surnamed Henry Hotspur of the North. With the humorous conceits of Sir Iohn Falstaffe. Newly corrected by W. Shake-speare*. London: Andrew Wise, 1599.

————. *Supplement to Henry IV, Part 1*. Edited by G. Evans (New Variorum edition). *Shakespeare Quarterly*, for the Shakespeare Association of America, 1956.

————. *The Second part of Henrie the fourth, continuing to his death, and coronation of Henrie the fift. With the humours of sir Iohn Fal-staffe, and swaggering Pistoll. As it hath been sundrie times publikely acted by the right honourable, the Lord Chamberlaine his seruants. Written by William Shake-speare*. London: Andrew Wise and William Aspley, 1600.

————. *The Second Part of Henry the Fourth*. Edited by M. Shaaber (New Variorum edition). Philadelphia: J. B. Lippincott Co., 1940.

————. *The Second Part of the History of Henry IV*. Edited by J. Wilson (New Cambridge edition). Cambridge: University Press, 1946.

————. *The Second Part of King Henry the Fourth*. Edited by R. Cowl (Arden edition). London: Methuen & Co., 1923.

————. *The Cronicle Historie of Henry the fift, With his battell fought at Agin Court in France. Togither with Auntient Pistoll. As it hath bene sundry times played by the Right honorable the Lord Chamberlaine his seruants*. London: Thomas Millington and John Busby, 1600.

————. *Henry V*. Edited by J. Wilson (New Cambridge edition). Cambridge: University Press, 1947.

————. *King Henry V*. Edited by J. Walter (Arden edition). London: Methuen & Co., 1954.

————. *The First part of the Contention betwixt the two famous Houses of Yorke and Lancaster, with the death of the good Duke Humphrey*. London: Thomas Millington, 1594.

_____. *The First Part of King Henry VI*. Edited by A. Cairncross (Arden edition). London: Methuen & Co., 1962.

_____. *The First Part of King Henry the Sixth*. Edited by H. Hart (Arden edition). London: Methuen & Co., 1909.

_____. *The First Part of King Henry VI*. Edited by J. Wilson (New Cambridge edition). Cambridge: University Press, 1952.

_____. *The Second Part of Henry VI*. Edited by A. Cairncross (Arden edition). London: Methuen & Co., 1957.

_____. *The Second Part of King Henry VI*. Edited by J. Wilson (New Cambridge edition). Cambridge: University Press, 1952.

_____. *The Third Part of King Henry the Sixth*. Edited by H. Hart (Arden edition). London: Methuen & Co., 1910.

_____. *The Third Part of Henry VI*. Edited by A. Cairncross (Arden edition). Cambridge, Mass.: Harvard University Press, 1964.

_____. *The Third Part of King Henry VI*. Edited by J. Wilson (New Cambridge edition). Cambridge: University Press, 1952.

_____. *King Henry VIII*. Edited by R. Foakes (Arden edition). London: Methuen & Co., 1957.

_____. *Julius Caesar*. Edited by J. Wilson (New Cambridge edition). Cambridge: University Press, 1949.

_____. *Julius Caesar*. Edited by T. Dorsch (Arden edition). Cambridge, Mass.: Harvard University Press, 1961.

_____. *The Tragedy of Julius Caesar*. Edited by G. Kittredge. Boston: Ginn and Co., 1939.

_____. *King Lear*. Edited by H. Furness (New Variorum edition). Philadelphia: J. B. Lippincott & Co., 1880.

_____. *King Lear*. Edited by J. Wilson and G. Duthie (New Cambridge edition). Cambridge: University Press, 1960.

_____. *King Lear*. Edited by K. Muir (Arden edition). London: Methuen & Co., 1952.

_____. *M. William Shake-speare, His True Chronicle History of the life and death of King Lear, and his three Daughters. With the unfortunate life of Edgar, sonne and heire to the Earle of Glocester, and his sullen and assumed humour of Tom of Bedlam. As it was plaid before the Kings Maiesty at White-Hall, vp-pon S Stephens night, in Christmas Hollidaies. By his Maiesties Seruants, playing vsually at the Globe on the Banckside.* N.p.: Nathaniel Butter, 1608.

_____. *The Tragedy of King Lear*. Edited by G. Kittredge. Boston: Ginn and Co., 1940.

_____. *The Tragedy of King Lear*. Edited by W. Craig (Arden edition). London: Methuen & Co., 1901.

_____. *Macbeth*. Edited by H. Furness (New Variorum edition). Philadelphia: J. B. Lippincott & Co., 1873.

_____. *Macbeth*. Edited by J. Wilson (New Cambridge edition). Cambridge: University Press, 1947.

_____. *Macbeth*. Edited by K. Muir (Arden edition). London: Methuen & Co., 1951.

_____. *Othello*. Edited by H. Furness (New Variorum edition). Philadelphia: J. B. Lippincott & Co., 1886.

_____. *Othello*. Edited by J. Wilson (New Cambridge edition). Cambridge: University Press, 1957.

_____. *The Tragedy of Othello*. Edited by H. Hart (Arden edition). London: Methuen & Co., 1905.

298)

————. *King Richard II.* Edited by J. Wilson (New Cambridge edition). Cambridge: University Press, 1951.

————. *King Richard II.* Edited by P. Ure (Arden edition). London: Methuen & Co., 1955.

————. *The Life and Death of King Richard the Second.* Edited by M. Black (New Variorum edition). Philadelphia: J. B. Lippincott Co., 1955.

————. *Richard II.* Edited by G. Kittredge. Boston: Ginn and Co., 1939.

————. *The Tradgedie of King Richard the second. As it hath beene publikely acted by the right Honourable the Lorde Chamberlaine his Seruants.* London: Andrew Wise, 1597.

————. *Richard III.* Edited by J. Wilson (New Cambridge edition). Cambridge: University Press, 1954.

————. *The Tragedy of King Richard the Third.* Edited by A. Thompson (Arden edition). Indianapolis: Bobbs-Merrill Co., 1907.

————. *The Tragedy of King Richard the third . . . As it hath beene lately Acted by the Right honourable the Lord Chamberlaine his seruants.* London: Andrew Wise, 1597.

————. *The Tragedy of Richard the Third: with the Landing of Earle Richmond, and the Battell at Bosworth Field.* Edited by H. Furness, Jr. (New Variorum edition). Philadelphia: J. B. Lippincott Co., 1908.

————. *The True Tragedie of Richarde Duke of Yorke, and the death of good King Henrie the sixt: With the whole contention betweene the two Houses, Lancaster and Yorke; as it was sundry times acted by the Right Honourable the Earle of Pembrooke his seruantes.* London: Thomas Millington, 1600.

————. *An Excellent conceited Tragedie of Romeo and Iuliet, As it hath been often (with great applause) plaid publiquely, by the right Honourable the L. of Hunsdon his Seruants.* London: John Danter, 1597.

————. *Romeo and Juliet.* Edited by E. Dowden (Arden edition). London: Methuen & Co., 1900.

————. *Romeo and Juliet.* Edited by G. Kittredge. Boston: Ginn and Co., 1940.

————. *Romeo and Juliet.* Edited by H. Furness (New Variorum edition). Philadelphia: J. B. Lippincott & Co., 1871.

————. *Romeo & Juliet.* Edited by J. Wilson (New Cambridge edition). Cambridge: University Press, 1955.

————. *Timon of Athens.* Edited by K. Deighton (Arden edition). London: Methuen & Co., 1905.

————. *The Lamentable Tragedy of Titus Andronicus.* Edited by H. Craig (Arden edition). London: Methuen & Co., 1904.

————. *The most lamentable Romaine Tragedie of Titus Andronicus. As it hath sundry times beene played by the Right Honourable the Earle of Pembrooke, the Earle of Darbie, the Earle of Sussex, and the Lorde Chamberlaine theyr Seruants.* London: Edward White, 1600.

————. *Titus Andronicus.* Edited by H. Baildon (Arden edition). London: Methuen & Co., 1904.

————. *Titus Andronicus.* Edited by J. Maxwell (Arden edition). Cambridge, Mass.: Harvard University Press, 1961.

————. *Titus Andronicus.* Edited by J. Wilson (New Cambridge edition). Cambridge: University Press, 1948.

————. *Troilus and Cressida.* Edited by H. Hillebrand and T. Baldwin (New Variorum edition). Philadelphia: J. B. Lippincott Co., 1953.

————. *Troilus and Cressida.* Edited by K. Deighton (Arden edition). London: Methuen & Co., 1906.

Simpson, C. *The British Broadside Ballad and Its Music.* New Brunswick, N.J.: Rutgers University Press, 1966.

Spitzer, L. *Classical and Christian Ideas of World Harmony: Prolegomena to an Interpretation of the Word "Stimmung."* Edited by A. Hatcher. Baltimore: Johns Hopkins Press, 1963.

Sternfeld, F. "The Dramatic and Allegorical Function of Music in Shakespeare's Tragedies." *Annales Musicologiques* 3:265–82.

————. "Lasso's Music for Shakespeare's 'Samingo.' " *Shakespeare Quarterly* 9:105–16.

————. "Music and Ballads." *Shakespeare Survey* 17:219–22.

————. *Music in Shakespearean Tragedy.* London: Routledge & Kegan Paul, 1963.

————. "Ophelia's Version of the Walsingham Song." *Music & Letters* 45:108–13.

————. "Shakespeare's Use of Popular Song." In *Elizabethan and Jacobean Studies Presented to Frank Percy Wilson . . .*, pp. 150–66. Oxford: Clarendon Press, 1959.

————. "A Song from Campion's *Lord's Masque*." *Journal of the Warburg and Courtauld Institute* 20:373–75.

————. *Songs from Shakespeare's Tragedies.* New York: Oxford University Press, 1965.

————. "Le Symbolisme musical dans les pièces de Shakespeare présentées à la cour d'Angleterre." In *Les Fêtes de la Renaissance*, edited by J. Jacquot, pp. 319–33. Paris: Éditions du Centre Nationale de la Recherche Scientifique, 1956.

————. "*Troilus and Cressida*: Music for the Play." In *English Institute Essays—1952*, pp. 107–37. New York: Columbia University Press, 1954.

Stevens, J. *Music & Poetry in the Early Tudor Court.* Lincoln: University of Nebraska Press, 1961.

————. "Shakespeare and the Music of the Elizabethan Stage: An Introductory Essay." In *Shakespeare in Music*, edited by P. Hartnoll, pp. 1–48. London: Macmillan and Co., 1964.

Stroup, T. "Cordelia and the Fool." *Shakespeare Quarterly* 12:127–32.

Thompson, M. "Uses of Music and Reflections of Current Theories of the Psychology of Music in the Plays of Shakespeare, Jonson, and Beaumont and Fletcher." Ph.D. dissertation, University of Minnesota, 1956.

Thorndike, A. *The Influence of Beaumont and Fletcher on Shakespeare.* Worcester, Mass.: O. B. Wood, 1901.

Tillyard, E. *The Elizabethan World Picture.* New York: Macmillan Co., 1944.

————. *Shakespeare's History Plays.* London: Chatto & Windus, 1948.

Titcomb, C. "Baroque Court and Military Trumpets and Kettledrums: Technique and Music." *The Galpin Society Journal* 9:56–81.

————. "The Kettledrums in Western Europe: Their history outside the orchestra." Ph.D. dissertation, Harvard University, 1952.

Turberville, G. *The Noble Arte of Venerie or Hunting . . . (1575).* Folger Shakespeare Library (STC 24328).

Walker, A. "Popular Songs and Broadside Ballads in the English Drama 1559–1642." Ph.D. dissertation, Harvard University, 1934.

Wallace, K. *Francis Bacon on Communication, or: The Art of Applying Reason to Imagination for the Better Moving of the Will.* Chapel Hill: University of North Carolina Press, 1943.

Ward, J., ed. *The Dublin Virginal Manuscript.* Ph.D. dissertation, Wellesley College, 1954.

————. "Fragments at Western Reserve University." In *Aspects of Medieval*

and Renaissance Music: A Birthday Offering to Gustave Reese, edited by
J. LaRue. New York: W. W. Norton, 1966.
————. "Music for 'A Handefull of pleasant delites.' " *Journal of the
American Musicological Society* 10:151–80.
Wells, S. "Tom O' Bedlam's Song and *King Lear.*" *Shakespeare Quarterly*
12:311–15.
Weston, J., ed. *The Chief Middle English Poets: Selected Poems.* Boston:
Houghton Mifflin Co., 1914.
Wey, J. "Musical Allusions and Songs as Part of the Structure of Meaning of
Shakespeare's Plays." Ph.D. dissertation, Catholic University of America,
1957.
Wilson, J. *What Happens in Hamlet.* Cambridge: University Press, 1951.
Woodfill, W. *Musicians in English Society from Elizabeth to Charles I.*
Princeton, N.J.: Princeton University Press, 1953.
Wooldridge, H., ed. *Old English Popular Music* (a revision of W. Chappell's
Popular Music of the Olden Time). 2 vols. London: Chappell & Co., 1893.
Wright, T. *A History of Caricature & Grotesque in Literature and Art.* London:
Virtue Brothers & Co., 1865.
————, ed. *Songs and Carols.* London: Richards for the Percy Society, 1847.

Index